KT-157-238

The Business Policy Game Corporate Charter

Firm Name _____ World _____

Company _____

Corporate Officers

Name	Position
_____	_____
_____	_____
_____	_____
_____	_____
_____	_____

Authorized by: _____ Date _____

(Simulation Administrator)

The Business Policy Game, 4th Edition

CONTENTS

The Business Policy Game, 4th Edition

PREFACE

A significant number of changes have been made in the Fourth edition of this book to enhance its educational value.

1. A strong international component has been added to the simulation. It includes the addition of a separate, realistic national economic environment with realistic cost and demand relationships and CPI and GDP measures. The national environments are related with relevant exchange rates.

2. Financial reports are now structured by market, with a separate subsidiary in each market. Thus firms can assign the subsidiary in each market area to an individual member who has responsibility for the performance of that subsidiary and its market.

> **IMPORTANT NOTE**
> The disk packaged with this manual contains *The Business Policy Game* programs (described in Appendix A) and spreadsheet templates for a decision support system (see Appendix B). Before starting to install *The Business Policy Game* programs, please check to see that you have the disk for the correct version (IBM compatible or Apple Macintosh). It should be the same version that will be used by your simulation administrator. If you require a different version or a different size disk, please ask your administrator to contact one of the authors. Their addresses and contact numbers are listed in *The Business Policy Game: Instructor's Manual* and in a file named README on the administrator's disk.

3. Sales offices have been added to each market area. The sales office in an area is responsible for managing its own inventory and the sales force. During any quarter, current inventory plus the units ordered and received by the office are available for sale. If the office does not place an order, sales will be limited to the amount of inventory on hand in the market area.

4. If a firm decides it no longer wants to compete in an area, it may close and sell its sales office and leave the area. It may later decide to reenter the area by establishing a new sales office.

5. If a firm decides it has too much productive capacity, it may close its plant in any area and sell the plant to a developer. A new plant may be built in the area later if additional productive capacity is desired.

6. The graphing program is now a stand-alone program instead of a spreadsheet macro. It is much faster and easier to graph the performance of the teams in a world over the number of years of play or the number of quarters of play.

7. The game may be simplified by limiting competition to one country or by reducing the number of market areas in which the firms compete.

8. Sales force resignations now are reported so that teams can more easily keep track of their sales forces.

9. Construction lead times have been shortened to make the simulation easier to use when operating on the quarter system.

10. All computer-generated reports may be viewed on the computer screen and any (or all) of the reports may be printed as needed.

11. An industry world now may have from three to eight teams competing. The larger limit on number of teams provides more flexibility in fitting the simulation to varying class sizes.

12. The menus for the programs follow common user interface guidelines.

Several features which we believe to be particularly user friendly are:

1. The context sensitive help feature available on command when entering decisions.

2. Thorough checking of decision values when they are entered, with informative messages notifying players when errors or invalid entries are made.

3. An expanded decision support system is available for use with a variety of spreadsheet programs.

4. The decision form in the manual matches the form displayed on the computer screen when decisions are entered.

5. Versions of the program are available to run on both IBM-compatible and Macintosh computers with nearly identical interfaces.

The Business Policy Game is a general management simulation that provides students with a challenging decision-making exercise. It has been used successfully with groups of upper-class undergraduates and graduate students in business administration and in executive development programs. The simulation also has been used successfully for many years in the International Collegiate Business Policy Competition.

Each simulation participant requires *The Business Policy Game: Player's Manual* which includes computer programs and spreadsheet templates on a floppy disk. An instructor's manual is available. The simulation software is available in two versions, for use on IBM and compatible computer systems or on Apple Macintosh systems.

The Business Policy Game has been patterned, in part, after similar games which preceded it. Particular acknowledgment is given to Dr. John E. Van Tassel, whose "Boston College Decision-Making Exercise" inspired the senior author to become interested in business simulation and influenced the development of the model of this game and the player's manual. This revision is the result of experiences with the first three editions, as well as numerous other simulations and discussions with Association for Business Simulation and Experiential Learning (ABSEL) members and colleagues. We would like to thank all of those authors and friends for their contributions.

Particular thanks are extended to each of the teams and advisors who participated in a beta test of the current international revision for the thirtieth anniversary of the International Collegiate Business Policy Competition in Las Vegas during April, 1994. Teams from the following schools were accompanied by their faculty advisors who have provided much feedback that has helped to improve this version:

Undergraduate student teams from the following schools participated with their faculty advisors:

Jon Ozmun, Northern Arizona University (Flagstaff)
Warren Brown, University of Oregon (Eugene)
Andrew Klein, Groupe de Bissy Management School (France)
Tom English, Boise State University (Idaho)
Colleen Mullery, Humboldt State University (Arcata, California)
Don Mann, University of San Diego (California)
David Tucker, Harding University (Searcy, Arkansas)
Bernard Malamud, University of Nevada, Las Vegas
Mohsen Attaran, California State University, Bakersfield
Andrew Klein, Ecole Des Praticiens Du Commerce International (France)
Larry Mills, Southern Nazarene University (Bethany, Oklahoma)
William D. Biggs, Beaver College (Glenside, Pennsylvania)
Steven Achtenhagen, San Jose State University (California)
Abe Harraf, Embry-Riddle Aeronautical University (Daytona Beach, Florida)
L. T. Snyder, University of West Florida (Pensacola)
Charlene Coe, California State University, Fresno
Chike Okechuku, University of Windsor (Ontario, Canada)
Don Negri, Willamette University (Salem, Oregon)
C. H. Barnes, Gonzaga University (Spokane, Washington)
Don Springer, University of Portland (Oregon)

Hassan Setoodeh, Embry-Riddle Aeronautical University (Prescott, Arizona)
Michael Hergert, San Diego State University (California)
Glenn Gomes, California State University, Chico
Edmundo Gonzales, Instituto Tecnologica Y De Estudios Superiores De Monterrey
        (Mexico)

Graduate student teams from the following schools participated with their faculty
advisors:

Don Mann, University of San Diego (California)
Joe Walka, Northern Arizona University (Flagstaff)
Stephen Achtenhagen, San Jose State University (California)
Greg Frazier, University of Oregon (Eugene)
James Cross, University of Nevada, Las Vegas
Mohsen Attaran, California State University, Bakersfield
Ronald Salazar, Idaho State University (Pocatello)
Gerry Huybregts, Eastern New Mexico University (Portales)
Ralph Pope, California State University, Sacramento
Allen Nash, Murdoch University (Perth, Western Australia)

Special thanks are due to several colleagues who have helped the authors with beta tests
of the fourth edition in the classroom:

Jon Ozmun, Northern Arizona University (Flagstaff)
Bill Busby, Northwood University (Midland, Michigan)
Stephen Achtenhagen, San Jose State University (California)
Tom Leonard, Bryant College (Smithfield, Rhode Island)
Michael Hergert, San Diego State University (California)
Rocky Waters, Humboldt State University (Arcata, California)

Most of all, we each want to thank our spouses, Carolyn Cotter and Nan Fritzsche, respectively, for their patience and counsel. Without their assistance, and the help and cooperation
of our children, Sonja and Tanya Fritzsche; and Kate and David Cotter, this project could never
have been completed.

The Business Policy Game, 4th Edition

AN OVERVIEW OF *THE BUSINESS POLICY GAME*

Educational objective. An instructional supplement for courses dealing with strategic management and business policy, both domestically and internationally. Formulation of mission, objectives and strategy are emphasized, with opportunity to implement strategies and policies that will lead to the realization of objectives. A premium is placed on successful integration of functional area concepts. The model is challenging to upper-division undergraduate and graduate business students.

The simulation. A computer-based simulation of a manufacturing firm with domestic and international subsidiaries. Student teams compete with each other as members of the management of simulated companies producing and selling a consumer durable good. Includes marketing, production and finance decisions. The model is interactive so that marketing decisions, for example, may influence the sales of competitors as well as the sales of the firm making the decision.

Course use. Strategic management and business policy at the upper-level undergraduate or graduate level; suitable for use independently or as supplementary material. Seminars for management development. Variations of the model have been used successfully in the classroom and in intercollegiate competition for nearly three decades.

Number of participants. Twelve or more. An industry world may contain from three to eight firms (student teams), with each firm's management consisting of four to eight participants. For more than eight teams, separate industries may be run concurrently.

Time required. Sixteen to twenty sessions of about fifty minutes each (later sessions typically may require less time). Outside preparation will reduce the time required in group sessions. Initial preparation by participants may require six to eight hours each.

Space required. Ideally, each company might have a separate "board room" for decision-making sessions. Grouping of teams in different parts of a large room works satisfactorily.

Materials and equipment needed. A copy of *The Business Policy Game: Player's Manual* for each participant and *The Business Policy Game: Instructor's Manual* for the administrator. The administrator should arrange to have the computer programs and history files installed on a personal computer system or local area network. Access to a computer system by players is recommended, but not required. A spreadsheet program is useful for student analysis and a decision support system.

Administrator's role. To provide an environment which maximizes the learning experience; and to arrange for materials, physical facilities and computer processing of student decisions. Instructions and suggestions for classroom use and for all phases of the simulation are provided in the instructor's manual.

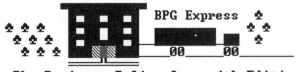

CHAPTER 1

INTRODUCTION

The Business Policy Game was designed as a strategic management simulation to provide a challenging, complex decision-making exercise. As a strategic management simulation, it requires participants to define and articulate their corporate missions, set objectives, develop strategies to realize the objectives and create operating policies to ensure that operating decisions support the strategy. Participants are also responsible for making quarterly operating decisions for each of the functional areas of finance, marketing and production and to integrate those decisions for the purpose of meeting the firm's overall goals and aspirations. Participation in the simulation requires that a student of business administration review information and techniques that have been learned in other courses and/or in practical on-the-job experience, and put into practice many of the principles of management decision making and strategic planning. To be successful, participants need to adopt the viewpoint of top management in the simulated business firm which they operate. They must specify carefully the goals and objectives which guide their firm's operation. The participants are required to make quarterly decisions concerning the operations of their manufacturing firm as they compete with the management teams of other firms in the industry.

The Business Policy Game is not intended to duplicate any actual industry. Rather, the simulation model was designed to include general relationships that might exist in any competitive industry. One might say it is generic. Participants need to utilize their knowledge and experience in order to make certain deductions about the economy in which they are operating and about general relationships which exist within the simulation. These deductions must be combined with knowledge about specific relationships and with the participants' beliefs about the actions that competitors are likely to take. A set of decisions ideally would follow from utilizing a combination of different types of data analysis, forecasting techniques and development of strategies and policies to meet the goals and objectives of the firm. (See Figure 1-1.)

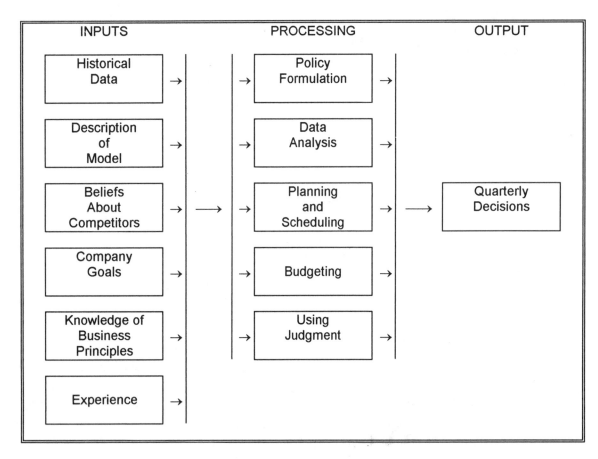

FIGURE 1-1
Flow Chart of Activities in Preparation for
Making Decisions in *The Business Policy Game*

The Simulated Environment

You will be a member of the management team of a simulated manufacturing company. Your company's corporate headquarters is located in one of three domestic market areas. Three subsidiaries handle operations in the other two domestic areas and in Sereno, a simulated country in Latin America. Each of the two countries has a different economic environment reflected in differing growth rates of gross domestic product (GDP). Different inflation rates are reflected in separate consumer price indexes (CPI). A different social and legal environment results in different demand characteristics for your product, different tax structures and different employment practices.

The computer program used to process the decisions made by competing teams includes definitions of certain relationships that have been abstracted from the economic environment of the business world. This abstraction, or model, does not purport to include all of the relationships that exist. To do so would make the simulation too complex to handle. The relationships included are those that contribute significantly to the degree of realism required to provide a plausible simulation. These relationships are outlined and described in subsequent sections of this manual. A description of the rules which must be followed in order to participate successfully in the simulation also is included.

Some of the relationships that exist in the simulation and the rules for dealing with the relationships will be described only in general terms. These relationships are comparable to those in the business world that are subject to uncertainty and thus not completely specified. For example, if a manufacturer lowers the price of a product, sales of the product normally increase. The magnitude of the sales increase cannot be known with certainty. Thus, only the general relationship between price and sales volume will be described in this manual. The actual effect of a specific price change must be estimated by observing the relationship between price and sales volume which exists in historical data and by experimentation with the price variable during the course of the simulation.

Other relationships will be described in more precise terms in later chapters. These relationships are subject to less uncertainty in the business world. Cost functions, accounting relationships and methods of deriving various entries in the income statement, cash flow statement and balance sheet are included in this group. The cash balance at the end of the quarter, for example, is equal to the previous quarter's cash balance plus total cash receipts less total cash payments. Explicit descriptions concerning the constraints required by the simulation model also are provided, which the participants may consider to be "rules of the simulation." One such rule, for example, states that only one plant may be built in any marketing area.

During the course of the simulation, the participants will encounter a variety of business and economic situations and administrative problems. In order to cope successfully with these problems, the participants will find it necessary to engage in economic forecasting, sales forecasting and profit planning. Cash flow analysis and capital budgets must be prepared. Production planning and scheduling must be accomplished. Cost analysis, pricing, policy formulation and the development and implementation of marketing programs will be necessary. In addition, participants must prepare and analyze financial reports, cash flow statements, cost and sales analyses reports and informational reports regarding competitors and the economic situation. Most participants will find it necessary to review basic textbooks and materials from this and other courses, and to draw from their past experiences in order to complete these activities effectively.

Preparing for Action

The Business Policy Game will require a heavy investment in time on the part of the participant—TANSTAAFL. (There ain't no such thing as a free lunch.) This investment should be a prudent one, however, as participation in the simulation should significantly increase overall understanding of the operation of business enterprises. The more you put into the exercise, the more you will get out of it.

In order to participate effectively in the simulation, one must understand the relationships within the simulation model as well as its rules and constraints. Sample historical data from the previous two years of the firm's operation, prior to your management team's tenure, are shown in Appendix C.

These data also are found in Historical Data for Years 1 and 2 (Report J) of your firm's reports for Year 2, Quarter 4, which will be provided to you by your game administrator. The historical data in your Year 2, Quarter 4 reports will differ from that in Appendix C if your game administrator is using a different economic environment.

Study the data thoroughly for relationships which will help the firm in managing its resources. Economic forecasts and sales forecasts must be made, and plans must be formulated for the firm's continued operation. It should be obvious that these tasks require the delegation of specific responsibilities to different team members. Thus, members of each firm should organize to perform the management function effectively.

Getting Ready for the First Decision

Before preparing the first set of decisions and after carefully reading this manual, you and your colleagues are urged to complete the following set of activities and planning reports:

1. Organize your management team. You should assign members of your team to corporate offices and other critical posts, decide upon specific decision-making procedures to be followed, and divide the work load among the various members of your firm. Unless the simulation administrator prescribes an organizational structure, you may design the organization of your management team. Your organizational structure and your ability to work together as a management team will be important ingredients in the success of your firm.

You should weigh the advantages and disadvantages of various organizational structures when designing your organization. Company officers for a functional organization might include president; vice-presidents of finance, marketing and production; vice-president for economic and sales forecasting; and corporate secretary for recording policies and decisions. A geographical structure might replace the functional heads with subsidiary managers for each of the market areas.

Some teams find centralized decision making to work well. Various company officers will normally make recommendations to the president regarding the operations of their particular departments. However, the final decision-making authority rests with the president. Other teams prefer to vest their decision-making authority in the management team as a group. Recommendations are provided by the various officers of the firm, but the actual decisions are made by the officers as a group. Still other teams find a decentralized form of organization to be effective. Final decision-making authority is vested with the head of the unit responsible for the decision. Under a decentralized functional organization, the marketing decisions would be made by the vice-president of marketing, production scheduling decisions by the vice-president of operations, etc. Alternatively, decisions for each market area would be made by the general manager of the subsidiary in the area. Coordination of overall decision making would be undertaken by the president, and conflicts would be resolved by the president of the firm.

You should prepare an organization chart that shows the lines of authority in your firm's organization and the position in the organization of each member of your firm. Then, fill in the Corporate Charter, located on page iii in the front of this manual, with your company name and the name and position title of each member of your team. The Corporate Charter should be turned in to your simulation administrator.

2. <u>Prepare a forecast of expected levels of economic activity by country</u>. Your firm's sales will be affected by the general level of economic activity in each country in your industry world. As real gross domestic product (GDP) rises, you can expect sales to rise, too, and as real GDP falls, sales are likely to fall at the same time. GDP forecasts for each country are included in your quarterly reports. A forecast of real GDP will be helpful in estimating future sales. Specific suggestions for preparing such a forecast are contained in Chapter 6.

3. <u>Prepare a sales forecast by market area</u>. Production scheduling, plans for investment in new plant(s) and in equipment, expected cash receipts and selling expenses all are affected by the volume of sales your firm realizes. Suggestions for preparing sales forecasts by market area using the Sales Forecast Work Sheet can be found in the "Forecasting Sales" section of Chapter 6.

4. <u>Prepare a production schedule</u>. Production must be scheduled for the first decision period as well as planned for subsequent quarters of business operation. Production planning will depend upon your firm's expectations of sales volume. The completed plan will provide the basis for determining production facility requirements. Suggestions for preparing production plans using the Production Plan Work Sheet, together with descriptions of production costs and production possibilities, are found in the "Operations Planning and Scheduling" section of Chapter 7.

5. <u>Prepare an investment plan</u>. Alternative methods of expanding productive capacity and their associated costs may be analyzed using numerous financial tools. See Chapter 8 for a description of the alternatives. The nature of the expansion that your firm undertakes will depend upon your production plan.

6. <u>Prepare a capital budget</u>. Capital is required to finance any planned expansion. The Capital Budget Work Sheet, discussed in the "Capital Budgeting" section of Chapter 9, may be used to analyze alternate sources of funding for your firm.

7. <u>Prepare a cash budget</u>. Sufficient funds must be provided to finance the expenses and cash outlays required by your operations and investment plans. Sources of funds and cash requirements are outlined in Chapter 9. Suggestions for preparing the Pro Forma Cash Flow Work Sheet also are included under the "Cash Budgeting and the Cash Flow Statement" section of Chapter 10.

8. <u>Prepare *pro forma* financial statements</u>. Your projected balance sheet may be used to analyze how the composition and levels of assets and liabilities affect your financial condition.

Your expected level of profitability is an important means of judging the success of your firm's planned operation. You should evaluate your decisions prior to submitting them by preparing a *pro forma* income statement and balance sheet. Income Statement and Balance Sheet work sheets, along with suggestions for their preparation, are found in the "Profit Planning and the Income Statement" and "The Balance Sheet" sections of Chapter 10.

    9. <u>Formulate mission and objectives and outline initial strategies and policies</u>. As you complete the planning activities outlined above, tentative policies should be developed for the operation of your firm and for the decisions which must be made on a quarterly basis. We suggest that you state these policies explicitly in written form for future reference. As the simulation proceeds, you probably will decide to revise your policies based upon the experience gained from the operation of your firm and the changing conditions of the dynamic business environment.

    We recommend that your firm be very specific in the formulation of mission, objectives, strategy and operating policies. A corporate objective to "maximize profits" is laudable but provides little guidance for strategy and policy formulation and is of little value as a standard for achievement. At the end of the first year of the simulation, or any other year for that matter, you will have little idea whether profits were in fact maximized or whether you fell short. It would be better to seek an objective of, say, "15 percent after-tax return on equity." Then you could judge your achievement more adequately after a year's experience and take corrective action where necessary.

    You may view many of your operating policies as decision rules to be followed in specific situations. An example of a specific policy might be: "Ignore price reductions by competitors when they amount to less than ten cents per unit, but when the reductions are greater, match their price immediately." Avoid such generalizations as "charge a fair price that is consistent with production costs and with competitors' pricing policies." That's pure cotton. The clear formulation and statement of your policies will help to assure the consistency and stability of your firm's operations and will save you a considerable amount of preparation time during the decision periods as you participate in the simulation. See Chapter 4 for additional help in the development of mission and objectives and the formulation of strategies and policies.

    The simulation administrator may require written reports on some or all of the above activities as part of the material used to evaluate team performance. Work sheets, contained in Appendix D, can be used to facilitate the preparation of some of the reports. It is suggested that a most effective way to present the work sheets is to develop a decision-support system. The work sheets in spreadsheet template format are available on the disk enclosed with this manual. When we refer to work sheets, we are referring to the paper forms in this manual. When we refer to spreadsheets, we are referring to the spreadsheet templates of the paper work sheets. A decision-support system can be developed relatively easily by using these spreadsheet templates.

    Your initial reports will provide a good basis for a more extensive strategic business plan and policy manual that the administrator may require after you have gained some experience with the simulation.

Submitting Decisions

The next step is to formulate and submit an actual decision set for the first period of your firm's operation under new management, Year 3, Quarter 1. The simulation administrator will specify the **date** and **time** when your decisions are due. It is important that your firm's decisions be submitted prior to that time. Failure to do so may hold up the simulation run. More likely it will result in the decision submitted for your firm during the previous period being used as the decision for the current period. Such action normally would not be in the best interests of your firm. Chapter 2 outlines the decisions that must be made and describes the decision form. Copies of the decision form are included in Appendix D.

We hope that the experience of participating in *The Business Policy Game* will be both enjoyable and rewarding. More importantly, though, it should be a meaningful and challenging educational experience. The amount of serious effort that you put into the analysis, planning, and decision-making activities of the simulation will determine how much the simulation will contribute to your education. Remember TANSTAAFL!

CHAPTER 2

QUARTERLY DECISIONS

The management of each simulated firm must make a number of decisions for each quarter of simulated operations. This chapter summarizes the decisions that are required and provides instructions for their entry on the decision form as well as indicating certain limits and restraints that have been placed upon specific decisions. Some restraints are a result of the limitations of the simulation model, and some are imposed to add realism to *The Business Policy Game*. More detailed information about each type of decision will be provided in later chapters of this manual to assist participants in formulating their strategy and decisions. Blank decision forms are found in Appendix D. These should be detached, and one copy submitted to the simulation administrator for each decision. You and your teammates may need to share some of these and other blank forms.

IMPORTANT NOTE

If you submit your decisions on a floppy disk, also submit a written copy of your decision form. If your disk becomes damaged or, for some reason, the computer is unable to read the disk, the simulation administrator will have a hard copy of your decision and it can be re-entered. Otherwise, your last previous decision may have to be used for the current decision period.

The simulation administrator will specify the date, time and place where each simulation decision set is due. Timely submission of simulation decisions (on computer disk and/or on the decision-entry form as specified by your administrator) is **extremely important**. If your decision set is not submitted promptly, the processing of the simulation will be delayed, causing lost time and possible hardships for your competitors and the simulation administrator. Failure to submit a decision set by the appointed time will most likely result in your most recent previous period's decision set being used for the current quarter, with adjustments for decisions that may not be legal for the current quarter (*i.e.* constructing another plant in the same area would be outside of the constraints of the model).

The mode of data entry will be specified by the simulation administrator.

1. You may be asked to enter your own decisions via personal computer, saving them on a floppy disk. Each team should create a Decision/Data Disk which is a format-ted, blank disk with the following label:

    > BUSINESS POLICY GAME
    > Decision/Data Disk
    > Company c, World w
    > Company Name

    where c is your company number and w is your world number. The disk must be initialized by the simulation administrator with several data files necessary to run the program. The decision set is entered by using the BPG computer program. See Appendix A for installation instructions and program documentation.

2. You may be asked to enter your decisions via a local area network (LAN) using the decision-entry program. Decision data then would be saved on the LAN sys-tem. See Appendix A for program documentation. The program may have been installed on the system already.

3. The administrator may arrange to have all data entered centrally from information that your firm submits on decision forms from Appendix D. Completion of the decision form is discussed later in this chapter.

After the simulation has been run on the computer, you will receive a set of reports (see Appendix C for an example) showing the results of your operations and those of your competi-tors. The report may be given to you in the form of a computer printout or you may be asked to print it yourself from a floppy disk or from the computer system that you used to enter the deci-sions.

If the first or second mode is utilized, you will be told where to find microcomputers which can be used to enter your decision set or you may use your own computer if it is compat-ible with the one used to run the simulation. Follow the instructions for using the decision-entry program, found in Appendix A. Don't forget to submit your decision form to show the values that have been entered. This will guard against Murphy's law: "If something can go wrong, it will."

If the third mode is specified, submit your decision forms by the specified time for data entry. Invalid entries may be edited by the simulation administrator and/or the computer program. Even though adjustments to invalid entries may not reflect your intentions, the decisions of the administrator are not subject to appeal. **You** are responsible for the implementation of your decisions by correct entries on your decision form.

Decision Form

Data are entered to the computer directly from the decision form. **Always** be sure to fill it in completely prior to data entry. Then check it carefully. Incorrectly completed forms may result in incorrect data entry and thus simulation results which are somewhat different from what your firm anticipated. We suggest that you refer to the sample decision form in Figure 2-1 as you read this chapter.

The figure illustrates the completed decision form for Company 1, which was used to generate the historical data for Year 2, Quarter 4 in Appendix C. Values for other companies were the same, except for advertising and production scheduling. In these two cases, the entries shown for Area 1 were made in each firm's home area instead. The home area for Company 2 is Area 2, and for Company 3 is Area 3. If there are more than three companies, the home areas for Companies 4, 5, 6, 7 and 8 are Areas 1, 2, 3, 1 and 2 respectively.

As you complete the decision form, be sure to enter values within the limits shown below (including a minus sign where appropriate) in each entry block. If no sign is entered, the numbers are assumed to be positive. When entering decisions with the decision-entry program, if you attempt to enter too many digits for a field, your computer may beep to indicate an error. If you enter a value outside of the limits noted below, an error message will appear in the middle of the screen requesting a valid entry. If no decision entry is made, the default value from the previous period's decision set will be used.

Company, World, Year, Quarter

Enter your Company, World, Year and Quarter numbers on the decision form, as well as your company name. If you are using the decision-entry program to enter your decisions via personal computer, check the decision-entry screen to be sure that the proper values are displayed.

Company _1_ World _1_ Year _2_ Quarter _4_ Company Name _____

Marketing Decisions

Marketing strategy is discussed in Chapter 5, along with additional information about each of the marketing decisions and the costs associated with them. Figure 2-3 at the end of this chapter summarizes the initial costs and expenses for *The Business Policy Game*.

DECISION FORM
THE BUSINESS POLICY GAME, 4th Edition

Company _1_ World _1_ Year _2_ Quarter _4_ Company Name _____

Marketing / Salespeople / Finance (000s)

	Price	Adv(000s)	Hire	Transfer	Comm	Salary
Area 1	$ 10.00	$ 46	#	#	20 ¢	$ 3000
Area 2	$ 10.00	$ 40	#	#	20 ¢	$ 3000
Area 3	$ 10.00	$ 40	#	#	20 ¢	$ 3000
Sereno	Ps 75	Ps 105	#	#	60 ¢	Ps 8971

Finance (000s)

Bank Loan	$
Bond Issue	$
Stock Issue	#
Dividends	$
Time CDs	$ 1000

R&D/Training (home currency)

R&D	$ 72
Trng	$ 68

Sales Office Orders (000s)

Area 1	# 87
Area 2	# 75
Area 3	# 75
Sereno	# 75

Model/Quality

Model	# 1
Quality	# 2

Production Schedule / Capacity Adjustment / Construction

	Lines	Hours	Layoff	Deac-tivate	Reac-tivate	New Lines	New Add'n	New Plant
Area 1	# 6	# 40	#	#	#	#	#	#
Area 2	#	#	#	#	#	#	#	#
Area 3	#	#	#	#	#	#	#	#
Sereno	#	#	#	#	#	#	#	#
2nd Shift	#	#	#	#	#	#	←	←

Copyright © 1995 by Richard V. Cotter and David J. Fritzsche

FIGURE 2-1
Decisions for Year 2, Quarter 4

Price

The wholesale price of your product must be set each quarter in each of the market areas in which your firm is operating. During the last quarter of Year 2, each firm charged $10.00 per unit for its product in each of the three Merican market areas and Ps 75 in Sereno. For price, as for all other decision variables, last period's value will be used if there is no entry for the current quarter. Company policy (and the simulation model) limits price changes to a maximum of 30 percent per quarter in domestic markets and 40 percent in foreign markets. Because the product price was $10.00 in domestic areas during Year 2, Quarter 4, the highest price that your company may charge in these areas in Year 3, Quarter 1 is $13.00 and the lowest is $7.00. A price change as large as this is discouraged because of the unknown effect that such changes may have on the market. Management may specify different prices for different areas. If your price is in whole dollars, enter zeros for the cents so that there is no question of whether you forgot to enter the cents figures.

The Sereno market area price is set in pesos rather than dollars. Decimal fractions for pesos are not required. See the current exchange rate (found in each quarter's financial reports) to translate pesos to dollars and cents.

Maximum change, Areas 1 to 3:	30 percent in any quarter.
Maximum change, Sereno:	40 percent in any quarter.
Exception:	If the sales office is closed (see below) the price is 0
Limits, domestic areas:	1 to 99.99 (in dollars and cents)
Limits, Sereno:	1 to 99999 (in Pesos)

	Price
Area 1	$ 10.00
Area 2	$ 10.00
Area 3	$ 10.00
Sereno	Ps 75

Advertising

Advertising expenditures must be allocated to each of the market areas in which your firm is operating. Enter the amount (in thousands of dollars or pesos) to be spent in each area. The amount must be specified even though no change is desired, and the default values from the previous quarter will be used if you make no entry.

Limits, domestic areas: 0 to 999 (in thousands of dollars)
Limits, Sereno: 0 to 9999999 (in thousands of Pesos)

	Adv(000s)
Area 1	$ 46
Area 2	$ 40
Area 3	$ 40
Sereno	Ps 105

Salespeople

The number of active salespeople and the number of salespeople in training are reported by area in the Sales Force Analysis section of the Operating Information Report each quarter.

1. Hire Salespeople. To hire and begin training new salespeople, enter the number of people to be trained in each area under Salespeople–Hire. A new salesperson must spend one quarter in training in an area prior to being sent to the field to sell. Salespeople in training will be assigned automatically to their area when training is complete. No further decision entry is necessary after the salespeople are hired. If you make an entry in the following quarter, you will hire additional salespeople to begin their training period in that quarter.

Limits :   0 to 99

	Salespeople			
	Hire	Transfer	Comm	Salary
Area 1	#	#	20 ¢	$ 3000
Area 2	#	#	20 ¢	$ 3000
Area 3	#	#	20 ¢	$ 3000
Sereno	#	#	60 ¢	Ps 8971

2. Transfer Salespeople. If your firm desires to transfer a salesperson from one area to another, this can be accomplished by making the appropriate entries under Salespeople–Transfer on the decision form. To transfer salespeople, you should enter a negative number for the area from which the salespeople are leaving, indicating the number of salespeople you are moving out

of the area. This must be balanced by one or more positive numbers in the area(s) to which the salespeople are moving.

Your positive moves into some areas may not exceed the total value of negative moves out of other areas. To do so would indicate an increase in the size of your sales force, and an increase only may be accomplished by hiring new salespeople and training them (See paragraph 1 on the previous page). If your negative values total more than your positive values, the additional salespeople will be fired (see paragraph 3 below).

In order to limit the entries in this field to transferring salespeople (and not firing them), all individuals who move out must have a place to move to, and all individuals who move in must have come from another market area. You may transfer salespeople from several areas at the same time. However, you may not transfer salespeople in and out of the same area in one quarter. They must either go into an area or out of an area. Not both. Remember, the sum of the negative (people moving out) and the positive (people moving in) numbers must equal zero. If the value of negative entries exceeds the value of positive entries, the extra negative values will result in discharging that number of salespeople.

Transfers take place immediately. A transferred salesperson, however, may not be very effective until he or she has moved and settled into a new market area. The salesperson will, however, continue to draw a salary. In addition, the salesperson will be provided with a moving allowance paid by the subsidiary in the area from which the individual moves.

Make sure you leave at least one sales person in each area unless you want to close a sales office. The sales office in an area will be closed if there are no sales people remaining in the area (see paragraph 4 on the next page).

Maximum: to be transferred out: number of active salespeople
Subject to: the sum of positive numbers may not exceed the sum of negative numbers
Limits: -99 to 99

3. Discharge Salespeople. You may fire salespeople by entering a negative value for the number of people you want to fire under Salespeople–Transfer. You indicate that the salespeople are to be fired by entering a negative number in the area where they are working, with no balancing positive number in another area indicating a transfer to a new area. Thus, if you decide to fire 2 salespeople in Area 3, enter -2 under the Salespeople–Transfer column for Area 3.

Make sure you leave at least one sales person in each area unless you want to close the sales office in the area. The sales office in an area will be closed if there are no sales people remaining in the area (see paragraph 4 on the next page).

Maximum to be discharged: Number of active salespeople
Limits: -99 to 0

4. <u>Closing a sales office</u>. If all salespersons in a subsidiary sales office are transferred or discharged by entering a negative number under Salespeople–Transfer that is equal to the total number of active salespeople, then the sales office in that area will be closed. All salespeople that are discharged will receive severance pay. Sales executives will be discharged and will receive severance pay. The sales office will be sold to a real estate developer for and there will be no more sales in the area. Any cash balances will be transferred to the parent corporation. If there is not enough cash to meet all obligations, the parent corporation will supply it by purchasing more stock in the subsidiary—like money down a rat hole.

At the same time that a sales office is closed, you must set the following marketing decision variables to 0 in the area affected. With no sales office there will be no one available to accommodate further sales in the area.

Price
Advertising
Sales Salary
Sales Commissions
Sales Office Orders

See "Leaving and Entering Market Areas" in Chapter 5.

5 <u>Opening (re-opening) a sales office</u>. To open a new sales office in an area where there is none (*i. e.* the sales office was previously closed), transfer at least one salesperson from another area and hire as many salespersons as you wish to be available next quarter when sales may begin. A new sales office will be built and executives hired to supervise construction and preparation of the office. The transferred salesperson will supervise and coordinate sales training and executive orientation. Construction of the office takes one quarter, and sales may begin immediately in the quarter following the decision to open the office by transferring one or more salespeople into the area. See "Leaving and Entering Market Areas" in Chapter 5.

Changes in Sales Force Compensation

The compensation rates for salespeople in each market area may be changed by entering the new compensation levels on the decision form. If no entries are made, default values (rates from the previous quarter) will be used.

1. <u>Salary</u>. The salary for each active Merican salesperson at the end of Year 2 amounted to $3,000 per quarter. Salary for Sereno salespersons was Ps 8971. Sales salaries may be increased or decreased. Enter the total amount of the desired salary level, in dollars or pesos per quarter, under Salespeople–Salary on the decision form.

Limits, Areas 1 to 3: 0 to 9999 (in dollars)
Limits, Sereno: 0 to 9999999 (in Pesos)

2. Commissions. Sales commissions are paid to salespeople in addition to their basic salary. Commissions in domestic areas amounted to 20 cents per unit sold at the end of Year 2. Sereno commissions were 60 centavos (Ps 0.60) per unit. Sales commissions may be increased or decreased during any quarter. Enter the new amount for the desired commission rate in number of cents per unit for Merica, or centavos per unit for Sereno, under Salespeople–Commission on the decision form.

Limits, Areas 1 to 3:   1 to 99 (cents per unit)
Limits, Sereno: 1 to 99999 (centavos per unit)

Model Number

Enter the model number to be produced during the quarter. For Year 3, Quarter 1 the only model available is Number 1 and you are producing it at Quality level 2 (see below). The latest model number developed by the research and development department, together with the applicable labor and materials costs, will be reported in the Operating Information Report each quarter.

		STANDARD COSTS PER UNIT for Next Quarter			
		Merica Area 1 $	Merica Area 2 $	Merica Area 3 $	Sereno Ps
Model 1 Quality 2	Labor Cost	2.88	2.88	2.88	8.90
Savings Level 0	Material Cost	1.23	1.23	1.23	5.72
Note: for Quality 1 add 10%. For Quality 3 subtract 10%					

Model numbers are sequential (Models 1, 2, 3, etc.). Your company's Model 2 (when it becomes available for production) will have different marketing characteristics than another company's Model 2. If a new model is available and your company wishes to put it into production, enter the new model number. Otherwise, enter the same model number that was produced in the previous quarter. If model number 4 is reported to be available, and your firm decides to introduce it, enter 4 on the decision form. Production of a new model begins immediately. Sales of the new model begin next quarter unless your firm stocks out of the old model this quarter. In that case, when all units of the old model have been sold, the new model is substituted to fill any further demand.

> **IMPORTANT NOTE**
> The demand during the first quarter of a new model's production is for the OLD model—not the new model. The new model will not officially go on sale until it has been in production for one calendar quarter to build inventories.

Maximum: Highest model number reported to be available from the R & D Department.

Minimum: Same model number as was produced last quarter. Once a new model has been placed in production, an earlier model may not be reinstated.

Limits: 1 to 12

Model/Quality	
Model	# 1
Quality	# 2

Model Quality

When a new model is introduced, its quality level must be specified. You may choose from three levels of quality:

(1) deluxe
(2) standard
(3) economy

The quality level of a model is determined when the model is introduced and may not be changed during the production run. The choice of quality level is yours. Quality level is determined by manufacturing tolerances and the quality and quantity of raw materials used. Features of the product are important, too. Deluxe quality may signify extra features that are not available in a standard quality model, and economy quality may signify fewer features than for the standard model. It is not related to whatever you may have spent on research and development in order to bring the new model to market. When introducing a new product, enter the desired quality level in the Quality space on the decision form. If you continue to produce the same model as last quarter, you must also continue the same quality level.

Limits: 1, 2 or 3
May be changed only when introducing a new model

Sales Office Orders

This is a very important decision variable which **must** be used to obtain goods for your firm's sales offices to sell. If a sales office does not place an order with your firm's headquarters, it will only be able to sell the stock it has on hand in inventory. **The product is not shipped to an area unless an order is placed by a sales office**. The only exception is for a sales office in an area which also has a producing plant. The sales office may obtain additional stock from the plant in its area if the plant still has inventory remaining after filling all of the sales orders from the other sales offices.

IMPORTANT NOTE

Customer orders refer to the actual customer demand by market intermediaries (wholesalers, large retailers, etc.) for your product in each market area. They are the orders which customers place with your sales offices for the purchase of your product. Your firm does not sell to the end consumer.

The sales office in each area must submit an order to your firm's headquarters each quarter. Your firm (by way of the BPG computer program) will then determine how many units of product are shipped and from what locations, according to a pre-approved policy. Units not sold during the quarter in which they are purchased will be placed in inventory. Inventory carried over from one quarter to the next by a sales office is stored in a public warehouse. Sales offices in an area which also has a manufacturing plant may store up to 300,000 units in the plant's warehouse facility.

Your firm has developed a set of policies to guide product allocation. The allocation priorities are as follows:

1. Goods held in inventory by a sales office **will not be shipped** to another area or country but will be held for sale in the area where they already are located.

2. Sales office orders will be filled only from your firm's current-quarter production. Shipments will be allocated to fill sales office orders **before** filling any additional customer orders. These shipments include those to **all** sales offices, both in areas with manufacturing plants and in areas without a plant. For sales offices in producing areas, "shipment" constitutes setting goods aside in the warehouse area of the plant for sale to local area customers.

3. If a plant's production exceeds the number of units in the local sales office order, the excess production will be made available for shipment to other area sales offices **after** the local sales office order has been completely filled (not customer orders). In other words, sales offices in producing areas are given priority and will have their total order filled (given sufficient production in the area), even if there is not enough production to fill orders of other sales offices.

4. If an area's production is less than the local sales office order, the shortage will be entered in a request for shipment from a plant in another area (if there is one).

5. Then, goods available for shipment from all plants are matched with unfilled sales office orders from all areas. If goods available for shipment equal or exceed orders from sales offices in non-producing areas plus unfilled orders from areas producing less than their sales office has ordered, all orders are filled. Otherwise, they are pro-rated according to the size of the orders.

6. If goods are available for shipment from more than one plant, sales office orders are filled first from non-home area plants beginning with Sereno, then from domestic non-home areas and finally from the home area.

The bottom line is that the sales office in each market area must manage its own inventory. Failing to do so may result in stockouts even though other areas have inventory left over.

Limits: 0 to 999 (in thousands of units)

	Sales Office Orders (000s)
Area 1	# 87
Area 2	# 75
Area 3	# 75
Sereno	# 75

Finance Decisions

Surplus subsidiary funds are paid to your parent firm in the form of dividends to the parent corporation for investment or reallocation to other expenditures.

As a matter of company policy, all external financing, including bank loans, will be undertaken only by the parent company. Financing needs of subsidiaries (including Sereno) will be filled by the parent company purchasing additional common stock in the wholly-owned subsidiaries. Stock purchased in the Sereno subsidiary will be paid for in dollars, which will be converted to local currency at the exchange rate in effect at the time of the purchase.

Financial strategy is discussed in Chapter 9, along with additional information about each of the finance decisions and the costs associated with them. Figure 2-3 at the end of this chapter summarizes the initial costs and expenses of *The Business Policy Game*.

Bank Loan

If your firm wishes to take out a short-term bank loan by drawing against your $2.5 million line of credit, enter the amount desired (in thousands of dollars) under Bank Loan on the decision form. Short-term loans are made for a period of one quarter, and repayment is automatic during the quarter following that in which the loan is made. The annual interest rate will be the

A 40051086   338.4

short-term rate that is available during that quarter to a company with your credit standing. Your account will automatically be charged one-fourth of the annual rate during the quarter in which the loan is outstanding.

Bank loans are secured by inventory and receivables, and may not exceed 50 percent of the value of receivables plus inventory at the end of the previous quarter. Your line of credit requires an annual cleanup, so a loan request will be denied if there has been a loan outstanding during each of the past **three** consecutive quarters.

Bank loans are available **only** to the parent company.

Maximum loan: 50 percent of receivables plus inventory
Maximum loan: 0 if a loan was outstanding in each of the previous three quarters
Limits: 0 to 2500 (in thousands of dollars)

Finance (000s)	
Bank Loan	$
Bond Issue	$
Stock Issue	#
Dividends	$
Time CDs	$ *1000*

Sale or Redemption of Bonds

1. Bond issue. Your parent company may incur additional long-term debt by issuing new bonds in amounts that are **multiples of $1,000,000**. New bond issues are callable ten-year bonds carrying the long-term rate of interest that will be available to a company with your credit rating during the quarter of issue. In the financial markets, there is some uncertainty in planning a bond issue regarding the actual rate that will be available at the time of issue. This amount isn't normally known very much in advance. In the simulation, the investment banker doesn't fix the rate until the first day of the quarter in which the bonds are to be sold.

Bonds must be secured by plant and equipment. The value of existing bonds plus new bonds to be issued may not exceed 75 percent of net fixed assets. Furthermore, your investment banker will consider an issue too risky to underwrite if the existing bonds, plus new bonds to be issued, exceed 50 percent of total equity (consisting of the previous quarter's total equity plus the proceeds of new shares to be sold simultaneously with the bonds—see "Sale of Common Stock" on the next page). Enter the amount of new bonds to be sold (in thousands of dollars) on the decision form under Bond Issue. If you decide to issue $1,000,000 worth of bonds, enter 1000 on the decision form. Do **not** include commas in your entry. Bonds can be issued only by the parent company.

Maximum issue: 50 percent of equity or 75 percent of net fixed assets, whichever is less

Limits: 0 to 9000 (in thousands of dollars), in million dollar lots

     2. <u>Bond redemption</u>. Bonds that are outstanding may be called and redeemed in amounts that are multiples of $100,000 except that there is a restriction in the bond indenture that prohibits the redemption of more than $500,000 of the face amount of bonds in any one quarter. A call premium is required, amounting to 5 percent of the face value of the repurchased bonds. If your firm has more than one bond issue outstanding, the bonds carrying the highest interest rate will be redeemed first. If bonds are to be redeemed, enter the face amount of the bonds for which redemption is desired (in thousands of dollars), **preceded by a minus sign**, under Bond Issue on the decision form. If you decide to redeem $500,000 worth of bonds, for example, enter -500 on the decision form. The 5 percent call premium will be charged automatically. Bonds can be redeemed only by the parent company.

Maximum redemption: Total amount of bonds outstanding (if less than $500,000)

Limits: -500 to 0 (in thousands of dollars) in hundred thousand dollar lots

Sale of Common Stock

     1. <u>Stock issue</u>. Your parent firm may issue new shares of common stock through an investment banker in multiples of 100,000 shares, provided the new issue will be large enough to raise at least **$1 million**. The investment banker will make a firm offer at any time of a price that will be determined by the following formula:

$$\text{Issue price} = \frac{\text{(shares outstanding)} \times \text{(latest market price)}}{\text{(shares outstanding)} + \text{(shares to be issued)}}$$

     If your firm's credit rating is 2, this is the issue price. If your firm's credit rating is 3, subtract 10 percent of the formula value from the issue price. If your credit rating is 1, add 10 percent.

     Enter the number of new shares to be issued (in thousands of shares) on the decision form under Stock Issue. If your firm decides to issue 4,000,000 shares of stock, for example, enter 4000 on the decision form. Do **not** include commas in your entry.

     External sale (or repurchase) of common stock will be undertaken only by your parent company, in thousands of dollars. Subsidiaries may issue stock only to the parent company, and only to meet financing requirements due to working capital shortages, plant construction or purchase and installation of new equipment. Sales of subsidiary stock will occur automatically when additional funds are required, and no decision entry is necessary.

Minimum issue: Enough shares to raise $1 million
Limits: 0 to 9000 (in thousands of shares) in 100,000-share blocks

2. Stock repurchase. Shares of your parent firm's common stock may be repurchased by placing a purchase order with the firm's stockbroker. The shares will be purchased at a price that is 10 percent above the market price reported at the end of the previous quarter. Stock is repurchased by entering the number of shares to be repurchased, preceded by a minus sign, in the Stock Issue section of the decision form. Repurchase must be made in multiples of 100,000 shares. If your firm decides to repurchase 500,000 shares of stock during the current quarter, for example, enter -500 on the decision form. Your corporate charter requires that there be at least 3 million shares outstanding so repurchases are limited to an amount that would leave at least 3 million shares after the repurchase. Shares may not be repurchased if the balance of the Accumulated Earnings account is not sufficient to fund the repurchase.

Maximum repurchase: to leave at least 3 million shares outstanding
Limits: -500 to 0 (in thousands of shares) in 100,000 share blocks

Dividends

Cash dividends may be paid by your parent company to external stockholders. A restrictive bond covenant, however, provides that the dividends paid in any quarter, taken together with dividends paid in the previous three quarters, may not exceed the total amount of earnings in the previous four quarters of operations. In addition, the board of directors of your company has decided that even if all bonds should be repurchased, this restriction on dividend policy would be maintained. Thus, if total earnings in the previous four quarters amounted to $200,000 and dividends already paid in the previous three quarters amounted to $190,000, the maximum dividend that could be paid in the current quarter would amount to $10,000. Enter the amount of cash dividends to be paid (in thousands of dollars) under Dividends on the decision form.   If your firm decided to declare the permissible amount of $10,000 in dividends in the above example, you would enter 10 on the decision form. Dividends may not be declared if the Accumulated Earnings account on the balance sheet has a negative balance.

Subsidiaries may declare dividends only to the parent company (these are not recorded on the decision form but paid automatically when funds are eligible to be transferred).

Maximum: Net profits earned in the last 4 quarters minus dividends paid in the last 3 quarters
Maximum: 0, if retained earnings are negative
Limits: 0 to 9999 (in thousands of dollars)

<u>Certificates of Deposit</u>

Three-month time Certificates of Deposit (CDs) may be purchased by your parent firm in multiples of one hundred thousand dollars. Purchases may be made at the beginning of any quarter. CDs mature at the beginning of the next quarter, three months later. Interest will be earned on deposits at the rate reported in the industry report for 3-month time CDs during the quarter in which they will be invested. Interest (but not principal) will be credited to your account on the last day of the quarter in which the deposit is made (and thus is available to meet that quarter's expenses), with quarterly interest calculated at one-fourth of the annual rate.

IMPORTANT NOTE

While interest is credited on the last day of the quarter that the deposit is made, the funds from the deposit itself are not available until the next day—the first day of the subsequent quarter. Thus, if your firm should need emergency cash during the quarter in which the funds are invested in CDs, the funds will not be available to meet the need.

To purchase time CDs, enter the amount of the purchase in thousands of dollars on the decision form under Time CDs. If your firm decides to purchase $400,000 worth of CDs, for example, enter 400 on the decision form. Do not include commas in your entry. Repayment of the CDs, as well as crediting your account with earned interest, will be done automatically by the bank.

Limits: 0 to 9900 (in thousands of dollars), in hundred thousand dollar lots

Production Decisions

Production planning, scheduling and costs are discussed in Chapter 7, along with additional information about each of the production decisions and their associated costs. Production capacity changes are discussed in Chapter 8. Figure 2-3 at the end of this chapter summarizes the initial costs and expenses of *The Business Policy Game*.

<u>Research and Development Expenditures</u>

Your parent firm is responsible for all research and development work. Research and development expenditures fund your R & D department which develops new models of your product. The department also is involved in adapting the latest manufacturing techniques for use in producing the new products. Enter the amount (in thousands of dollars) to be spent for R & D.

Limits: 1 to 999 (in thousands of dollars)

R&D/Training	
(home currency)	
R&D	$ 72
Trng	$ 68

Production Employee Training

Training of production employees enhances employee productivity by upgrading skills and preparing individuals for more complex job assignments. It also helps maintain current productive efficiency by sharpening ongoing production processes. Thus, training of production employees can lead to savings in unit labor costs because the employees are more productive. Savings in unit materials costs may result because of more efficient materials handling and less materials wastage.

The employee training costs are completely funded by the parent company and are paid in dollars, even though some of the training may take place in manufacturing facilities located in other domestic market areas or in Sereno.

Enter the amount to be spent (in thousands of dollars) on production training.

Limits: 1 to 999 (in thousands of dollars)

Production Scheduling

At the beginning of Year 3, a manufacturing plant with six production lines is available in your home area. No production facilities are currently available in the other areas. However, a plant may be built in any other area using the area's working capital and additional funding, if required, from the parent company. There are no restrictions on foreign investment of firms producing low cost durable products in Sereno.

On each quarterly decision form, all available production lines in each plant and for each shift must either be scheduled for production, idled or deactivated. See Chapter 7 for certain restrictions on production scheduling and temporary layoffs.

1. Schedule production lines and hours. Production lines to be scheduled for first-shift operation should be entered on the decision form for the area in which they are located. Enter the number of production lines that are to be producing (not more than the maximum available) and the number of hours that are to be scheduled per week (from 40 to 48). Make sure your entry is for the area or areas in which you have a plant. The decision-entry program will not accept an entry for an area where no production lines are available.

IMPORTANT NOTE

If new lines are desired, an entry **must** be made under New Lines one quarter before production may be scheduled. See paragraph 1 under "Investment in Production Facilities and Equipment" below.

Limits: Lines: 0 to maximum number of lines available
          Hours   0, 40 to 48

Note: Lines scheduled + lines idled + lines deactivated must be equal to the number of lines available.

2. <u>Second shift</u>. Production on a second-shift operation is possible only in a firm's home-area plant (see Chapter 7). Enter the number of production lines that will be producing on the second shift and the number of hours that are to be scheduled per week (see paragraph 1on the previous page).

Limits, Lines: 0 to maximum number of lines available in home area

Note: Lines scheduled + lines idled + lines deactivated must be equal to the number of lines available.

Limits, Hours: 0, 40 to 48

	Sales Office Orders	Production Schedule	
	(000s)	Lines	Hours
Area 1	# 87	# 6	# 40
Area 2	# 75	#	#
Area 3	# 75	#	#
Sereno	# 75	#	#
2nd Shift		#	#

> **IMPORTANT NOTE**
> Second-shift lines are not available and may not be sched-
> uled until workers for the shift have been trained according
> to paragraph 2 under "Investment in Production Facilities
> and Equipment" below. An entry **must** be made under New
> Lines in the Construction section of the form one quarter
> before second-shift lines may be scheduled for production.

Capacity Adjustment.

1. Temporary Layoff (for one quarter only). Production lines that are available but not scheduled for production, and have not been deactivated, must be idled by laying off employees. Enter the number of lines which you plan to idle through layoffs on the decision form under Capacity Adjustment–Layoff. Be sure that all lines (both first-shift lines and second-shift lines) are accounted for. If you idle a first-shift line, a corresponding second-shift line must be idled or deactivated unless there remain at least as many first-shift lines as second-shift lines. A second-shift line may not continue operating unless there is a corresponding line on the first shift. Check to be sure that your entry is for the area in which you want to idle lines.

Limits: 0 to maximum number of lines available

Note: Lines scheduled + lines idled + lines deactivated must be equal to the number of lines available.

2. Deactivate first-shift lines. Any line that is available for production may be deactivated and removed from production until such time as you choose to reactivate the line. Enter the number of lines that you desire to deactivate in the appropriate area on the decision form under Capacity Adjustment–Deactivate. Deactivated lines may not be scheduled for production until they have been reactivated (see paragraph 4 on the next page).

Limits: 0 to the number of lines available for production

Note: Lines scheduled + lines idled + lines deactivated must be equal to the number of lines available.

3. Deactivate second shift. Production lines available for second-shift production may be deactivated by entering the number of lines you desire to deactivate under the Capacity Adjustment–Deactivate column for the 2nd Shift area on the decision form. Second-shift-lines must be deactivated if the corresponding lines on the first shift are deactivated.

Limits: 0 to number of second-shift lines available

Note: Lines scheduled + lines idled + lines deactivated must be equal to the number of lines available.

	Sales Office Orders	Production Schedule		Capacity Adjustment		
	(000s)	Lines	Hours	Layoff	Deac-tivate	Reac-tivate
Area 1	# 87	# 6	# 40	#	#	#
Area 2	# 75	#	#	#	#	#
Area 3	# 75	#	#	#	#	#
Sereno	# 75	#	#	#	#	#
2nd Shift		#	#	#	#	#

4. Reactivate deactivated lines. Production lines that have been previously deactivated may be reactivated and made available for production. In order to reactivate a second-shift line a first-shift line must be available or in the process of being reactivated. Both first and second-shift lines may be reactivated at the same time. The number of lines available for reactivation, if any, are shown in the Production Capacity Status section of your Operating Information Report.

PRODUCTION CAPACITY STATUS				
	Merica Area 1	Merica Area 2	Merica Area 3	Sereno
Production Lines Currently Producing	6	0	0	0
Space Available for New Lines	2	0	0	0
Lines Available for Reactivation	2	0	0	0
Second-Shift Lines for Reactivation	2	0	0	0

Reactivation requires one quarter of preparation before a line may be scheduled for production. Enter the number of lines to be reactivated under the appropriate area on the decision form. Lines may not be scheduled for production until the following quarter.

Limits: 0 to number of lines previously deactivated

Note: A second-shift line must be supported by a first-shift line. You may not reactivate a second-shift line unless you have a supporting first-shift line either available, being built or reactivated.

Investment in Production Facilities and Equipment

Investment in new facilities or equipment may take the form of construction of new lines in existing plants, training workers for second-shift operation, constructing a new addition to an existing plant or constructing a new plant. For details on these alternatives, see Chapter 8.

1. <u>New First-Shift Lines</u>. Plant space that is available for new line construction is reported in the Production Capacity Status section of your Operating Information Report.

```
                                    PRODUCTION CAPACITY STATUS

                                    Merica    Merica    Merica
                                    Area 1    Area 2    Area 3    Sereno
Production Lines Currently Producing   6         0         0         0
Space Available for New Lines          2         0         0         0
```

Construction and preparation of new lines requires one quarter before the lines become available for production. In Year 3, Quarter 1, space is available to add as many as two new lines in the existing home area plant. If a new addition or a new plant is under construction, the construction of new production lines may be undertaken as early as one quarter before completion of the new plant capacity (see paragraphs 3 and 4, below). In this way, production lines may be made available for production as soon as the new addition or new plant is completed.

Enter the number of new lines to be added in the area where a plant with additional capacity is located. After the construction has begun, no further entry is necessary (that is, enter 0 in subsequent quarters) unless you want to build additional lines. Positive entries in subsequent quarters will result in starting **additional** new lines at that time (if space is available). When ready for production, and not before, new lines must be scheduled for production, idled or deactivated.

Limits: 0 to space available

	Sales Office Orders (000s)	Construction		
		New Lines	New Add'n	New Plant
Area 1	# 87	#	#	#
Area 2	# 75	#	#	#
Area 3	# 75	#	#	#
Sereno	# 75	#	#	#
2nd Shift		#	← ← ← ←	

2. <u>New Second-Shift Lines</u>. In a **home area plant**, second-shift operations can be added to producing first-shift lines. You may also add second-shift lines at the time you build first-shift lines. The key is that there must always be a first-shift line to support each second-shift line. To add second-shift lines, enter the number of second-shift lines you wish to add on the decision form in the New Lines column under 2nd Shift. The line(s) will be available for production during the **next** quarter.

Limits: 0 to number of 1st-shift lines operating in home area

3. New Additions. Additions may be constructed by adding new structures to existing plants. Capacity may be added in units of **two** production lines per addition unless the maximum plant size of twelve lines already has been reached. Two quarters are required to construct an addition. An addition may be added to a plant under construction if it is not started prior to the last 2 quarters of plant construction. To begin construction, enter 2, the number of lines of capacity, under New Add'n on the decision form in the area in which you wish to construct the new lines.

After construction has begun, no further entries are necessary (that is, enter 0 in subsequent quarters unless space is available within the 12-line maximum and you wish to begin construction of another addition). If you wish, you may begin construction of production lines (paragraph 1, above) so that the lines will be available for production when the new addition is completed. New line construction may be started as early as one quarter after construction of the new addition is begun.

Limits: 0 or 2 lines (to a maximum of 12 lines in a plant)

4. New Plant. To begin construction of a new plant, enter the number of lines of capacity that are desired (2, 4, 6, 8 or 10) in the area in which the new plant is to be located. Only one plant per company is permitted in each of the four market areas. It takes three quarters to complete the construction of a new plant. After construction has begun, no further entry is required except to begin construction of new lines (see paragraph 1 on the previous page) prior to the start of production. New production lines may be started during the third quarter of plant construction.

Limits: 0 in home area; 0, 2, 4, 6, 8, 10 lines in other areas
New plants may only be built in areas where there is no existing plant.

5. Plant Closing. To close a plant in an area, enter -1 under new plant construction for the area. See Closing a Plant in Chapter 8 for details on plant closing. This is an important decision and should be considered carefully before it is implemented. If you enter -1 to close a plant, you also must deactivate all available production lines at the same time. The plant and production equipment then will be sold.

Limits: 0 or -1, -1 closes the plant in the area

Once a plant is closed, it will be sold and may not be reopened! A new plant must be built in order to produce again in the same area.

Entering Decisions & Printing Reports

You may be asked to use a computer to enter your decisions directly, saving them on a floppy disk or on a hard disk (which may be part of a PC network), and to print your firm's reports. These options are explained in Appendix A, "Installing and Using the BPG Computer Program."

Your decision set will be stored in a file on the disk and saved for use when the simulation program is run by the administrator. If your decision set is stored on a floppy disk, you will need to submit your disk to the simulation administrator prior to the time the simulation is to be run.

Before entering your decision on the computer, the following tasks should be performed:

1. Complete the decision form. The decision form always should be completed before entering decisions on the computer. The decision form helps to organize your firm's decision set in the order in which the values will be entered. The form centralizes the decision variables in one place, thus easing the chore of checking for decision completeness. The form also serves as the original record of your team's decision. It is recommended that you turn in a copy of your decision form (if you use floppy disks) in case the computer has trouble reading your disk.

2. Enter and save the decision file. Your firm's decision set will be stored on magnetic disk. The simulation administrator will tell you the type of computer system, the type of disk you will use (floppy or hard) and how to access the disk. Appendix A contains information about installing and running the programs on the Player's Program Disk. If you are using an IBM or compatible computer system, read the first section, titled "IBM and Compatible Users." If you are using a Macintosh computer system, skip to the second section labeled "Macintosh Users."

Summary

Steps for entering decisions and printing output.

1. Complete Decision Form

2. Run BPG computer program

3a. Print Reports   3b. Enter New Decisions   3c. Change Decisions

4. Quit

FIGURE 2-2
QUICK-REFERENCE GUIDE
DECISION-VARIABLE DEFINITIONS AND LIMITS

PRICE Amount to be charged for your product Maximum change, Areas 1 to 3: 30 percent Maximum change, Sereno: 40 percent Limits, Areas 1 to 3: 1.00 to 99.99 (dollars and cents) Limits, Sereno: 1 to 99999 (pesos) If there is no sales office, price must be 0	**ADVERTISING** Amount to be spent for advertising in each marketing area Limits, Areas 1 to 3: 0 to 999 (thousands of dollars) Limits, Sereno: 0 to 9999999 (thousands of pesos)
HIRE NEW SALESPEOPLE Number of new salespeople to be hired. Those hired now will be in training for one quarter, then become active salespeople in the following quarter. Limits: 0 to 99	**TRANSFER OR DISCHARGE SALESPEOPLE** Number to be transferred or discharged Negative values: discharge or transfer out. Positive values: transfer in. A negative balance will be discharged. Maximum: Number available minus 1 Limits: -99 to 99
CLOSING A SALES OFFICE Transfer **out** or discharge of **all** salespeople will cause the sales office in that area to be closed and executives discharged. Maximum negative entry: Number of active salespeople Limits: -99 to 0	**OPENING (REOPENING) A SALES OFFICE** Transfer **in** of one or more salespeople to an area where there is no sales office will cause an office to be built and executives to be hired. Limits: 0 to 99
COMMISSION Commission per unit to be paid to each sales person Limits, Areas 1 to 3: 1 to 99 (cents per unit) Limits, Sereno: 1 to 99999 (centavos per unit) If there is no sales office in an area, the value must be 0.	**SALARY** Quarterly salary to be paid to each salesperson Limits, Areas 1 to 3: 1 to 9999 (dollars) Limits, Sereno: 1 to 9999999 (pesos) If there is no sales office in an area, the value must be 0.
BANK LOAN Short-term loan to parent company, for one quarter. Maximum: 50% of consolidated receivables plus inventory Maximum: 0, if loan outstanding in each of the last 3 quarters. Limits: 0 to 2500 (in thousands of dollars)	**BOND ISSUE** Sold in million-dollar lots by parent company Positive numbers: sell new 10-year bonds Maximum: the lesser of 50% of equity or 75% of net fixed assets Limits: 0 to 9000 (in thousands of dollars)
BOND REPURCHASE Redeem outstanding bonds in lots of $100,000 Negative numbers: amount of bonds to repurchase. Limits: -500 to 0 (in thousands of dollars)	**STOCK ISSUE** Sold in 100,000-share lots by parent company Positive numbers: Number of common shares to be issued, Minimum issue: enough shares to total $1,000,000 Limits: 0 to 9000 (in thousands of shares)
STOCK REPURCHASE Repurchased in lots of 100,000 shares Negative numbers: Number of shares to repurchase Maximum repurchase: to leave at least 3 million shares with positive accumulated retained earnings. Limits: -500 to 0 (in thousands of shares)	**DIVIDENDS** Declared and paid by parent company Amount to pay external shareholders from profits Maximum: Consolidated net income in last 4 quarters, minus dividends paid in last 3 quarters. Limits: 0 to 9999 (in thousands of dollars)
TIME CERTIFICATES OF DEPOSIT (CDs) Short-term 3-month investments by parent company, purchased in $100,000 lots. Limits: 0 to 9900 (in thousands of dollars)	**PRODUCT RESEARCH & DEVELOPMENT** Amount for parent company to spend on developing new models Limits: 1 to 999 (in thousands of dollars)

(Continued on next page)

FIGURE 2-2 (Continued)
QUICK-REFERENCE GUIDE
DECISION-VARIABLE DEFINITIONS AND LIMITS

TRAINING OF EXISTING PRODUCTION EMPLOYEES Amount for parent company to spend on training of existing production employees (to reduce production costs). Limits: 1 to 999 (in thousands of dollars)	**MODEL NUMBER** For production this quarter. Goes on sale next quarter. Minimum: Same model number as last quarter Maximum: Highest number reported to be available Limits: 1 to 12
QUALITY (of product) May be changed only on introduction of a new model. Enter 1 for deluxe quality Enter 2 for standard quality Enter 3 for economy quality	**SALES OFFICE ORDERS** Number of units to be shipped to each sales office. Units will be held there for resale. Unsold units will be placed in inventory. Limits: 0 to 999 (in thousands of units)
SCHEDULING PRODUCTION LINES (First Shift) Number of lines scheduled for production. Any lines not scheduled must be Idled or deactivated. New lines must be purchased and installed one quarter before they may be scheduled. Limits: 0 to number of lines available	**SCHEDULING PRODUCTION HOURS** (First Shift) Number of hours to schedule production per week. Number of lines must also be scheduled. Limits: 0, 40 to 48 (hours)
SECOND-SHIFT LINES (Home area plant only) Number of lines scheduled for second shift First-shift lines also must be scheduled. New lines must be prepared one quarter before production may be scheduled. Limits: 0 to number of first-shift lines scheduled for production.	**SECOND-SHIFT HOURS** (Home area plant only) Number of hours scheduled per week Number of lines must also be scheduled. Limits: 0, 40 to 48
TEMPORARY LAYOFF–IDLED (one quarter only) Number of lines to shut down for temporary layoff of employees . Lines subject to temporary layoff are automatically available for production one quarter later. Limits: 0 to number of lines available for production Lines that are available for production but not scheduled must be Idled(temporary layoff) or deactivated.	**DEACTIVATE PRODUCTION LINES** (Permanent Layoff) Number of lines to be deactivated (and not available for production until reactivated). If a plant is closed all lines must be deactivated, and none will be available for reactivation later. Limits: 0 to number of lines available Lines not scheduled for production must be Idled or deactivated.
REACTIVATE PRODUCTION LINES Number of previously deactivated 1st or 2nd-shift lines to be prepared for production next quarter. 1st-shift lines must be available in order to reactivate 2nd-shift lines. 1st and 2nd-shift lines may be reactivated at the same time. Limits: 0 to number of previously deactivated lines	**NEW PRODUCTION LINES** Number of new lines to be purchased and installed, ready to begin production the following quarter 1st-shift lines must be available to install new 2nd-shift lines. Limits (1st shift): 0 to space reported as available Limits (2nd shift): 0 to number of 1st-shift lines
NEW ADDITION Number of lines capacity to add to the plant Construction takes 2 quarters. This is an addition to the building in which new lines may be installed. Only one new 2-line addition may be started in any quarter, but another could be started the following quarter so that two additions are under construction at the same time. New lines must be installed separately during the last quarter of construction (or later). Limits: 0 or 2 (to a maximum capacity of 12 lines)	**NEW PLANT** Number of lines capacity for a new plant to be constructed May only be built in areas where there is no existing plant. This is a new building in which production lines may be installed during the last quarter of construction (or later). New lines must be installed separately. New additions may be built later, to a maximum capacity of 12 lines in any area. An entry of -1 causes the plant to be closed and sold for 90% of book value. All lines must then be deactivated at the same time. No further production in such a plant is possible. Limits: -1 (to close plant) 0, 2, 4, 6, 8 or 10 (number of lines capacity)

FIGURE 2-3
SUMMARY OF *THE BUSINESS POLICY GAME* COSTS — Year 3, Quarter 1
(Costs change over time because of inflation and changes made by management.)

Marketing Expenses

Salespeople	Salaries and commissions:	$3,000 or Ps 8971 per quarter + 20 cents or 60 centavos per unit
	Training:	$10,000 or Ps 36,000 per trainee
	Moving expense:	$5,000 or Ps 30,000 per salesperson transferred
	Severance expense:	$5,000 or Ps 30,000 per salesperson fired

Inventory storage: In-plant warehouse: 10 cents or Ps 0.60 per unit up to 300,000 units

                       Public warehouse: 30 cents or Ps 1.80 per unit

Transportation Expense:

Shipments from:	To:	Cost per unit in dollars convert to pesos at current rates
Sales office or plant	Customer in same area	$0.10
Plant (Merica)	Sales office in another Merica area	$0.60
Plant (Merica)	Sereno sales office	$0.90
Plant (Sereno)	Merica sales office	$0.90

General Selling Expense: Each Merica area: $37,500 + $4,000 x number of salespeople + $0.20 x number of units sold

                                 Sereno: Ps 225,000 + Ps 24,000 x number of salespeople + Ps 1.20 x number of units sold

Production Costs

Labor costs/line for Model 1, Quality 2 (other models as reported):

				Standard costs/unit	
Straight time:	$288 or Ps 890 per hour for Model 1		Labor	$2.88	Ps 8.90
Second shift:	110% of straight time		Materials	1.23	5.72
Overtime:	150% of straight time (200% in Sereno)		Maintenance	0.25	1.50
			Total (Qual 2)	$4.36	Ps 16.12
Maintenance:	$25 or Ps 150 per hour per line		(Qual 1) + 10%		
			(Qual 3) − 10%		

Layoff standby cost: $52,000 or Ps 312,000 per quarter per line

Deactivation cost: $100,000 or Ps 600,000 per line

Reactivation cost: $50,000 or Ps 300,000 per line

Construction Costs:

     New 2nd Shift: $100,000 per line worker training (home area only)

     New line: $500,000 or Ps 3,000,000 per line + Worker training: $100,000 or Ps 600,000 per line

     New addition to plant: $900,000 or Ps 5,400,000 per 2-line addition

New plant construction:	2 lines capacity	$1,200,000 or Ps 7,200,000
	4 lines capacity	$1,900,000 or Ps 11,400,000
	6 lines capacity:	$2,600,000 or Ps 15,600,000
	8 lines capacity:	$3,300,000 or Ps 19,800,000
	10 lines capacity	$4,000,000 or Ps 24,000,000

Finance Expenses

Bank loan: Interest at the short-term interest rate during the quarter the loan is issued

Bonds: Existing bonds, at 10% annual interest, new bonds at long term interest rate in quarter of issue

       Interest paid quarterly. Bonds are callable at a 5 percent call premium

Common stock: Issue price determined by formula in text

Income tax: 39% of net income; paid quarterly

Value Added Tax in Sereno: 10% of net sales to customers, paid quarterly

Other Expenses

Executives' salaries: $50,000 or Ps 300,000 per manufacturing plant, $25,000 or Ps 150,000 per sales office, each quarter

Plant depreciation: $26,000 per quarter (existing plant)

       Straight-line basis over 31.5 years, no salvage value (0.7937% per quarter)

Equipment depreciation: $107,000 in Year 2, Quarter 4 (existing equipment)

       Straight-line basis over 7 years, no salvage value (3.5714% per quarter)

CHAPTER 3

THE BUSINESS ENVIRONMENT

As *The Business Policy Game* begins, you and your fellow team members are assuming the management of a simulated corporation that has been in existence for a number of years. Your firm's principal business activities are the production and distribution of an unnamed product that has the general marketing characteristics of a consumer durable good. The product's characteristics represent a composite of the characteristics of a number of products in the "business world" and thus cannot be accurately described by any unique existing product. The same product type is also manufactured and sold by other firms in direct competition with your firm. However, these products are differentiated in the minds of consumers.

The firms in your industry have surprisingly similar histories during past years. An examination of the historical data and financial statements presented in Appendix C will highlight the fact that there has been little, if any, difference among the operations of the various companies in your industry. Each company has maintained substantially the same level of sales; production levels for each company have been about the same; the pattern of financing has been similar; and profits have differed by a relatively small amount. One almost could guess that the various companies have been operating under the same management, unless collusion were present. This is an unlikely assumption in view of the antitrust laws that exist in our simulated world.

As the simulation develops, you may be sure that the different operating strategies that will be developed by your firm and its competitors will cause a divergence among the production, sales, financing, and profit performance of the various competing companies. Furthermore, as you and your competitors place new models on the market, you will find that there is a difference between the way your product is received by the market and the way in which your competitors' products are received. Consumers will demonstrate brand preference. You may prefer to think of the differences as akin to the differences between a new IBM and a new Compaq computer or perhaps even an Apple Macintosh.

The firms in your industry are conducting business in two simulated environments, Merica and Sereno. Merica is a North America country and Sereno is a Latin America country. A short background discussion of each follows.

Merica

Merica is located on the North American continent in the Western Hemisphere. Its land area stretches approximately 9.4 million square kilometers. Nearly every type of climate can be found in Merica from tropical to polar. Deserts and major mountain ranges are found in the West. While the West is rather arid, with the exception of the Northwest, the East and most of the Midwest receives sufficient rainfall to support farming. Farming in the west generally requires irrigation. As you would expect, temperatures vary widely over the country.

Merica's population is approaching 260 million people. More than half of the people live in the South and West. Approximately twenty-five percent live in the Midwest and the remainder live in the Northeast. More than three quarters of the population live in cities, towns and suburbs. The capital city of Columbia is located on the east coast. The growth in population is low with approximately 25 percent of the growth occurring through immigration.

Merica is a leading industrialized country. Its work force is highly skilled and mobile. The citizens generally enjoy a high standard of living. Median family income is over $35,000 per year, and professional and middle-management salaries begin around $30,000 and climb rapidly upward. Eighty-nine percent of the households own a motor vehicle.

The common language in Merica is English. Many other languages are spoken in various ethnic areas, but English is the common language of communication. English dialects vary in different parts of the country, but each is generally understood throughout the country. Primary and secondary education are provided free of charge by local school districts within each state. Most states require children to attend school until they reach their 16th birthday. Nearly half of the graduates of high schools enroll in college. Approximately 25 percent of the population is college educated.

Exporting

Merica offers tax and nontax incentives for the export of goods produced in the country. Unfortunately, your firm is not able to take advantage of tax incentives due to the special nature of its products. Nontax benefits of interest to exporters include special financing set up through export-import banks, credit programs and financing assistance programs for foreign buyers and promotion of export programs both within Merica and in foreign markets.

Importing

Consumer durables imported to Merica are subject to duty based upon their classification in the country's import tariff schedules. The duty rate depends upon the country of origin and the type of product, as well as numerous other factors. Certain countries are given preferential rates due to trade agreements. Most products are subject to most-favored-nation or general rates of duty. However, imports from some countries are subjected to the highest rates when normal trading relations have not been developed.

A product's tariff classification is based primarily upon the product's description. The product's value is based upon the transaction value which includes the actual sales price plus certain commissions and other expenses. Transaction values may be documented using commercial invoices, country of origin certificates, bills of lading and foreign assembly declarations.

According to tariff agreements, the duty rate for your company's durable good is 0 percent. However, you will have to pay a user fee of 0.19 percent which is charged on all imports. If you ship by water, your goods will be subject to a 0.125 percent harbor maintenance fee.

When your imported goods arrive in Merica, you or your agent must file the required documents with the customs service. The documents include a bill of lading, airway bill or carrier's certificate, a commercial invoice showing the value of the shipment, an entry manifest and a packing list.

Local representation is not required, but licensed customs consultants are readily available through accounting firms and customs brokers. Sales agents may also be helpful in meeting the administrative requirements of the import process. Establishing a sales subsidiary causes no problems from a Merica customs standpoint. However, numerous other Merica government agencies should be consulted prior to establishing a sales subsidiary.

Your staff will have prepared the appropriate documents and cleared them with the Customs Service prior to the importation of goods. The processing and importing fees are not shown separately on your accounting reports, but you can safely assume they have been paid and included with other costs of purchase.

Investing

Merica has no restrictions on foreign ownership of firms producing low cost consumer durables. There are no limits imposed on monetary exchange or the entry of foreign funds into the country. Both capital and profits may be repatriated as desired. Foreign firms are required to meet the same requirements as domestic firms when obtaining loans or funds from the capital markets. The federal government holds a neutral policy with respect to encouraging foreign investment.

State and local governments follow quite a different course. They offer extensive incentives to attract foreign-owned plants to their area. Incentives are also provided for joint ventures and licensing arrangements with foreign investors. Their objective is to create jobs, reduce unemployment and welfare costs and to enlarge the tax base. Incentives are in the form of grants, such as tax breaks, direct loans and loan guarantees. Additional help may be provided in the form of recruiting and training services, plant location assistance, etc.

The country has a well-educated, skilled work force. Workers tend to be highly paid including substantial fringe benefits. The benefits are not required by law, but they are included in most union contracts and are generally provided in varying degrees by all employers. The benefits normally include health insurance, life insurance, sick pay and vacation time. Profit sharing and pension plans are commonly offered. Fringe benefits account for approximately 28 percent of total compensation. A 40-hour work week is common with overtime paid to industrial employees for time over 40 hours. Ten paid holidays normally are observed in all parts of the country. Two weeks of paid vacation are commonly provided for new employees with vacation time increasing with employee tenure to a maximum of four or six weeks. It is unlawful to discriminate on the basis of age, sex, religion, veteran status, handicap, national origin or race.

A social security program provides limited health and pension benefits for people aged 65 and over. Both employees and employers contribute 8 percent of the employee's pay to the program. An unemployment tax of 7 percent on the first $7,000 of wages is also paid by the employer. In addition, employers contribute to state workers' compensation funds which provide benefits when employees are injured, contract a disease or die as a result of their employment. The requirements and contribution amounts differ by state. Labor costs represent a significant portion of total production costs in Merica. As a percentage, labor costs are among the highest in the industrialized world.

Federal taxes in Merica currently amount to 39 percent of corporate income. There is no value added tax in Merica nor is there a capital tax on corporations. Other taxes which are assumed by the simulation to be included in the stated level of costs include:

> Import and export taxes
> Payroll taxes, principally social security
> State and local taxes
> Taxes on real property

Sereno

Sereno is a large country in Latin America. It covers approximately 1,800,000 square kilometers, almost one-fourth the size of Merica. The greater part of the country is on a high plateau. Almost half of the country is arid or semiarid. Rain generally falls between May and October with very little rain being received during the rest of the year. Temperatures are generally moderate most of the year. However, there are mountainous regions in the country which have quite different climates.

Sereno's population of approximately 80 million people is growing at the rate of 2.1 percent per year, one of the highest rates in the world. There has been a large shift in the population from rural to urban areas since 1940. Today more than 60 percent of the population lives in urban areas. The largest city is the capital city of San Jose which is located at 5,500 feet above sea level.

The distribution of wealth within the country is very uneven. At the higher income levels, which include upper and middle management, the standard of living is comparable to that found in industrialized countries. However, only about 20 percent of the population is wealthy enough to afford this type of lifestyle. Earnings for office, skilled, semiskilled and unskilled workers are substantially below those in industrialized countries. It should be noted that wages are rising, and these latter groups are becoming significant markets for low cost durable goods. They tend to be young and many have young families. One of the country's major problems is to find jobs for members of these groups which represent a large share of the rapidly increasing population.

A recent article in *Fortune* argues that people in developing countries tend to buy more durable goods than they would with the same income in a developed country. Products mentioned included TVs, refrigerators, etc. Thus you might estimate that between 50 to 75 percent of the population of Sereno would be financially able to purchase your product.

The national language of Sereno is Spanish. Education is provided free through six years of primary school and three years of secondary school. The government funds public universities, which provide an additional three years of pre-college education through preparatory schools. While all students have a right to attend school, many in the rural areas are not able to attend school on a regular basis. In recent decades, a major effort has been made to reduce illiteracy.

Exporting

Both tax and nontax benefits are provided to encourage exports of locally produced goods from Sereno. Firms exporting from Sereno can claim a value added tax credit for all export sales. Nontax benefits include shipments being given top priority in customs clearance and special promotional assistance in Sereno and in foreign markets. An import drawback provision provides for a refund of import duties paid on imported merchandise that is later incorporated into exported goods.

Importing

Sereno has no import restrictions on low-cost consumer durable goods. The country uses the Harmonized System for Merchandise Classification and Codification which makes classification of goods compatible with that of most of its trading partners. Merchandise is valued at its commercial invoice price in determining its dutiable value. Duties range from 0 to 20 percent, with most duties running between 0 to 10%. The duty rate for your company's durable goods is 0 percent.

Industry protectionism is gradually being phased out since Sereno joined GATT several years ago. Most imports of tangible items are subject to a value added tax at the same rate that applies to domestic sales. The documents required to import goods include the import declaration completed by a customs broker or forwarding agent, a detailed packing list and a commercial invoice showing all charges made by the seller in connection with the sale. The invoices must be stamped by the Sereno consul in the country from which the shipment is made. A customs services processing fee is payable with the import declaration.

Your staff will have prepared the appropriate documents and obtained consular approval for importing goods to Sereno. The customs service processing fees are not stated separately in your financial reports, but you can assume that they will have been taken care of and included with other costs of purchase.

Delivery of goods made to a customer within Sereno is subject to income and value added taxes. A local agent must be used to withdraw merchandise from a Sereno customhouse.

Investing

Sereno allows up to 100 percent foreign ownership of consumer durable manufacturers. Foreign investment normally is made by establishing a Sereno corporation. Prior authorization by the Ministry of Foreign Affairs is required. The formation of a corporation with minority foreign ownership usually requires about three or four weeks. A majority ownership takes about twice as long. The cost is relatively minor. A notarized deed must be obtained which represents a combined charter and bylaws.

A Sereno subsidiary may pay dividends to its parent equal to the entire amount of current-quarter profits, with the following restrictions:

1. Twenty percent of the profits must be set aside in an equity reserve (part of retained earnings) until the reserve has accumulated to an amount at least equal to 50 percent of capital stock.

2. Dividends may only be paid if, after payment, there will be a minimum cash balance of one million pesos (held in Sereno banks).

The availability of local financing is very limited. It also is very expensive. Short-term commercial credit, when available, commands interest rates of approximately 30 to 40 percent per annum. There are no restrictions on repatriation of capital. However, foreign currency must be obtained in foreign currency markets. Sereno is not a low-tax country, and it offers no special tax treatment to foreign investors.

Skilled and managerial personnel are generally in short supply. However, trainable unskilled and semiskilled workers are readily available. Labor costs are low compared to developed countries, although they are rising. Labor unions are becoming widespread. Sereno labor law requires that all employers provide their employees with a minimum of training.

Minimum wages are established for separate regions of the country. The minimums are raised each calendar quarter to mirror closely the rate of inflation. The maximum work week is six eight-hour days for a total of 48 hours, although a 44 or even a 40 hour work week is not uncommon, particularly in offices. Double time must be paid for overtime (more than 40 hours per week). Triple pay is required for work on any of the seven legal holidays.

The social security program includes current medical expenses, workmen's compensation and old age and disability pensions, which cost employers from 14.6 to 20.9% of their employee's pay. In addition, a payroll tax of 5% is levied to cover a national low-cost housing program. Labor contracts often provide for additional benefits. Seniority premiums are paid to all workers who are fired, die or retire with at least 15 years of service. Under the Sereno constitution, it is unlawful to discriminate against an individual on the basis of race, religion or sex.

Employers must provide transportation for employees when a plant is located outside of an area served by reasonable public transportation. Many firms have established company-supported cafeterias which offer meals at reduced prices. Total fringe benefits, including benefits mandated by labor law, cost employers between 70 and 100 percent of base wages.

Taxes that must be paid in Sereno include:

> Taxes on income—the general corporate rate is 39 percent of net income
> Value added taxes—10 percent of net sales

Value added taxes are assessed against total sales. Since your company imports all of its merchandise or manufactures it from imported raw materials, there are no deductions. The amount of the tax is deductible for purposes of income tax assessment in Sereno. Income and value added taxes are calculated and reported separately in simulation reports. In addition, other taxes are assumed by the simulation model to be included in the stated level of costs:

> Import & export taxes
> Payroll taxes, principally social security
> Local taxes
> Taxes on real property
> Taxes on salaries

Market information in Sereno is neither as abundant or as readily available as in industrialized countries.

Economic Environment

The firms in your industry are conducting business in two simulated environments, Merica and Sereno. Merica represents a developed country, and Sereno represents a developing country. One of the environments is likely to be similar to the economy of your country during recent years. Because of this similarity, a knowledge of the characteristics of your nation's economy will enable your firm to make certain inferences about one of the simulated economic environments. Your country's gross domestic product (GDP) for example, has generally increased over time. However, unless your country is highly unusual, this growth has not been constant over time as indicated by the historical record. The GDP index, as well as other economic time-series indexes, has fluctuated considerably.

The current-dollar and current-peso GDP indexes for *The Business Policy Game* are reported in the Quarterly Industry Report, **unadjusted** for inflation. In addition, a four-quarter forecast of real GDP, adjusted for changes in the Consumer Price Index in each country, is purchased every three months by your marketing department and reported each quarter in the Quarterly Industry Report. A four-quarter forecast of expected exchange rates is included in the forecast.

```
                    REAL GROSS DOMESTIC PRODUCT FORECAST
          Actual Values, Last 4 Quarters    Forecast Values, Next 4 Quarters
          Qtr  5  Qtr  6  Qtr  7  Qtr  8    Qtr  9  Qtr 10   Qtr 11   Qtr 12

Merica  102.17  102.66  100.93   99.90      99.57   97.94    98.79    94.46
Sereno   94.87   97.05   98.20  100.00     104.76  107.08   109.14   115.87
---------------------------------------------------------------------------
                         EXCHANGE RATE FORECAST

Sereno    5.99    5.97    5.97    6.00       6.09    6.02     6.08     6.18
```

As you might expect, the quality of the forecast is best for the quarter immediately ahead, with a wider range of possible values as time becomes more distant. These are, in fact, excellent forecasts and may be relied upon as the best data available at the time.

Other economic data also are included in *The Business Policy Game* reports. The impact of price level changes is shown by the Consumer Price Index (CPI), also reported for each country quarterly. The Stock Market Index, reported only for Merica, may be considered as roughly comparable to the Dow Jones Industrial Average, the Tokyo Stock Exchange Nikkei 225 average, the Frankfurt Stock Exchange FAZ index or the Sydney Stock Exchange All Ordinaries index. Interest rates in the simulation will rise and fall in much the same manner as rates in developed countries during the last several years. You will find that knowledge of these economic times series data is helpful as you forecast future levels of simulated economic activity. Suggestions for using techniques to forecast future economic activity are found in Chapter 6.

```
                      FINANCIAL MARKET DATA
                     Merica  Sereno  |          ---Credit Rating---
GDP Index (Nominal)   99.90  100.00  | Interest Rates:  No. 1  No. 2  No. 3
Consumer Price Index 100.00  100.00  |   Long-Term       8.40   9.10  10.60
Stock Market Index   100.00          |   Short-Term     11.00  11.20  12.30
3-Month Time CD Rate   9.50          |
```

Inflation Adjustments

All prices that your firm must pay for goods and services are subject to inflation. Inflation varies over time and is reported via the CPI for each country. It is important to note that inflation rates vary by country. Most costs and expenses shown in this manual are those facing your firm during Year 3, Quarter 1 as you begin the competition. As the competition continues, you will need to estimate changes in costs during subsequent quarters as price levels change.

To calculate the cost in any subsequent quarter, multiply the cost given for Year 3, Quarter 1 by an inflation multiplier. After you have received the reports for the quarter previous to the one for which you are estimating costs, divide the country's CPI in that quarter by the CPI in the same country for Year 2, Quarter 4 (or estimate the previous quarter's CPI if the reports are not available yet). The resulting value is the inflation multiplier to use. Prices are always adjusted using the previous quarter's inflation rate as we do not know next quarter's inflation rate until the quarter is over.

For example, the Year 3, Quarter 1 cost of a 2-line plant in Sereno is given in Chapter 8 as Ps 7,200,000. If the reported (or estimated) CPI in Sereno for Year 4, Quarter 3 is 145 and the CPI in Sereno for Year 2, Quarter 4 is 100, the inflation multiplier is calculated as

$$145 \div 100 = 1.45$$

Then multiplying the Year 3, Quarter 1 price by 1.45 will result in an estimated peso cost during Year 4, Quarter 4 of

$$\text{Ps } 7,200,000 \times 1.45 = \text{Ps } 10,440,000$$

Similarly, if the Merica CPI in the same quarter turns out to be 124 (a much lower rate of inflation), the price of a 2-line plant in Merica will be

$$\$1,200,000 \times 1.24 = \$1,488,000$$

Notice that the cost of building in each area is **not** affected by the then-current exchange rate. Costs in each country are determined by the different way that prices behave in Sereno and Merica. But because consolidated financial statements are prepared using dollars, the currency of the parent corporation's country, the costs (and revenues) will be stated in dollars, translated at the exchange rate of the quarter in which the financial statements are prepared.

Exchange Rate Calculations

Continuing the example discussed under "Inflation Adjustments" above, you need to translate the Sereno plant cost to dollars to determine how the cost of the plant will be reported in your consolidated financial statements. We will have to estimate this amount using the forecast of exchange rates in the Quarterly Industry Report for Year 4, Quarter 3. If the forecast for Year 4,

Quarter 4 turns out to be 25.20 pesos to the dollar, the translated value of the cost in dollars can be estimated as $414,000:

$$Ps\ 10,440,000 \div 25.20 = \$414,286$$

IMPORTANT NOTE

This is not the same amount that it would cost to build a similar plant in Merica in the same quarter. The relationship between costs in the two countries will change over time because of the different rates of inflation and the different rates of change in the exchange rate. This example shows an exaggerated difference in the rates and should not be taken as a typical case—only one that is possible. But it does illustrate the way the relationship may change dramatically over time.

Market Areas

There are four market areas in *The Business Policy Game*. Three are located in Merica, and one is in Sereno. For purposes of identification, numerical designations have been given to each Merica area. The Eastern portion of Merica is known as Area 1, the Southern portion as Area 2 and the Western portion as Area 3. Sereno is the fourth market area. The level of economic activity in each of these areas is growing although the rate of growth differs between the two countries.

The numerical designations for the first three market areas correspond to the home areas of the companies that are competing in the simulation. At the end of Year 2 (when your management team takes over your firm), each company has one production plant which is located in its home area. All home areas are located in Merica. Company 1 has a production plant located in its home area, Area 1. Company 2 is located in Area 2 and Company 3 in Area 3. If more than three teams are competing, Company 4 has Area 1 for its home area along with Company 1. Company 5 is located in Area 2, Company 6 is located in Area 3, Company 7 is in Area 1 and Company 8 is in Area 2. As yet, no company has located any production facilities in Sereno, but all have been exporting from their Merica manufacturing plants to Sereno. The administrator of the simulation will assign team numbers to each company and will let you know how many companies are competing.

Distribution, Research and Development, Production

While each company has been producing goods only in its home area, each firm has sales offices and an operational sales force in all four areas and has been marketing its product actively in each market area. During the fourth quarter of Year 2, each company posted a wholesale price of $10.00 per unit in market areas 1, 2 and 3 and Ps 75 in Sereno. During that quarter, selling and distribution expenses (including advertising, salespeoples' compensation, transportation, administration and depreciation) averaged approximately $2.12 per unit sold in Merica and about

3. Optional supplementary reports that may be distributed by the simulation administrator:

   a. Your simulation administrator has the option of distributing evaluation and scoring reports showing the relative performance of the teams in your industry world on a variety of evaluation measures.

   b. Vignettes that develop situations and problems outside the scope of the computer model, and that may require a response from your team or a discussion among class members.

Data that are reported in the various reports are described in subsequent chapters.

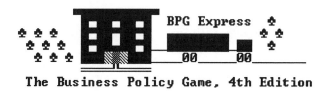

CHAPTER 4

DEVELOPING THE STRATEGIC PLAN
AND SELECTING STANDARDS OF SUCCESS

Your simulated firm may be viewed as a single business corporation or as a strategic business unit (SBU) of a diversified corporation. In either case, you are calling the shots without interference from above. Your responsibility is to stake out the direction the firm will take in terms of its mission, develop realistic goals and objectives, create a strategy which will enable your firm to attain its stated goals and successfully implement its strategy. Your reward could be mega-salaries and a golden parachute.

Mission

The firm's mission serves as the crystal ball for the organization. It describes the business of the firm and the type of business it is aspiring to become. The mission deals with the scope of activities performed and the purpose of the activities. The mission statement may focus upon products and/or services being provided, major ingredients in a line of products, central technology of an organization, customer groups served, customer needs, etc. (Thompson and Strickland, 1992). Be sure to leave your rose-colored glasses home when you develop the mission statement. This one requires some realistic thought.

Defining Goals and Objectives

The manner in which the performance of your simulated firm is evaluated will depend, in part, upon your ability to meet the goals and objectives that your firm has set. We recommend that your firm explicitly develop a written set of goals upon which your management can agree very early in the simulation. The simulation administrator may require your firm to submit a written document defining your goals and objectives, along with the strategies and policies which you have formulated to achieve these goals and objectives.

Many students, and business managers as well, tend to define their goals and objectives in very general terms. For example, an objective might be "to make a satisfactory profit on a minimum investment in physical and financial assets." While this may sound fine on the surface, a closer examination reveals that this statement really doesn't provide very much guidance for the operation and evaluation of your company.

Explicit Definition

Strategic goals and objectives should set the hurdles for your firm to jump when pursuing its mission. They provide the specific level of accomplishment desired. If you don't know the exact height of the hurdle, how high should you jump? Imagine the glory and fame obtained from jumping five feet to clear a one-foot hurdle, or consider the possibility of jumping three feet to clear a ten-foot brick wall.

We think of goals as desired long-term performance levels and objectives as short-term performance targets. Both goals and objectives state **what** is to be achieved and **when** it is to be accomplished (Quinn, 1980). Your strategic goals and objectives should contain the following four components (Hofer and Schendel, 1978):

"1. the goal or attribute sought

2. an index for measuring progress toward the goal or attribute

3. a target or hurdle to be achieved

4. a time frame within which the target or hurdle is to be achieved."

We urge your firm to provide explicit definitions of your goals and objectives. An explicit definition can be made either in absolute or in relative terms. Examples of absolute definitions include:

1. Maintain a rate of return on stockholders' end-of-Year 2 investment in your company's stock (goal) of at least 20 (hurdle) percent (index) through Year 7 (time).

2. Maintain a growth rate for assets (goal) of at least 5 (hurdle) percent (index) each year (time).

3. Generate sufficient sales to maintain a share of the market (goal) equal to at least 30 (hurdle) percent (index) by year five (time).

Examples of comparative statements of objectives (relative to competitors) include:

1. Attain a larger (hurdle) share (implicit index) of the market (goal) than any of our competitors by Year 5(time).

2. Maintain a net return on the book value of owners' investment (goal) at least equal (hurdle) to the median return (index) of the industry through Year 7 (time).

Your firm's objectives and goals may be defined in terms of some of the quantitative measures that have been described or in some other terms that your management may prefer. They should, however, be related to the variables that actually are included in the simulation model. Realizing a company objective of "maintaining high morale," while a noble objective, could only be partially inferred from reported results by examining, perhaps, the turnover rate in salespeople. Your firm does not actually have overt control over most working conditions which affect employee morale.

After goals and objectives have been set for your business, goals and objectives need to be set also for the functional areas of your firm. The goals set for the finance, marketing and production functions must reinforce and be consistent with the goals set for the business. Similarly, the functional-area objectives should lead toward the realization of the functional-area goals.

Your goals and objectives should appear reasonable, and their realization should be possible in light of the historical data available to you. It is possible that your firm may wish to revise its hurdles after you have gained several quarters of experience with the simulation. However, give your goals some time to work before you give up on them. Changing goals every quarter will lead you in circles, and you run the risk of becoming the last of the big wheels with no destination!

Formulating Strategies

Once your objectives and goals have been defined, it is important to formulate strategies for attaining those objectives. Operating without a clear strategy is like driving in an unfamiliar state without a road map. Both are only recommended for the extremely faithful. A strategy is a **plan** for utilizing the firm's resources to attain your stated goals. Your firm's strategy should be set forth explicitly so that it will provide guidance for day-to-day operations by your management team and its subordinates. One test of the clarity of your strategy is to ask yourself how another management team would operate your firm if the other team was provided with only your firm's written statement of its goals, objectives, strategies and policies. Would they make similar sets of decisions in your absence? If the answer is affirmative, your document probably is acceptable. If not, it's back to the drawing boards.

You may want to think of strategy as (Hofer and Schendel, 1978):

the fundamental pattern of present and planned resource deployments and environmental interactions that indicate how the organization will achieve its objectives.

The four components of strategy which follow from this definition are:

1. Scope: products offered and market segments served.

2. Resource deployments: planned use of funds, equipment, materials, personnel, etc.

3. Competitive advantage: unique position created relative to competition by the scope and resource deployment decisions.

4. Synergy: added advantage obtained by the specific combination of resources and/or scope decisions.

As you develop your strategy, include all four components to strengthen your final plan. Interrelationships which might go unnoticed when simply planning for resource utilization become important elements. The resulting strategy should enable your firm to interact successfully with its environment.

There are a number of generic strategies which your firm may follow. The strategies consist of the combinations of the following three dimensions: scope of your market, types of competitive weapons used and segmentation of the market (Chrisman, Hofer and Boulton 1988). The scope can either be narrow (serving one market) or broad (serving more than one market). The competitive weapons consist of price, user benefits and some combination of price and user benefits. User benefits are created through product development, product availability and promotion. The market may either be segmented (using different competitive weapons in different markets) or unsegmented (using the same competitive weapons for all markets).

To develop your firm's strategy, select a generic strategy and then tailor the dimensions to your specific environment. For example, scope will specify the market areas in which you plan to compete. Your competitive weapons consist of price, product model, product quality, advertising and sales force. You may choose to segment your markets or treat all market areas alike.

In addition to general business strategy, your firm needs to develop functional-area strategies in finance, marketing and production. The guiding forces behind functional-area strategies are functional-area goals. Functional-area strategies consist of the plans made by the functional areas to meet the functional goals discussed above. Functional-area strategies taken together determine the success of your firm's overall business strategy.

Setting Policy

Company policies are the internal, working rules of the organization. They are guidelines developed by management to set limits for, or otherwise control, day-to-day tactical decision making and other actions of subordinates. Policies may be used to simplify the decision-making process by eliminating specific alternatives from consideration. For example, if your company has a policy of not introducing a new product until at least two new models are available, no time would be spent debating whether to introduce a new product if only one new model were available.

We again want to caution you against using vague generalities when developing policy. "Maintaining a reasonable price for our product in relation to production costs and competitors' pricing activities" does not provide much guidance for your marketing department as it sets product prices. A more useful policy might be "to maintain a markup of 50 percent over production cost, with the constraint that in no event should the wholesale price exceed that of the highest-priced competitor by more than 5 percent." Other examples of an explicit pricing policy might be "to maintain a markup of 40 percent over production costs plus transportation costs to each market area without regard to competitors' pricing policies," or "to match competitors' prices in each market area without regard to markup over production cost." Hopefully these examples will provide you with a starting point for the development of your firm's specific policies.

Keep in mind that the purpose of developing policies is to enable your firm to meet the objectives which the management team has set for the firm. Policies are tools for management to use in the day to day operation of the firm. Policies should be formulated for each of the decision areas for which your firm will be responsible (described in Chapter 2). As the simulation progresses and your firm obtains additional information concerning conditions in the industry and the activities of competitors, you may wish to revise your existing policies.

Even though your initial policies may be revised during the simulation, they will be valuable in providing guidance and direction to your management team and subordinates as decisions are being made. Policies serve as management's stabilizer. Your firm will discover that establishing clearly defined policies will save much time in the decision-making process. If top management decides to adopt a specific policy when faced with a management issue, the next time the issue arises the decision will simply follow the established policy. Management can spend its time on analysis and the development of new policies rather than rehashing the same issues over and over.

Strategic Plan

The simulation administrator may ask your firm to submit a written strategic plan. The plan may be due prior to the start of the simulation, may be developed during the course of the simulation or may be considered as part of a term project for your firm's management.

In order to complete a strategic plan, your firm must conduct a situation analysis. This consists of a thorough examination of the industry, the competition and your firm. The plan then flows from the findings of the situation analysis. We like to include this analysis as a supporting part of the strategic plan. However, your administrator may decide to include only the actual plan itself. The components of our full strategic plan (including the situation analysis) follow:

I. Situation Analysis

   A. Industry

      1. stage of life cycle
      2. structure: description of important factors which shape the industry
      3. driving forces: forces which change the industry structure
      4. economics: cost, price and profit relationships
      5. key success factors: key requirements for success in the industry
      6. problems: current or potential problems facing the industry

   B. Competition

      1. intra-industry

         a. rivalry among existing competitors
         b. threat of new competitors - existing products & services
         c. threat of competitors in other industries offering substitute products & services
         d. bargaining power of suppliers
         e. bargaining power of customers

      2. individual competitor

         a. company 1: position in industry
         b. company 2: position in industry
         c. etc.

      3. forecasted changes in competitive conditions

   C. Company

      1. past performance - significant ratios

      2. current conditions

        a. external opportunities
        b. external threats
        c. internal strengths
        d. internal weaknesses

    3. significant issues and problems which must be faced

II. Strategic Plan

    A. Mission statement

    B. Business level

        1. goals & objectives
        2. strategy

    C. Functional level

        1. finance

            a. goals & objectives
            b. strategy
            c. policies

        2. marketing

            a. goals & objectives
            b. strategy
            c. policies

        3. production

            a. goals & objectives
            b. strategy
            c. policies

    D. Implementation plan and action timetable. Include *pro forma* financial statements showing your expectations of achieving your goals and objectives.

At a minimum, the plan should consist of your mission statement; your business-level goals, objectives and strategy; your functional-area goals, objectives, strategies and policies; and an implementation plan. Each element of the plan should be well thought out and should be integrated with all of the other elements of the plan. The plan serves as your operations map.

Your firm's performance will be judged according to how well your management team competes with the management teams of the other firms in your industry. This evaluation will be based, in part, upon your firm's ability to set and achieve reasonable goals. During the evaluation process, comparisons will be made with other companies in the industry regarding profitability, efficiency and financial standing. Certain ratios and quantitative measures will be received regularly in the computer-generated quarterly reports. These will be described below.

There also is a subjective element to performance evaluation requiring a judgment of the quality of planning and goal-setting activities, the quality of the plans and goals themselves, the faithfulness of the company's management in meeting goals and objectives, and the ability to submit successfully to board or shareholder reviews. Some of these qualitative factors are discussed in the last section of this chapter.

Avoid End Play

At times, teams involved in a simulation exercise such as *The Business Policy Game* are tempted to adopt an unofficial strategy which is referred to as "end play." This strategy calls for the allocation of the firm's resources in such a manner as to build the best relative position among the competitors during the final period of the simulation. This procedure ignores the quarters preceding and following the final quarter of the competition. In fact, the firm often is left in a position from which it would be impossible to continue. As end play involves only the final quarter or two of play, it really does not have much impact upon final team standings given the total number of quarters upon which evaluations are based. Thus, it is basically a fruitless exercise. A word to the wise! As "end play" is unrealistic in the business world, it is frowned upon and likely will result in a penalty during the final evaluation of a firm's performance.

Even though you have been told that the simulation will continue only for a definite number of quarters, you should take the attitude that your firm's operations will continue well beyond that time. Even if you plan to sell your interest in the company when you retire, you are likely to receive the greatest return on your investment if your firm's plans have been laid out in such a manner as to take maximum advantage of the situation existing at the end of the period. If this is done, successors will continue to have a commanding position in the industry and the greatest likelihood of continued, profitable operations. Again, we emphasize that an end-of-play strategy is unwise and is likely to hurt your relative position in the industry as well as downgrade your firm's performance when final evaluations are made.

Profitability

The profits of a business firm usually are considered to be for the benefit of the firm's owners or stockholders. If a firm is profitable, it is reasonable to expect that the wealth of individual stockholders should increase as a result of that profitability. The wealth of a stockholder can be increased in two ways: through appreciation in the market value of stock and/or through receipt of dividend payments. Realization of a satisfactory growth in stockholders' wealth requires the firm's management to conduct its activities in such a manner that the combination of dividend payments and appreciation of the firm's stock meets the financial requirements of the firm's stockholders.

Rate of Return on Stockholders' Investment (Investor ROI)

Given that the firm stays healthier when stockholders are willing to invest in its stock, one overall goal of your firm ought to focus on providing some level of additional incremental wealth to your stockholders. This especially should be the case if we assume that you and other members of your management team purchased a majority interest in your firm's common stock at the end of Year 2 in order to gain control of its management. Obviously, then, dividend payments and stock price appreciation would benefit your management team as stockholders in your firm. Dividends and appreciation can be considered as incremental returns on your initial investment at the end of Year 2. One way to compare the incremental return on your stock investment with those of stockholders in other competing firms is to compute and compare the rate of stockholder return on initial investment. You may wish to set a goal of a minimum rate of return on your stock investment or to attempt, at least, to realize a rate of return for your stockholders as great or greater than stockholders of competing firms may realize.

This rate of return may be considered as an overall measure of profitability to your stockholders on their initial investment. In addition, it should be noted that the ability of a firm to pay regular dividends and maintain an increasing stock price is dependent upon its ability to show regular earnings. Potential stock purchasers in *The Business Policy Game*, as in the business world, will put a premium on earnings growth and thus will tend to bid up the market price for a fast-growing company's common stock.

The rate of return on stockholders' initial investment will be computed at the end of each quarter and will be reported as Investor ROI in the Quarterly Industry Report. Investor ROI assumes a purchase of common stock at the end of Year 2, Quarter 4, and shows the time-adjusted return (stock price appreciation plus dividends) to the end of the quarter of the report. The computation is made by solving the following equation for r, the time-adjusted rate of return:

$$P_8 = \frac{P_n}{(1+r)^{(n-8)}} + \sum_{t=9}^{n} \frac{D_t}{(1+r)^{(t-8)}}$$

where D_t is equal to the dollar amount of dividends paid in quarter t, P_n is equal to the price of your company's common stock at the end of the most recent quarter, n. P_8 is the price at the end of Year 2 (the eighth quarter of historical data) when you began the simulation. The rate, r, is that discount rate that equates the discounted value of dividends and current stock price (discounted quarterly) to the initial stock price. The rate then is annualized by multiplying it by 4 and reported as Investor ROI. The relevant period for the calculations begins in Quarter 9 (Year 3, Quarter 1) when you take over the management of your firm.

Other Ratios

While the rate of return on stockholders' investment provides an overall measure of profitability, it is by no means the only one. Profitability can be considered in relation to the historical, or book value, of the owners' investment in a business or in relation to the dollar value of sales that the business has made in a given period of time. These profitability ratios will be reported quarterly in the industry reports.

The net profit margin on sales (Income to Sales) shows the percentage of profit from each sales dollar. The return on equity (Income to Equity) reflects the percentage return on funds invested by stockholders and earnings retained in the business. Quarterly income and sales are used for ratios in Quarterly Industry Reports. The ratios are restated using annual income and sales for the Annual Industry Report.

Other ratios are reported regularly. These reflect such things as efficiency of asset use, efficiency of operations and soundness of financial condition. See the Quarterly Industry Report in Appendix C for examples.

Ratio analysis can be a useful way to compare a firm's performance with some standard. Standards of performance that may be used include absolute norms, criteria reflecting the performance of other firms in the same industry, or standards derived from the historical performance of the firm for which the ratios are computed. Some analysts use rule-of-thumb standards with which to compare ratios of different companies. For purposes of *The Business Policy Game*, however, it probably will be more useful to you (and to those who will judge your firm's achievement) to compare your company's performance with your own historical record and with the performance of other companies in your industry. Your ability to increase your firm's rate of return on invested capital, for example, and to increase it more rapidly than that of the other companies in your industry will reflect favorably upon the quality of your management.

Financial Standing

Three different credit ratings are possible for firms competing in *The Business Policy Game*: superior (Number 1), preferred (Number 2) and average (Number 3). Credit ratings are reported in the Quarterly Industry Report. Each firm starts the simulation with a preferred credit rating (Number 2). During the course of the competition, this rating may be improved to a superior rating or reduced to an average rating according to the way the firm handles its financial affairs. The credit rating is a composite figure that reflects demonstrated ability to meet a company's financial obligations and the likelihood of continuing to meet those obligations in the future. Interest rates on bank loans and new bond issues, as well as the selling price of new common stock issues, are determined, in part, by a firm's credit standing.

In *The Business Policy Game*, credit analysts normally recompute and assign new credit ratings only once each year, at the end of the fourth quarter. A shortage of cash which necessitates emergency borrowing, however, usually will result in the immediate reduction of a firm's rating during the quarter in which the emergency borrowing occurs.

Factors Affecting Credit Ratings

Many factors normally are considered by a credit analyst in judging the financial standing of a business firm. Among those that will be used to determine your firm's credit rating are the demonstrated ability to:

1.   Meet repayment obligations on bank loans and other commitments, and avoid emergency borrowing.

2.   Show significant growth of total resources as reflected in the value of total assets.

3.   Increase the market acceptance of your product as shown by an increasing share of the market.

4.   Show a reasonable return on the book value of owners' investment in the firm (Income to Equity).

5.   Pay a reasonable proportion of profits to stockholders in the form of dividends. *The Business Policy Game* stockholders expect to receive a growing stream of dividends amounting to between 30 and 60 percent of earnings.

6.   Maintain a capital structure that shows a reasonable relationship between borrowing and net worth (Bonds to Equity).

7.   Generate sufficient profits so that there will be a comfortable margin over and above the bond interest requirements (Interest Coverage).

The Business Policy Game analysts will consider your performance on these measures over an extended period, rather than just looking at a single quarter's performance. As in the business world, the management of your simulated firm will have no direct control over the determination of its credit rating. You may, however, influence the analysts' decision by control of the various items shown above. The precise way that these various factors actually influence the determination of credit ratings in the simulation will have to be determined by experimentation and observation.

Qualitative Standards

Successful performance in the various quantitative measures that commonly are considered as reasonable standards for business success is important, but by no means the only way in which success can be measured. In addition, your management team probably will be judged on the way in which you are able to accomplish your goals and the manner in which you may have reached the level of performance shown by the quantitative measures. These latter judgments are more qualitative and subjective in nature.

At the beginning of this chapter it was suggested that you should prepare a written statement of your strategic business plan. The quality of these statements is important, and the way in which you utilize your knowledge and understanding of management theory and are able to integrate your knowledge of the functional areas of business will contribute to development of superior reports. You likely will be judged on the quality of the reports themselves, including how realistic your goals and objectives may be in the light of the economic environment in which you are operating. In addition, you may be judged on your success in actually realizing the goals that you have set for yourself.

How well has your management group done in developing an effective organization and in working together as a team? This is a question that must be asked after you have completed the simulation and one that should be addressed by your group from the beginning. In a very real sense, your ability to work together effectively will tend to determine how well you are able to accomplish your goals and how you are likely to stand in relation to the quantitative measures of success. There can be a real synergistic effect when several individuals can become a community working together toward common goals.

An overall strategy for your firm is important and your ability to integrate strategies for marketing, production and finance is a hallmark of success. But also you need to ask these questions, because those who judge your success will almost surely ask them:

1. "Is your marketing strategy effective and well-implemented?"

2. "Are your production plans and strategies effective and well-implemented?"

3. Is your financial strategy effective and well-managed?"

Finally, appearances are critically important to those who look at your work and are likely to be judging your performance. This applies in business organizations as well as to almost any form of interpersonal or inter-organizational relationship. The style and professionalism of your reports will have a marked impact on the way in which you will be judged. The poise and professionalism of your team members as they relate to others are important. Team members need to be able to relate professionally to each other, to members of other teams (your competitors), to the simulation administrator and to others who may be judging your performance. Your written and oral communications with each other, and with those outside of your management team, will be used to form the bases of many kinds of judgments about you and how well you have done.

References

Chrisman, J. J., Hofer, C. W. & Boulton, W. R. (1988) "Toward a System For Classifying Business Strategies," *The Academy of Management Review*, 13(3), 413-428.

Hofer, C. W. & Schendel (1978) *Strategy Formulation: Analytical Concepts.* St. Paul: West Publishing Company.

Quinn, J. B. (1980) *Strategies for Change: Logical Incrementalism.* Homewood, IL: Richard D. Irwin.

Thompson, A. A. & Strickland, A. J. (1992) *Strategy Formulation and Implementation* (5th ed.). Plano, TX: Business Publications, Inc.

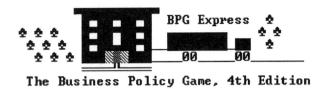

CHAPTER 5

MARKETING: STRATEGY

Your firm's marketing department is responsible for providing an attractive product at a convenient location for consumer purchase. The product's price should be equal to or less than the perceived value of the product. The department needs to communicate this information to make consumers aware of your desirable product offered at a fair price. In short, the role of your marketing department is to serve the consumer. If it fails this responsibility, your firm is likely to fail in its mission!

The marketing function in the simulation has been simplified somewhat from that found in the business world so that the simulation will be tractable. A sufficient number of elements have been included so that you can deepen your understanding of the role marketing plays in the firm and in the business world.

Your firm's marketing management should begin the simulation by setting marketing (functional level) goals and objectives and developing marketing strategy to accomplish these goals (see Chapter 4). Marketing goals should support the overall goals developed at the business level. The goals should focus upon what marketing can contribute to achieving the business-level goals. The following business-level goal was used as an example in Chapter 4:

> Generate sufficient sales to maintain a share of the market (goal) equal to at least 30 (hurdle) percent (index) by Year 5 (time).

Marketing goals and objectives that could support this business-level goal might be:

Goal: Sell only product models (goal) which represent the current state (hurdle) of technology (index)(time implicit).

Objective: Introduce a new model (goal) at the beginning (hurdle) of each
               (time) calendar year (index).

Goal: Increase sales (goal) 10 (hurdle) percent (index) faster than our
               nearest competitor during our management tenure (time).

Objective: Increase sales (goal) by 15 (hurdle) percent (index) per year (time).

Other marketing goals and objectives may focus upon selling expense reductions, transportation cost control, sales forecasting, etc.

Marketing strategy should be designed to enable your marketing department to attain its goals and objectives. The strategy should plan for the allocation of marketing resources to gain a competitive advantage and to achieve a synergistic impact. The strategy for the model goal might focus upon the timing and size of research and development expenditures. The effects of inflation should be taken into account. The strategy for increasing sales would involve the size, timing and geographical allocation of resources for promotion, distribution and pricing. An effective marketing strategy should include **all** of the marketing decision variables which require resources.

The quarter to quarter tactical decisions which your marketing management must make are described below. These decisions are guided by your marketing strategy and company policy. The decisions regarding the product to sell, the wholesale price to charge, the distribution of product among the sales offices, the level of advertising expenditures to commit and the size and compensation of the sales force are the responsibility of your marketing department. In addition to managing your firm's marketing mix, your marketing department is responsible for forecasting sales. Accurate sales forecasts are critical to the success of your firm. Sales forecasts will be the basis for estimating cash receipts, variable costs, plant expansion requirements, production requirements and inventory levels. An inventory that is too small results in lost sales and lost customers. An inventory that is too large results in excessive storage and financing costs.

This chapter contains a description of the marketing activities found in *The Business Policy Game* and the costs and expenses associated with these activities. The next chapter contains suggestions to assist in forecasting sales and economic activity. A careful reading of both chapters will help you understand the marketing function as it relates to *The Business Policy Game*. This knowledge, together with careful planning, will enable your firm to design and maintain an effective marketing mix which will provide a synergistic boost to your firm. Keep in mind, however, that customers' needs and desires change over time. An optimal mix will not necessarily remain optimal over your entire management tenure.

Your firm has a sales office located in each of your three domestic market areas, as well as in Sereno. Each office contains an area sales force manager plus staff. All customer orders generated in the area flow through the office. The office also is responsible for training and administrative duties required to keep the sales force operating effectively. This includes hiring and training additional salespeople to compensate for losses through normal attrition and terminating people when they are no longer needed. Finally, the product inventory for each area is managed by the sales office. To increase inventory, sales office orders **must** be placed with headquarters so that goods can be shipped.

Costs and Expenses

Unless otherwise noted, the costs described in this and subsequent chapters are those that were in effect at the beginning of Year 3, Quarter 1. The costs in Merica and Sereno are subject to inflation, but the rates of inflation for each country are generally different. For example, the general selling expenses for each sales office are described below as consisting of a fixed component, a semi-fixed component and a variable component:

	Dollar Cost	Peso Cost
Fixed component for each sales office	$37,500	Ps 225,000
Semi-fixed component for each salesperson	$ 4,000	Ps 24,000
Variable component for each unit sold	$ 0.20	Ps 1.20

If in Year 3, Quarter 1 your sales office, say in Area 2, had 10 salespeople and sold 100,000 units, the general selling expense for the area would be:

Fixed component for each sales office	$37,500
Semi-fixed component for 10 salespeople	$40,000
Variable component for 100,000 units sold	$20,000
Total general selling expense	$97,500

These costs will rise as the price level rises due to inflation in Merica. If the Consumer Price Index should rise by 10 percent, the general selling expense then would be:

Fixed component for each sales office	$41,250
Semi-fixed component for each salesperson	$ 4,400
Variable component for each unit sold	$ 0.22

and the total general selling expense for the same number of sales and salespeople would rise to $107,250.

If the Sereno sales office employed the same number of salespeople and sold the same number of units in Year 3, Quarter 1 (before the 10 percent price level rise), the general selling expense would be:

Fixed component per sales office	Ps 225,000
Semi-fixed component for each salesperson	Ps 240,000
Variable component for each unit sold	Ps 120,000
Total general selling expense	Ps 585,000

Now comes the kicker. If Sereno prices should rise by 20 percent, due to inflation (at twice the rate of Merica), the local currency costs also increase by 20 percent, and the total general selling expense for the same number of salespeople and the same number of units sold would be Ps 702,000.

It is important to remember when playing *The Business Policy Game* that you begin with information about costs and expenses in each country for Year 3, Quarter 1, but the relationships among these costs may change over time as each country experiences its own rate of inflation. All costs are subject to inflation, but they are subject to **different inflation rates in each country**. Current price levels and forecasts of future price levels are regularly reported in the Quarterly Industry Report as the Consumer Price Index.

Advertising

The role of advertising is to communicate with consumers. This communication may focus upon the product advantages and features that are stressed by your functional marketing strategy, or it may announce the availability of a new model. The specific message to be carried in your advertising is beyond the scope of this simulation. However, rest assured that the advertising agency that creates your advertising messages will promote your product in the best possible light.

The level of advertising expenditures is completely under the control of your firm's management. The marketing department is responsible for determining the advertising expenditure for each market area. The relative effectiveness of a firm's advertising in each area tends to follow an "S" shaped curve. Small expenditures will tend to have little effect on the market. (No one can hear you when you whisper.) As expenditures are increased, advertising effectiveness tends to increase at an increasing rate. At some level, the point of inflection on the curve is reached, and further increases in expenditures tend to yield relatively smaller benefits. As expenditures continue to be increased, a position is reached where additional expenditures yield no additional effectiveness. Expenditures beyond this level will eventually lead to a situation where additional expenditures will actually decrease advertising effectiveness. What would be your reaction to watching 24 advertisements for the same product during half an hour of television viewing?

The secret to successful advertising is to keep advertising expenditures at a level where the returns realized from each dollar spent on advertising significantly exceed the expenditure. The problem then becomes: "At what levels of expenditure do we realize this condition?" If your firm becomes somewhat frustrated in its attempts to find this ideal range, don't feel lonely. The major Fortune 500 firms don't know exactly where they are on the effectiveness curve either.

Advertising expenditures have a **carry-over effect** in that expenditures in one quarter will continue to affect sales for several quarters into the future. When planning your promotional campaign, be aware of this fact so that your firm can use it to best advantage. Your company may decide to engage in a constant or steadily increasing level of advertising each quarter. On the other hand, it may decide to engage in a seasonal strategy where expenditures are heavier in some seasons and lighter in others. Alternatively, your firm may decide to utilize a pulse strategy where it advertises heavily for several quarters, decreases expenditures for several quarters and returns to a heavy sequence for several quarters. You will want to avoid large fluctuations in advertising expenditures which we refer to as the "Yo-Yo strategy." Such expenditure patterns may only succeed in earning your firm the title of Yo-Yo Champion of the World.

Consolidated advertising expenditures for each of the firms in *The Business Policy Game* were $144,000 during the last quarter of Year 2, with about 15 percent more being spent in your home area and about 56 percent less (in dollar terms) in Sereno than in the other two areas.

On an annual consolidated basis, past advertising expenditures have averaged between $0.70 and $1.55 for each unit of product sold. However, keep in mind that the purpose of advertising is to stimulate sales; thus, past sales volume should not be used as a basis for setting future advertising expenditure levels. Advertising expenditures should be based upon the amount of sales the firm **wishes** to generate. This will depend upon the amount of inventory available, production capacity and time of year. Be sure to purchase advertising for **each** market area in which your firm is operating. This requires entering advertising expenditures on your decision form for each area. Remember, you aren't likely to sell much of your product if you don't advertise it. You also are not likely to sell as much as you expect if you advertise very little.

Enter the amount in thousands of dollars or thousands of pesos to be spent in each area. The amount must be specified even though no change is desired from the previous quarter.

Limits: 0 to 999 (in thousands of dollars) for Merica
        0 to 9999999 (in thousands of pesos) for Sereno

	Marketing	
	Price	Adv(000s)
Area 1	$ 10.00	$ 46
Area 2	$ 10.00	$ 40
Area 3	$ 10.00	$ 40
Sereno	Ps 75	Ps 105

Price

Your company's marketing department is responsible for setting the **wholesale price** for your firm's product in each of the market areas. There are no legal restrictions on charging different prices in different areas. Past prices charged by firms in your industry world have tended to hover around the $10 level in Merica although they have tended to fluctuate more in Sereno.

Econometric studies have indicated that prices tend to be somewhat elastic in this range. Thus, increases in price would tend to decrease total revenue while decreases in price would tend to increase total revenue, all other things remaining equal.

It should be obvious that your firm is part of an oligopoly, and your pricing actions should reflect this knowledge. Pricing in an oligopoly is somewhat treacherous. Each firm generally has a narrow range over which it may vary its price without competitor reaction. When your firm lowers its price beyond this range, your competitors are likely to follow suit. This may result in an expanded market with all firms sharing in the expansion. This movement could also set off a price war with rapidly falling prices (and profits). If the industry price continues to drop, there will come a point where one or more firms will be operating in the realm of profitless prosperity. As price drops below a certain level, consumers may view the product as being inferior and decide not to purchase it. A reduction in price may also decrease the funds your firm has available to spend on enhancing sales through other marketing activities.

As a general rule, firms in a mature industry tend to avoid price competition and instead develop a strategy to compete on the basis of product, promotion and distribution. Price competition can be met overnight. A change in the other three variables of the marketing mix takes more time to copy. Thus, a comparative advantage gained through altering one of the other variables of the marketing mix is longer lived than an advantage gained through a price change.

The wholesale price of your product must be set for each market area each quarter. Management may specify any price that it desires, except that company policy limits quarterly price changes to a maximum of 30 percent per quarter in Merica and 40 percent in Sereno. Large price changes are discouraged, given the unknown effect that they may have on the market. Different prices may be specified for each market area. If your Merica price is in whole dollars, enter zeros for the cents so that there is no question of whether you forgot to enter the cents' figures. Prices in Sereno are entered in whole numbers of pesos, with no decimal fraction.

Maximum change: 30 percent in any quarter in Merica
                    40 percent in any quarter in Sereno

Limits: 1.00 to 99.99 (in dollars) for Merica
        1 to 99999 (in pesos) for Sereno
        If there is no sales office in an area, the price must be 0.

Product

The products sold by the firms in your industry world are quite similar. However, there are quality and other perceived differences among the products which create customer preferences for each firm's product. Thus, firms may pursue a differentiation strategy. From time to time, a firm's research and development department may create a new model which it hopes will be more desirable than the older version of the firm's product. If the new model is introduced into the marketplace, the firm's market share will often increase given no other change in the marketplace.

Thus, companies that introduce new, innovative models will generally be more successful than firms that continue to rely upon their older, somewhat obsolete products. However, too frequent model changes will result in potential customers not knowing what product you are selling.

The model life cycle for the consumer durable good produced by your firm is relatively short. Thus, we advise your firm to engage in an aggressive R & D program so that it will have replacement products available when the sales of an existing model start to slide. The products developed by your R & D department may be entirely new models or they may be variations in features and/or packaging of existing products. A few years back, Quaker State introduced a packaging innovation with its new screw-on top containers of oil which gave it a packaging advantage in the marketplace. This packaging innovation (for motor oil) eliminated much of the mess of adding oil to a car and allowed the user to safely store the partly-used cans. Now most other brands have copied this innovation, but Quaker State held the competitive advantage for several years. Product innovation does not, however, guarantee success. Anheuser Busch brought out a new nonalcoholic drink a while back called Chelsea. It bombed badly! A word to the wise. If your new model turns out not to be a winner, it is advisable to be working on another to replace it quickly.

A major advantage of pursuing a differentiation strategy through product innovation is that it is difficult to copy. A classic example is the Volkswagen Beetle which was the envy of the automotive world for many years. It was a unique design which cornered a significant share of the new car market. Unfortunately for Volkswagen, its innovative Rabbit did not fare as well after several successful years due to the competition copying the product with improvements. While innovation may provide a temporal advantage, the advantage is not permanent. However, product innovation is much more difficult to copy than price changes. In turn, changes in promotion, distribution or in the sales force are generally easier to make than product changes. On the other hand, they are also more difficult to copy than price changes. As your marketing department considers making changes to your marketing mix, it should keep in mind the ease with which such changes may be matched by your competitors.

New Model

When a new model is released by your firm's research and development department, its availability together with its current savings level will be reported in the firm's Operating Information Report. For example, a new model number 5 might be shown as follows.

Each new model will have a different labor and material cost associated with it, which will be reported along with the release of the model. The costs that are reported are for Quality 2. The costs for other quality levels may be calculated easily, as shown below under "Model Quality." The inflation-adjusted standard costs reported for labor and materials will reflect any available cost savings that may have been achieved by your company's production and operations training program (See Chapter 7). These savings are referred to as savings levels and are shown in the report. The higher the savings level, the lower the cost. A new model may be introduced immediately or it may be held for introduction at a later date.

```
┌─────────────────────────────────────────────────────────────────────┐
│                   STANDARD COSTS PER UNIT                             │
│                     for Next Quarter                                  │
│                                                                       │
│                              Merica    Merica    Merica               │
│                              Area 1    Area 2    Area 3    Sereno      │
│                                $         $         $         Ps        │
│                                                                       │
│ Model  5 Quality 2   Labor Cost   3.35      3.35      3.35     16.65   │
│ Savings Level  4     Material Cost 1.73      1.73      1.73     10.80   │
│                                                                       │
│ Model  4 Quality 2   Labor Cost   2.88      2.88      2.88     15.75   │
│ Savings Level  4     Material Cost 1.50      1.50      1.50      9.45   │
│                                                                       │
│ Note:   For Quality 1 add 10%.   For Quality 3 subtract 10%           │
└─────────────────────────────────────────────────────────────────────┘
```

Each model released from the R & D department is assigned a sequential number with higher numbers indicating more recent releases. It is possible for the firm in the above example to be producing Model 3 and have Models 4 and 5 available for introduction. If more than one model number is available, there is no marketing advantage in skipping a model to produce the highest numbered model, unless your next model is two or three models behind those offered by competitors, making it technically obsolete.

If the firm decides to introduce Model 5, it will no longer be possible to introduce Model 4 in the future or to restart production of Model 3 as the tools and dies required to produce those earlier models will have been sold. In addition, the board of directors adopted a firm policy several years ago that older models of the company's product will not be produced once a newer model is introduced. The board wanted to avoid the potential negative image which could be created if consumers believed that the firm was producing and selling obsolete products.

IMPORTANT NOTE

While more than one firm may be producing a product with the same model number, the **model number is a unique identifier for each company**. The products will not be perceived to be identical by consumers. For example, both Lee and Levi Strauss make blue jeans. The jeans made by these two companies are perceived as unique products by consumers.

Your research and development department works closely with your marketing research department. Prior to the release of any new model, the marketing research department will assess the sales potential of the new model under development. The management of your firm has a long established policy that research studies of any new product released for production must indicate at least an 80 percent likelihood that the new model's sales will exceed sales of the model currently in production by as much as, perhaps, 20 percent. **Note**: Your management should be aware that research information is never totally accurate. Thus, there is up to a 20 percent probability that sales of the new model will not match the sales volume of the current product. In that event, it is unlikely that sales will decrease more than 5 percent from the current model sales level.

If a new model is available and your company wishes to put it into production during the current quarter, enter the new model number on the decision form. For example, if Model 4 is reported to be available, and your firm decides to introduce it, enter "4" on the decision form. Production of the old model ceases, and production of the new model begins immediately. Thus, the production costs in all plants for the current quarter will be those of the new model. However, the new model will not be sold in a market area until next quarter unless inventory of the old model in the area is exhausted. Sales for the current quarter in each area will be from the inventory on hand of the old model. Any units of the old model not sold during the quarter will be sold to a liquidation agent at the end of the quarter at a price equal to your firm's production cost (plus the 20 percent markup for units shipped to areas without production plants—see below). The liquidator's price does not include transportation costs your firm may have paid. All available inventory for next quarter will be of the new model.

If a sales office in an area has unfilled orders after it has exhausted its inventory of the old model, any shipments received by the sales office during the quarter will be substituted for the old model to satisfy the remaining orders. Because all production during the quarter is of the new model, all shipments from plants to fill sales office orders will be of the new model. As price is set only once a quarter, the new model will be sold at the same price as the old model. Thus, purchasers in the market area during the latter part of the quarter will get a bargain if your firm stocks out of the old model earlier in the quarter. Note that it is possible to sell units of the old model to a liquidator in one area which has a surplus of the old model while another area stocks out of the old model and must sell units of the new model to meet current quarter demand.

IMPORTANT NOTE
During the first quarter of production of a new model, customer orders are **all** for the previous model even if all previous-model inventory has been sold. Customers will not be aware of the new model until the following quarter.   Any perceived increase in benefits of the new model will not have an effect on sales until the new model is officially released.

Example of Introducing a New Model in Quarter Y			
	Quarter X	Quarter Y	Quarter Z
Old Model	Produce & Sell	Sell/Liquidate	
New Model		Produce/Sell only if old model stockout	Produce & Sell

Always enter the model number to be produced, even if it is the same as the last quarter. For Year 3, Quarter 1 the only model available is number 1.

Maximum: Highest model number reported available from the R & D Department
Minimum: Same model number as produced during the last quarter. Once a new model has
              been placed in production, an earlier model may not be reinstated
Limits: 1 to 12

Model/Quality	
Model	# 1
Quality	# 2

Model Quality

When a new model is put into production, the quality level at which the product will be produced and sold **must** be specified. A new model may be sold as a deluxe (superior quality), standard (average quality) or economy model. Your board of directors has a long standing policy that the quality level of a product model will not be changed as long as the model is in production. They wanted to prevent customer confusion and the potential ill will which could be created by selling different quality levels of the same product. Quality levels can be changed **only** when a new model is introduced.

Quality level is determined by manufacturing tolerances and the quality and quantity of raw materials used. Features of the product are important, too. Deluxe quality may signify extra features that are not available in a standard quality model, and economy quality may signify fewer features than for the standard model. It is not related to whatever you may have spent on research and development in order to bring the new model to market.

As you would expect, quality costs money. More costly material must be used and more care in assembly is required with each increase in quality. The relative costs for the three quality levels are:

```
Deluxe (Quality 1)      110% of standard cost for quality 2
Standard (Quality 2)    100% of standard cost for quality 2
Economy (Quality 3)      90% of standard cost for quality 2
```

Notice that the demand for your product is price-elastic, or sensitive to price changes. That is, a price increase can be expected, all other things being equal, to result in fewer units being sold. As you also might expect, the demand for higher quality products is less price sensitive than the demand for lower quality products. Therefore, if you change to a deluxe version (Quality 1) when you introduce Model 2, you can expect price increases to depress sales less than they would if you stayed with a standard version (Quality 2). Conversely, if you change to an economy version (Quality 3), you can expect demand to be more price sensitive than with the standard version (Quality 2).

IMPORTANT NOTE

If you change model quality when introducing a new model, the price sensitivity of the new quality will **not** take effect until the new model is officially released in the quarter **following** the initial production.

As a rule of thumb, higher quality products require more marketing effort than lower quality products. You will generally find that the higher price attached to higher quality products (normally yielding a higher margin) is also accompanied by higher promotion expenditures and higher cost distribution channels. Thus, to be successful, higher quality products tend to be marketed differently than lower quality products. Remember the difference in target markets.

When specifying the quality level of a new model on the decision form, enter the number of the quality level you have chosen:

> 1 -- deluxe
> 2 -- standard
> 3 -- economy

If you continue to produce the same model as in the previous quarter, you must also continue the same quality level.

Limits: 1, 2 or 3

May be changed only when introducing a new model

Salespeople

Your firm has a sales office located in each of your market areas, including Sereno. Each office contains an area sales force manager plus staff. All orders generated in the area will flow through the office. The office is also responsible for training and administrative duties required to keep the sales force operating effectively.

You have two decisions to make regarding the sales force. First, you must decide how many salespeople are required in each area. Second, you are required to develop a compensation package for the salespeople. This package consists of salary and commission rates.

Hiring Salespeople

The Operating Information Report for Year 2, Quarter 4, shows the number of salespeople working for the company during that quarter.

To determine the number of salespeople available for the next quarter, add the number of salespeople in training to those already active. Those who have resigned already have been subtracted from the reported number of active salespeople. The report does not show the number of salespeople fired. Your firm should know that information as it is part of the decision set that you submitted.

	Area 1	Area 2	Area 3	Sereno
Active Salespeople (number of)	12	10	10	13
Salespeople in Training	0	0	0	0
Salespeople Resigned	0	0	0	0
Memo: Sales Training Expense	0	0	0	0

Each firm can expect to lose salespeople over time through normal attrition. They may leave due to better career opportunities in other industries, retirement, illness or death or dissatisfaction with the compensation package being provided by the firm. Your firm has full control over the compensation package; however, you have no control over other factors which may cause a salesperson to leave the organization. We recommend that you plan for some resignations and maintain a sales force of sufficient size so that one or two resignations (or even more) during a quarter would not be devastating to the firm.

If your firm decides to hire additional salespeople, enter the number of salespeople to be hired under Salespeople–Hire on the decision form in the areas the salespeople are to work. A salesperson must be trained for one quarter prior to being assigned to sell in the field. Thus, if you hire 2 salespersons in Quarter 2, they will be available to sell in the field during Quarter 3.

	Salespeople			
	Hire	Transfer	Comm	Salary
Area 1	#	#	20 ¢	$ 3000
Area 2	#	#	20 ¢	$ 3000
Area 3	#	#	20 ¢	$ 3000
Sereno	#	#	60 ¢	Ps 8971

Training costs during the quarter amount to $10,000 in Merica at the beginning of Year 3, Quarter 1. Costs in Sereno for the same period are Ps 36,000. The costs will be subject to inflation at the rate of increase in the Consumer Price Index in each country.

Salespeople in training will be carried on the training roster for one quarter and will be automatically assigned to the area in which they are training in the following quarter. No further entry is necessary after the quarter in which the salespeople were hired. If you make an entry in the following quarter, you will hire additional salespeople to begin their training period in that quarter.

Limits: 0 to 99

Transferring Salespeople

Salespeople may be transferred from one area to another. If your firm hires a salesperson in Area 2 and decides that the salesperson is needed in Area 3 instead, it may transfer an **active** salesperson (not one still in training) to Area 3. The transfer can be accomplished by entering "–1" in Area 2 and "1" in Area 3 under Salespeople–Transfer on the decision form. Your positive "moves in" to other areas may not exceed the value of negative "moves out." That would signify increasing the size of your sales force, and an increase only may be accomplished by hiring new salespeople. If your negative values are larger than your positive values, the additional negative values will result in that number of salespeople being fired (see below).

You may transfer salespeople from several areas at the same time. However, you may not transfer salespeople in and out of the same area in one quarter. They must either go into an area or out of an area. Not both. In addition, you must maintain **at least one** salesperson in each area unless you are closing the sales office in the area. (If you close the sales office, you are leaving the area. See "Closing a Sales Office" on page 75.) Transfers take place immediately. A transferred salesperson may not be very effective until he or she has moved and settled into a new market area. The salesperson will, however, continue to draw a salary. In addition, the salesperson will be provided with a moving allowance of $5,000 (or Ps 30,000 in Sereno), shown under Other Expense for the area **from** which the individual moves.

Maximum negative (to be transferred out):	number of active salespeople
Maximum positive (to be transferred in):	the sum of positive numbers may not exceed the sum of negative numbers
Limits:	-99 to 99

Firing Salespeople

You may fire salespeople in an area by entering the number of people you want to fire under Salespeople–Transfer. You indicate that the salespeople are to be fired by entering a negative number in the area with no balancing positive number indicating a transfer to another area. Thus, if you decide to fire 2 salespeople in Area 3, enter -2 under the Transfer column for Area 3. A salesperson fired in a quarter is given $5,000 (or Ps 30,000 in Sereno) in severance pay (charged to Other Expense) at the beginning of the quarter and is no longer a member of the sales force. Remember, you must maintain at least one salesperson in each area if you intend to sell goods in the area. If you remove all salespeople from an area, the sales office in the area will be closed and sold. See "Closing a Sales Office" on page 75 .

Maximum to be discharged:	Number of active salespeople
Limits:	-99 to 0

Sales Salaries

It is the custom in your industry to pay salespeople a base salary plus a commission. At the end of Year 2, each salesperson was receiving a base salary of $3,000 (or Ps 8,971 in Sereno) per quarter plus commissions. Salespeople have no expense accounts. Increases or decreases in salaries will affect the performance level and job satisfaction of your salespeople. Higher salaries generally will tend to increase the loyalty of the sales force and result in lower turnover. Lower salaries usually lead to employee dissatisfaction, lower productivity and increased resignations. When developing your compensation program, heed Armand Hammer's sage advice, "If you pay peanuts, you'll get monkeys." However, at some point, diminishing returns will set in as salaries are increased. How loyal and happy can you make a sales force? The higher the salary, the less the need to earn a commission by selling.

The salary that your firm decides to pay its sales force must be entered for each area on the decision form in the Salespeople–Salary section. Each sales office determines the salary the salespeople in its area will receive. Salespeople in Sereno will be paid in pesos. Caution is urged when changing salaries. A Yo-Yo pattern here is likely to buy employee mistrust and resignations.

Limits: 1 to 9999 (in dollars) for Merica
　　　 1 to 9999999 (in pesos) for Sereno
　　　 If there is no sales office in an area, salary must be 0.

Sales Commissions

In addition to a base salary, salespeople recently have been paid a commission amounting to 20 cents for each unit sold, or 60 centavos in Sereno. Increases in the level of commissions will normally serve as a sales incentive, leading to an increase in the number of units sold. Decreases often have the opposite effect. As with advertising expenditures and sales salaries, the effect of increasing commissions is subject to the law of diminishing returns. The sales office in each area may adjust the level of sales commissions or change the relative emphasis on salary and commissions each quarter. Enter the amount of the desired commission in number of cents or centavos per unit under Salespeople–Comm for each area on the decision form.

Limits: 1 to 99 (in cents per unit sold) for Merica
　　　 1 to 99999 (in centavos per unit sold) for Sereno
　　　 If there is no sales office in an area, commission must be 0.

Managing the Sales Force

Managing the sales force involves resolving three questions:

　　1. How many salespeople should we employ?
　　2. Where should we deploy the sales force?

3. How should we compensate the sales force?

In order to determine the number of salespeople to employ, your firm must develop a sales forecast. Well-managed firms develop a sales quota which they expect their salespeople to meet. The number of salespeople to employ is then determined by dividing the forecasted sales for the quarter by the sales quota. During Years 1 and 2, salespeople have sold between 6,000 and 11,000 units per quarter, averaging about 8,000. Your salespeople may or may not match these figures depending upon the economic conditions in your industry, the aggressiveness of your competitors and your management skills.

If you develop a sales quota for your sales force, you can use the sales quota to allocate your salespeople among your market areas. Simply allocate your sales force by dividing the sales forecast for each area by the sales force quota and you have the required number of salespeople for the area. Unfortunately, your actual management activity is not quite that simple. You may already have recognized that salespeople are allocated in lumps of one person. Thus, if you forecast 104,000 units to be sold in an area and your sales quota is 10,000 units per salesperson, you're left looking for four-tenths of a salesperson. Here's what you get paid the big bucks to do: make wise decisions!

After your sales force is functioning in the field, it is wise to monitor the average number of units each person is selling in each area. You likely will find that all is not going according to plan. A quick calculation or two normally will show that salespeople in some areas are producing a much higher return than those in other areas. This would suggest that you transfer some salespeople out of the low producing areas into the high producing areas to balance more evenly the return obtained per salesperson in each area. Remember, though, that reducing the number of salespeople in an area will require the others to work harder if they are to maintain the same level of total sales. They may not be able to (or choose not to) work hard enough to do that.

While both salaries and commissions provide compensation for the salesperson, their uses are somewhat different. Salary provides security for the salesperson in that, regardless of the number of units sold, the salesperson is guaranteed a fixed salary. Salary is not a strong motivator to create additional sales. On the other hand, the commission is not paid unless a sale is made. It provides no security for the salesperson. It does provide a strong motivator for increasing sales. Each unit sold provides more money for the salesperson. Some mixture of the two compensation options is recommended. Your firm may want to place the emphasis of your compensation package upon one or the other of the two alternatives. However, be sure that your sales force can make a decent living, or they will be looking for another job. It should come as no surprise that some people work better when the emphasis is upon salary, and other people work better with the emphasis upon commission.

Promotional Balance

You spend your promotional budget on advertising and salespeople. What is the proper balance? Marginal analysis would call for shifting dollars from the lower contributing area to the higher contributing area. In effect, that is what we discussed previously when we suggested that you shift salespeople among areas to balance the number of units sold per salesperson. The proper allocation is more difficult when deciding whether to take money from advertising and put it into enlarging the sales force or vice versa.

There is a somewhat crude measure you can use to help determine whether you have the proper balance between your promotion tools. Calculate the number of dollars of sales obtained per dollar spent on advertising by area and the number of dollars of sales obtained per dollar spent on salespeople by area. However, don't shift dollars to balance these returns yet! The actions of your competitors can cause these returns per dollar spent to bounce all over the place while you hold your total expenditures constant. (We said this method was crude!) Calculate these returns for at least a year and take the average before you make any changes. Then you may decide to shift expenditures gradually in the indicated direction while continuing to monitor the resulting returns. Sorry folks, this is as close as we can get in an operational setting. (Of course you could always try some econometric techniques.)

Leaving and Entering Market Areas

Unless your simulation administrator has told you otherwise, at the beginning of Year 3, Quarter 1 your firm will be selling goods in all four market areas: Areas 1, 2 and 3 in Merica and in Sereno. While you **must** maintain a sales office in your home area, you may withdraw from or reenter any of the other three areas, including Sereno. Thus, your firm may decide to compete in all four areas or it may decide to concentrate its efforts in two or three market areas. The existence of a sales force is the key to maintaining a sales office. If there are no salespeople in an area, the sales office will be closed and sold, there will be no shipments to the area and no sales will be made to customers.

Closing a Sales Office

If your management team decides to leave a market area, it may do so by removing all salespeople from the area. This can be done by transferring salespeople to other areas and/or by discharging any remaining salespeople. Salespeople that are moved will require moving expenses and those who are discharged will receive severance pay. When the last salesperson leaves, the sales office in the area will be closed and the building sold to a local developer at 90 percent of book value. The developer's payment is made in the quarter in which the office is closed and the proceeds are available for your firm to use during that quarter. If there is no manufacturing plant in the area, any cash balances remaining at the end of the quarter will be transferred to the parent corporation. If there is not enough cash to meet all obligations, the parent corporation will supply it by purchasing more stock in the subsidiary.

When your firm closes a sales office, it will discharge all local administrative personnel. They will be paid a full quarter's compensation as severance pay, even though they are discharged at the beginning of the quarter. If you close a sales office in Year 3, Quarter 1 in Merica, executive severance pay for the quarter would amount to $25,000 (or Ps 150,000 in Sereno). When a sales office is closed, general selling expense for the area will fall to zero. Any unsold inventory will be purchased by a liquidator at your cost and the proceeds will be available for use during the quarter. The sale will be made under the same agreement used to liquidate unsold units of your old model when your firm introduces a new model.

As with any other business decision, you should plan for the closure of a market area. Inventory should be carefully controlled so your firm is not losing profit opportunities by liquidating units of product at cost. Salespeople should be integrated into other areas where possible to minimize firing. You have invested in the training of your sales force, an investment which will be lost if salespeople are fired. Firing employees who are performing well is also harmful to the morale and productivity of your remaining employees in other areas.

Opening a Sales Office

Your firm may decide to reenter a market area that it had previously abandoned. Alternatively, if your firm began the game competing in less than four market areas and expansion is allowed, it may decide to enter a new area. In either case, your company may enter an area in which it is not currently competing by transferring one or more salespeople into the area. When the salespeople are transferred in, the sales compensation level for the area, both salary and commission, **must** be specified on the decision form.

The key to opening a new market area is the transfer of at least one salesperson from another area. That will launch the process of creating the sales office in the area. A new sales office cost $400,000 in Year 1, Quarter 1 (or Ps 2,392,000 in Sereno, given a Year 1, Quarter 1 exchange rate of 5.98 pesos to the dollar). The current-quarter cost is determined by adjusting for the inflation rate of the country in which the sales office is to be built. For example, if the CPI in Merica is 115 for the most recent quarter, and the Year 1, Quarter 1 CPI was 85.8 (see Appendix C), the cost of a new sales office in Merica would be:

$$\$400,000 \times (115 \div 85.8) = \$536,130$$

If the office is to be built in Sereno, use the Year 1, Quarter 1 CPI in Sereno (74.8, for example) and the original cost of the Sereno sales office (Ps 2,392,000). If the CPI in Sereno for the most recent quarter happens to be 152, then the cost of a new sales office would be:

$$\text{Ps } 2,392,000 \times (152 \div 74.8) = \text{Ps } 4,860,749$$

At the beginning of the quarter, an administrator is hired to open the sales office. The administrator's initial duties include purchasing the sales office, hiring administrative personnel, supervising sales training and organizing sales operations in the new area. Using the above example, initial executive salaries for a sales office (Year 3, Quarter 1) are $25,000, and the Year 2 Quarter 4 CPI was 100. Therefore, administrative personnel costs for a new sales office in Merica would be:

$$\$25,000 \text{ x } (115 \div 100) = \$28,750$$

If the office is to be built in Sereno, the same costs would be:

$$Ps\ 150,000 \text{ x } (152 \div 100) = Ps\ 228,000$$

This amount will be charged to Executive Compensation on your income statement.

Typically a firm will transfer one or two of its salespeople into the area and hire several new salespeople for the area. The experienced salespeople who transferred into the area function as training coordinators. They will also assist the administrator in setting up the sales office.

Price and advertising expenditures must be specified during the following quarter when you begin to sell your product. Be sure to consider your competitor's prices and other elements of their marketing mix when introducing your product in an area.

When the sales office is opened, there are no units of product in inventory to sell. Don't forget to place a sales office order for the first quarter in which the sales force will be in operation. If the sales office is built this quarter, it will be in operation next quarter. Thus, a sales office order should be placed with next quarter's decision set. If you forget to place an order for the sales office, you have created a nice coffee house in which the area's new sales force can read poetry.

Other Marketing Expenses

Besides managing the advertising program and your sales force, your firm will incur several other types of expenses associated with the marketing function. These are shown in Figure 5-1. Most expenses related to selling and distribution activities will be reported as Selling Expense each quarter in the Consolidated Income Statement, partially illustrated in Figure 5-1. Other expenses are classified as Administrative and General Expense. Current levels of these expenses may be found in the reproduction of the reports for Year 2, Quarter 4 in Appendix C.

General Selling Expenses

Sales offices in each of the four areas incur General Selling Expenses. The entry on your firm's Income Statement for each office includes a fixed, a semi-fixed and a variable component. The fixed portion represents a quarterly charge for marketing, administration and overhead costs. The semi-fixed portion consists of a quarterly amount, over and above salary and commission, to support each active salesperson. The variable portion consists of an amount allocated for each unit sold related to administrative costs of selling the product. The Year 3, Quarter 1 costs for each sales office in Merica are:

$37,500 + $4,000 x number of salespeople + .20 x number of units sold.

The same costs in Sereno are:

Ps 225,000 + Ps 24,000 x number of salespeople + Ps 1.20 x number of units sold

These costs are subject to the particular country's inflation rate. All Sereno expenses are consolidated using current exchange rates.

The more units that are sold, the lower is the general selling expense per unit because the fixed and semi-fixed costs are spread over more and more units.

	Consolidated M$000s	Merica Area 1 M$000s	Merica Area 2 M$000s	Merica Area 3 M$000s	Sereno Ps000s
Selling Expense:					
Advertising Expense	144	46	40	40	105
Sales Salaries	116	36	30	30	117
Sales Commissions	79	24	22	22	65
General Selling Expense	406	107	97	97	629
Transportation Expense	196	12	54	54	455
Sales Office Depreciation	12	3	3	3	19
Other Selling Expense	0	0	0	0	0
Total Selling Expense	952	228	246	246	1390
Admin and General Expense:					
Research and Development	72	72	0	0	0
Total Training Expense	68	68	0	0	0
Storage Expense	43	6	13	13	66
Executive Compensation	145	73	24	24	142
Loan Interest	0	0	0	0	0
Bond Interest	50	50	0	0	0
Other Expense	0	0	0	0	0
Total Adm & Gen Expense	378	269	37	37	208

FIGURE 5-1
Partial Income Statement

Transportation Expense

There are two types of transportation expenses. One results from shipping goods from a manufacturing plant to a sales office in another area. The second results from shipping goods from the sales office (or a plant warehouse within the same area) to a customer. In areas where a sales office is associated with a plant, inventory is stored in a section of the plant warehouse. Thus, no costs are incurred for shipping goods to the sales office as shipments are made directly from the plant to customers when orders are filled. Shipping costs within Merica and to or from Sereno are invoiced in dollars, and those within Sereno are invoiced in pesos. Shipments to Sereno are paid by the Sereno subsidiary in pesos, with the pesos converted to dollars at current exchange rates. For Year 3, Quarter 1 the costs (subject to inflation) are as follows:

Shipments from	To	Cost per unit in dollars convert pesos at current rates
Sales office or plant	Customer in same area	$0.10 or Ps 0.60
Plant (Merica)	Sales office in another Merica area	$0.60
Plant (Merica)	Sereno sales office	$0.90
Plant (Sereno)	Merica sales office	$0.90

Shipments from your home plant to the sales office in another Merica area would cost $0.60 per unit. Shipments from the sales office to a customer would cost $0.10 per unit. Thus, the shipping cost from plant to customer would total

$$\$0.60 + \$0.10 = \$0.70 \text{ per unit}$$

A shipment from your home-area plant to the sales office in Sereno would be invoiced at $0.90, per unit and paid in pesos at Year 3, Quarter 1 exchange rates. A shipment from the Sereno sales office to the customer would be invoiced in pesos, with the cost for Year 3, Quarter 1 being Ps 0.60 per unit. The peso cost of a shipment from the home-area manufacturing plant to a customer in Sereno during Year 3, Quarter 1, with a forecast exchange rate of Ps 6.09 to the dollar, would be :

$$(\$0.90 \times 6.09) + \text{Ps } 0.60 = \text{Ps } 6.08 \text{ per unit}$$

All shipping costs are subject to inflation. Shipments to or from Sereno are invoiced in dollars, and thus are subject to the Merica inflation rate. However, the payment is made in pesos at the exchange rate for the quarter in which the goods are shipped. Shipments within Sereno are paid in pesos, and are subject to the peso inflation rate rather than the dollar inflation rate.

Sales Office Depreciation

A sales office was built in each market area in Year 1, Quarter 1 for $400,000 (Ps 2,392,000 in Sereno, with a Year 1, Quarter 1 exchange rate of 5.98 to the dollar). Each sales office is subject to depreciation on a straight-line basis over 31.5 years. This amounts to 0.7937 percent per quarter or $3,175 (rounded to $3,000) for Area 1, 2 and 3 offices and Ps 18,985 (rounded to Ps 19,000) for the Sereno office.

Training Expense

Training expense is incurred when new salespeople are hired. It costs $10,000 to train a new salesperson in Merica (or Ps 36,000 in Sereno). These sums include the salary paid to the salesperson during the training period. The cost of training new salespeople is recorded under

Total Training Expense on your firm's income statement during the quarter in which the training takes place. Because training is an administrative function, sales training expense is reported under Administrative and General Expense along with production and operations training expense and training expense of new production employees.

Inventory Storage Expense

Each production plant (whether in the home area, a nonhome area or Sereno) has internal warehouse space to store 300,000 units of finished product. Thus, your firm begins Year 3 with storage space for 300,000 units in your home-area plant. If additional plants are built, they also will include storage for 300,000 units. It costs 10 cents per unit (or 60 centavos in Sereno) to store unsold goods in your plant warehouse(s) for a quarter. If your inventory exceeds the available storage space in a plant, your firm will rent space in a public warehouse in the area to store the additional units of product. Units will **not** be shipped to other areas for storage. Public warehouse storage costs amount to 30 cents per unit of product (or Ps 1.80 in Sereno). Units in storage in the public warehouse will be sold prior to units stored in your plant warehouse. All storage costs for a quarter are invoiced and paid at the beginning of the quarter for goods in storage at the end of the previous quarter.

Storage costs are subject to inflation at the inflation rate of the country where the goods are stored. Note that storage of goods for a sales office in an area or country without any manufacturing facility is subject to the public warehouse storage rate of 30 cents per unit (or Ps 1.80 in Sereno) in Year 3, Quarter 1. These costs are paid by the subsidiaries for goods stored in their market area or by the parent company for goods stored in the home area.

Other Expense

Other marketing expenses include transfer costs for moving current salespeople and severance costs for fired salespeople. Transferred salespeople receive a $5,000 (or Ps 30,000 in Sereno) moving allowance. They also continue to draw their current salary. The moving allowance is paid by the area from which the salesperson is moving. Fired salespeople receive a $5,000 (or Ps 30,000 in Sereno) severance allowance. Both of these expenses are charged to Other Expense on your firm's income statement during the quarter in which they are incurred.

Implicit Cost of Stockouts

If your firm has sufficient inventory on hand to meet consumer demand, its sales will be limited by demand. On the other hand, if consumer demand in an area exceeds that area's inventory, production and sales office purchases, its sales will be limited by the volume of goods available for sale. Some of your customers who want to buy more units of your product than you can supply will become dissatisfied and are likely to take their business elsewhere. The demand for your product will tend to be reduced somewhat in the future over what it would have been if the stockout had not occurred. A stockout results not only in a loss of present sales, it generally results in the loss of a certain amount of future sales. Thus, when developing an inventory plan, your firm needs to weigh the costs of storing inventory vs. the costs of a stockout.

Maintaining a low inventory level reduces both the cost of funds required to finance the inventory and the storage costs incurred. However, low inventory levels increase the likelihood of stockouts which inflict an implicit cost that can be measured only in terms of lost sales and profits in the current quarter and lower levels of demand in subsequent quarters. Firms normally develop an inventory plan which includes some level of safety stock as a buffer to meet unexpected variations in demand. The level of safety stock selected is determined by balancing the cost of carrying the extra inventory with the cost of stocking out in the quarter.

Summary of Relationships

1. An increase in **advertising** expenditures usually will result in increased sales. Such expenditures are subject to the law of diminishing returns, and sharp fluctuations in expenditures are likely to harm your company's image.

2. The **price** that is charged will affect the level of sales and the amount of sales revenue. Your product is said to be price elastic, with price increases reducing the number of sales and the amount of sales revenue. Price competition is easily copied by competitors, as compared with other marketing focuses.

3. **New model introduction** is likely to increase your sales, with an 80 percent chance of an increase, perhaps by as much as 20 percent. This implies a 20 percent chance that sales may actually decline as a result of introducing a new model. A decline is unlikely to exceed 5 percent of current sales.

4. **Production of a new model** must be started one full quarter prior to selling the model. During the start-up quarter, sales of the old model will continue in each area until the inventory of the old model in the area is exhausted. If additional units are required to satisfy demand, units of the new model produced during the quarter will be substituted at the same price as the old model. All units of the old model remaining in an area at the end of the start-up quarter will be sold at the end of the quarter to a liquidator at cost.

5. **Model quality** affects the price elasticity of your product and the costs of producing it. Deluxe quality is less price elastic and production costs are 10 percent higher than standard quality. Economy quality is more price elastic and costs 10 percent less to produce.

6. **Training expenses** for new salespersons are $10,000 (Ps 36,000) each.

7. **Sales salaries** and **commissions** provide incentive for your salespeople. Usually increases in compensation will result in increased sales, subject to the law of diminishing returns. Higher-paying opportunities at competing firms may cause dissatisfaction on the part of some members of your sales force and increase turnover among salespeople.

8. **Closing a sales office** terminates your firm's sales operations in an area. An office is closed by removing all salespeople from the area. Administrative personnel are fired and given one quarter's severance pay. The sales office is sold and your firm receives ninety percent of the book value in proceeds. Any remaining inventory is sold at cost to a liquidator.

9. **Opening a sales office** in an area is accomplished by transferring one or more salespeople from another area into the area to be opened. This sets in motion the hiring of an administrator, the purchase of a sales office and the creation of a sales organization. A sales office cost $400,000 in Year 1, Quarter 1 (Ps 2,392,000 in Sereno with an exchange rate of 5.98 to 1). Executive compensation is $25,000 per sales office in Year 3, Quarter 1 (or Ps 150,000). A sales office order must be placed before the sales office will have any product to sell.

10. **General selling expense** includes both a fixed and a variable component. The total may be calculated as

$37,500 + $4,000 x number of salespeople + $0.20 x number of units sold (in Merica)
Ps 225,000 + Ps 24,000 x number of salespeople + Ps 1.20 x number of units sold (in Sereno)

11. **Transportation expenses** vary according to the originating point and destination. For goods shipped:

Shipments from	To	Cost per unit in dollars convert pesos at current rates
Sales office or plant	Customer in same area	$0.10 or Ps 0.60
Plant (Merica)	Sales office in another Merica area	$0.60
Plant (Merica)	Sereno sales office	$0.90
Plant (Sereno)	Merica sales office	$0.90

12. **Inventory storage costs** amount to 10 cents per unit (or 60 centavos) for the first 300,000 units in areas which have manufacturing plants. Beyond that, public warehouse space in the area is used at a cost of 30 cents per unit (or Ps 1.80) to store all inventory exceeding the 300,000 limit. For areas without plants, all inventory is stored in public warehouses. Quarterly storage costs are paid at the beginning of each quarter for goods stored at the end of the previous quarter.

13. **Other Selling Expenses** include:
      moving allowances: $5,000 (or Ps 30,000) per salesperson transferred
      severance costs: $5,000 (or Ps 30,000) per salesperson fired.

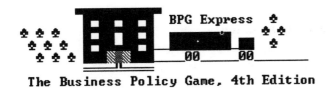

CHAPTER 6

MARKETING: SALES FORECASTING

The volume of new orders placed with your firm will depend upon a number of factors. Among the more important are:

Factors related to the economic environment

    1. the trend of economic activity in your market areas

    2. the season of the year

Factors related to your marketing activities and those of your competitors

    1. the wholesale prices charged by your firm and by competitors

    2. the level and mix of marketing expenditures

    3. the product introduction decisions

    4. the marketability of the models being sold.

In short, the number of new orders that will be generated for your firm's product in a quarter will be a result of the total effect of the economic environments, your marketing activities and the marketing activities of your competitors.

Economic Environment

Sales Levels and Gross Domestic Product

Econometric studies have shown a significant correlation between the level of demand for consumer durable goods and the level of economic activity as represented by real gross domestic product (real GDP). Nominal GDP, indexed in current dollars (or pesos, in Sereno), is unadjusted for price level changes. Nominal GDP and the Consumer Price Index (CPI) are reported for each country in the Quarterly Industry Report, together with other economic indicators. The GDP and the CPI indexes are indexed to equal 100 in Year 2, Quarter 4. Past levels of nominal GDP and CPI are shown in Appendix C.

```
                        FINANCIAL MARKET DATA
                     Merica  Sereno              ---Credit Rating---
GDP Index (Nominal)  100.00  100.00  Interest Rates:  No. 1  No. 2  No. 3
Consumer Price Index 100.00  100.00    Long-Term       8.40   9.10  10.60
Stock Market Index   100.00            Short-Term     11.00  11.20  12.30
3-Month Time CD Rate   9.50
```

An index of real GDP, adjusted for the impact of inflation, can be calculated by dividing the nominal GDP by the CPI, as follows:

$$\text{Real GDP Index} = \frac{\text{GDP}}{\text{CPI}} \times 100$$

In order to forecast demand effectively, your firm should become familiar with the historical GDP and CPI data for the simulation, as well as the available real GDP forecasts.

Your firm subscribes to ACCUDAT, a statistical service which provides forecasts of real GDP and exchange rates each quarter for the following four quarters. At the same time, they report actual values for the most recent four quarters. The ACCUDAT forecast is found on the first page of the Quarterly Industry Report (see Appendix C).

```
                  REAL GROSS DOMESTIC PRODUCT FORECAST
           Actual Values, Last 4 Quarters    Forecast Values, Next 4 Quarters
           Qtr 5   Qtr 6   Qtr 7   Qtr 8     Qtr 9   Qtr 10   Qtr 11   Qtr 12

Merica    102.17  102.66  100.93   99.90     99.57   97.94    98.79    94.46
Sereno     94.87   97.05   98.20  100.00    104.76  107.08   109.14   115.87
--------------------------------------------------------------------------
                        EXCHANGE RATE FORECAST

Sereno      5.99    5.97    5.97    6.00      6.09    6.02     6.08     6.18
```

This forecast may be used, reliably, for near-term economic forecasts. However, you are cautioned that while the historical data are accurate, the forecasted values are estimates obtained by pooling the results of a survey of leading economists. The forecast tends to be more accurate for the first quarter immediately ahead, with the accuracy decreasing with each subsequent quarter. The reported values represent the mean values for the next four quarters obtained from the survey of the group of economists.

Projecting the Trend of Growth

Changes in a country's overall level of economic activity from quarter to quarter may be separated for analytical purposes into three distinct types of effects: the overall trend, the cyclical effect and the seasonal effect. In preparing a forecast, we suggest that you separate the problem of forecasting economic growth from the problem of forecasting cyclical and seasonal fluctuations. A good first step is to project the average rate of growth in real GDP which has occurred in the country over the past eight quarters. The values that are shown below provide an example for Merica.

Quarter	GDP Index	CPI Index	Real GDP
1	84.0	85.8	98.0
2	86.3	86.5	99.8
3	89.7	88.2	101.7
4	91.9	90.0	102.1
5	94.1	92.1	102.2
6	96.6	94.1	102.7
7	98.1	97.2	100.9
8	100.0	100.0	100.0
			Forecast Real GDP
9			99.7
10			98.0
11			98.7
12			94.5

As you can see, the economy seems to have peaked out and may begin to slide in the coming year. Time will tell whether the forecasted decline will materialize. Even though the eight quarters of historical data, together with a four-quarter forecast, provide a relatively small base upon which to make a statistical projection, it still may be done. You probably will wish, however, to revise such a projection as additional data become available during the course of the simulation. Two relatively easy types of projections will be suggested, although you may wish to use other methods.

The first and simplest method, though not necessarily the most accurate, is to plot the observed data on a chart and connect the points of observed data. Then "eye-ball" the resulting chart and use a ruler to extend the general trend of the plotted line across the rest of the chart. A more sophisticated and, we might say, more statistically reliable method of projecting a trend is to compute a least-squares trend line based upon the observed historical values of GDP. This may easily be done using a spreadsheet package such as Excel, Lotus 1-2-3 or Quattro. The simple plot described above also may be done quickly with a spreadsheet program's graphing feature.

Projecting Economic Fluctuations

After estimating the overall trend of the GDP, the next step is to estimate how the GDP will fluctuate over the course of the business cycle. During periods of economic upturn, the GDP is very likely to grow at a rate faster than the overall trend; and during periods of economic recession, it is very likely to grow at a slower rate or even decline.

Durable goods demand has more pronounced cycles with greater fluctuations than the GDP. It also tends to have somewhat longer downswings and shorter upswings. Your biggest problem, as with forecasting in the business world, will probably be to correctly identify, in advance, the turning point in the business cycle. This involves prior identification of the exact quarter in which the GDP will change direction and move from a period of recession to one of economic upturn or vice versa. Your knowledge of the characteristics of economic fluctuations should help in estimating the likely length of any particular business cycle in your simulated world.

Leading Indicators

Forecasting accuracy may be improved by using economic time series data which forecasting experts consider to be "leading indicators." A leading indicator is a data series that has historically tended to change direction earlier than the change in the general level of economic activity. However, even though certain series tend to lead changes in the GDP most of the time, they do not always do so. Sometimes they change direction when the GDP does not follow suit. Thus, it is possible for leading indicators to signal "false starts." Other times they have been known to change direction after the GDP changes.

Data on several economic indicators are provided to you in *The Business Policy Game*. Appendix C includes historical information about the level of stock market prices and the behavior of interest rates. Current data on these variables will be reported each quarter throughout the course of the simulation.

If interest rates and the stock market index both turn downward, the possibility of an early downturn in the level of GDP should be considered. Such a signal by leading indicators, however, should not be considered in isolation. It will provide a clue, along with other data, about the possible future behavior of economic fluctuations in your simulated world. You probably will want to update your GDP forecast as additional information becomes available during the course of playing the simulation.

Forecasting Sales

Using the Sales Forecast Work Sheets

One sales forecasting approach is to view sales in a future quarter as being equal to the previous quarter's sales plus an incremental change in the number of units sold. Changes in the various individual factors that influence the level of sales will affect the level of total sales. This relationship might be expressed as follows:

Future sales = Previous sales + Incremental sales

where incremental sales are determined by changes in real GDP, seasonal factors, price, advertising expenditures, distribution, sales force activity, new model introduction and competitors' activities. Incremental sales may be either positive or negative. Mathematically,

Incremental sales = f(GDP, S, M1, M2, ... , Mn)

where GDP stands for real gross domestic product, S represents seasonal factors and M1, M2, ..., Mn represent the various marketing factors that affect the sales of a firm and its competitors.

Sales Forecast Work Sheets have been developed to assist you in forecasting your firm's future sales (see Figure 6-1). The Sales Forecast Work Sheets utilize this incremental model. To forecast sales for the coming year, begin by forecasting sales for each of the four quarters. Use one work sheet for each quarter to forecast quarterly sales by market area. After completing the quarterly forecasts, sum the quarterly sales forecasts to arrive at an annual forecast. We suggest that you follow the procedure indicated on the work sheet to develop your sales forecast. Copies of the work sheet are provided in Appendix D. The FORECAST.WK1 file on the Player's Program Disk packaged with this manual contains a spreadsheet template of the Sales Forecast Work Sheet.

We will use Merica, Area 1 to provide an example of using the work sheet to forecast sales. The real GDP forecast serves as the basis for the first entry on the Sales Forecast Work Sheet. Enter your forecasted **change in GDP** for the quarter (-.03 percent in our example, calculated from the ACCUDAT forecast shown above).

Previous Sales

The next step is to enter the actual sales (in thousands of units) from the previous quarter on the Sales, Previous Quarter line of the work sheet. For your first forecast this will be the sales figure for Year 2, Quarter 4 from the historical data in Appendix C or from a computer printout provided by your administrator for that quarter. If you plan to forecast total sales of your firm in a country or market area, enter the number of units your firm sold in that country or area during the previous quarter. For our example, shown in Figure 6-1, we will assume that sales in the previous quarter were 121,000 units.

GDP Changes

Sales of your simulated consumer durable product tend to be affected by changes in the level of economic activity in your simulated world. In an upturn, sales rise somewhat faster than the GDP; and in a downturn, they fall somewhat faster. You need to estimate the effect which changes in the level of economic activity will have upon your company's sales. Regression analysis of historical relationships between GDP and sales may give you some clues as to the amount of change to expect in your sales with a given change in GDP. If you undertake statistical analysis, remember that your price changes and other marketing activities, as well as the marketing activities of your competitors also will affect the level of sales. Allowance must be made for these factors in addition to the effect of changes in GDP. Alternatively, you may decide to make only rough estimates of the effect of GDP changes on the level of sales. All estimates should be refined as more data become available during the course of the simulation.

The ACCUDAT forecast of real GDP for Year 3, Quarter 1 indicates a decrease in the index from 100.0 to a mean value of 99.7 (about three-tenths of one percent). Suppose that you estimate that the sales of your durable good product will decrease by, perhaps, as much as twice the percentage decrease in real GDP. Your unit sales **decrease**, then, would be last quarter's sales times six-tenths of one percent, or

$$121,000 \times 0.006 = 726$$

This is rounded to 1,000 for our example and entered in the Sales Forecast Work Sheet (Figure 6-1) as -1.

Seasonal Factors

Next, an estimate should be made of the likely change in sales caused by seasonal factors. In *The Business Policy Game*, sales are highest during the second and fourth quarters of each year. During the first and third quarters, they are somewhat lower. ACCUDAT has developed a seasonal index for your world based upon an economic analysis of historical data. The index shows the following seasonal variation:

Quarter	Index
1	.92
2	1.01
3	.91
4	1.16

THE BUSINESS POLICY GAME SALES FORECAST WORK SHEET					
World _1_ Company _1_ Year __3_ Quarter __1__	Consoli-dated	Merica Area 1	Merica Area 2	Merica Area 3	Sereno
Forecasted GDP Change (percent)	----------	-0.3 %	%	%	%
Sales, Previous Quarter, thousands of units		121			
Estimated Sales Increments (thousands of units)					
From GDP Change		-1			
Seasonal Factors		-24			
Price Change		+5			
Advertising Change		+4			
Sales Salary Change		0			
Sales Commission Change		0			
Number of Salespersons Change		0			
New Model Introduction		-0			
Competitors' Actions		-2			
Total Incremental Change		-18			
Total Sales Forecast (thousands of units)		103			
Expected Average Price (per unit)	$.	$ 9.80	$.	$.	Ps
Expected Sales Revenue (thousands of local currency)	$	$1,009	$	$	Ps

Figure 6-1
Illustration of the Sales Forecast Work Sheet

These index values indicate that **with no change in any other factor affecting sales**, first-quarter sales are expected to be about 92 percent of the quarterly average, second-quarter sales about 101 percent and so forth.

Seasonal variations for Sereno are very similar to those for Merica.

Enter the expected **incremental change due to seasonal factors** on the next line of the work sheet. The decline from the fourth quarter (116 percent of average) to the first quarter of the next year (92 percent of average) might be expected to be quite large—about 20 percent:

$$(116,000 - 92,000) \div 116,000 = .207 \text{ percent}$$

If you estimate that seasonal factors would cause sales to decline by about 20 percent during the first quarter, other things being equal, multiply the previous quarter's sales of 121,000 units by 0.20 and enter -24

$$121,000 \text{ x } -.20 = -24,200$$

Changes in the level of GDP and the seasonal factors that affect your sales level are beyond the control of your company's management. However, the following factors that affect your sales can readily be influenced by your own decisions.

Marketing Activities

Changes in the price of your product, advertising expenditures, sales salaries, commissions, number of salespeople and the introduction of new models all will influence your levels of sales. The likely effect of your decisions in regard to each of these factors should be estimated and entered on the appropriate line of the Sales Forecast Work Sheet.

1. <u>Price Changes</u>. Other things being equal, a decrease in a company's wholesale price from the initial $10 (or Ps 75) will tend to result in the generation of sufficient additional sales to increase total sales revenue. Conversely, an increase in the price of the product will tend to cause a large enough reduction in the level of demand that total sales revenues will drop. It can be said, therefore, that the price elasticity of demand for your simulated consumer durable good is greater than one, or elastic. Product quality levels affect the degree of price elasticity. Higher quality products tend to be less sensitive to price changes than lower quality products. Deluxe quality (level number 1) is less price elastic than standard quality (level number 2) and economy quality (level number 3) is more price elastic than standard quality.

The level of demand for a company's product also will be affected by price changes of competitors. For example, if all companies in the industry were to reduce their prices from $10 per unit to $9.50 per unit, total industry sales would rise. The volume of sales for Company 1 would increase, but not by as great a factor as if Company 1 had been the only one to decrease its price. In other words, the **average price** charged by the firms in the industry will have an effect upon the level of demand for all firms in the industry, in addition to the effect of a price change by an individual company.

Enter the expected change in sales due to price changes on the work sheet. Suppose that you intend to decrease your unit price by 2 percent. After analyzing the historical relationship between sales and price changes, you might believe that a 2 percent price cut would produce a sales increase of 4 percent. Continuing our example, with the previous quarter's sales at 121,000 units, you would estimate an increase of about 5,000 units in the coming quarter and enter +5 on the work sheet:

$$121,000 \times .04 = 4,840$$

2. <u>Advertising</u>. Increases in the level of advertising expenditures will tend to increase the level of demand for your company's product and decreases generally will tend to reduce the level of demand. We suggest that you avoid sharp fluctuations in advertising expenditures. Stick to a well-planned strategy of resource allocations.

If you expect to increase advertising expenditures by 5 percent next quarter, you might anticipate a sales increase of 3 percent, or about 4,000 units in our illustration:

$$121,000 \times .03 = 3,630$$

The amount, +4, has been entered on the work sheet in Figure 6-1 to represent an increase of 4,000 units.

3. <u>Sales Force and Sales Compensation</u>. In addition to advertising, a company's promotion effort includes the activities of its sales force. The impact of this effort on sales is determined both by the number of active salespeople in the field and by the enthusiasm and perseverance of the salespeople. Again, other things being equal, an increase in your sales effort will tend to increase your volume of sales.

We suggest that you estimate the incremental changes in sales that are likely to result from changes in sales compensation and from changes in the number of active salespeople. In our illustration, we assume no change in compensation levels for the coming quarter and no additions to the sales force. If you hire additional sales people this quarter, you would want to include their incremental effect for next quarter.

4. <u>New Model Introduction</u>. Enter the incremental change expected to result from the introduction of a new model. This estimate should include the effect of the quality level of the model. Remember that a new model will go on sale in all areas during the quarter following the quarter that production was begun. Our illustration assumes no new models because R & D has not released a new model for introduction.

Competitors' Actions

The last item listed in the incremental change section of the work sheet is Competitors' Actions, another factor beyond your control. In many instances, you will have no way of anticipating what the activities of your competitors will be. You may have reason to believe, though, that your competitors will match a cut in price that you may have made in a previous quarter. If so, you know that such an action will partially negate the increased sales that you otherwise could expect from your own price cut. Any incremental effect that you can foresee as a result of competitors' activities should be entered on the work sheet.

In our illustration, we assume that our intelligence reports indicate that competitors are likely to cut prices, too, partially negating the effects of our price cut. If we assume that their action would reduce our sales by 2,000 units below what they would otherwise be, -2 should be entered on the work sheet.

Completing the Forecast

Completing the remainder of the Sales Forecast Work Sheet is a matter of simple arithmetic. The sales from the previous quarter plus the estimated total incremental change equals the forecasted total sales for the quarter. Total sales are multiplied by the average price that you expect to charge. The result is your estimate of expected sales revenue for the quarter for Merica, Area 1. Similar forecasts should be made for all market areas in which your firm is operating.

Don't be surprised if your actual sales during the first quarter of Year 3 deviate somewhat from your forecasts. And remember that the values estimated in the example are for purposes of explanation. They are not really inside information regarding the relationships between product demand and the various marketing factors. You may find that the actual relationships are somewhat different, and you are encouraged to make your own estimates. As you gain additional experience in forecasting, your estimates are likely to improve considerably. You will learn more about your industry, your competitors and the impact and results of the decisions that you make. However, your forecasts will never be totally accurate. Your management, therefore, should allow for a margin of safety to protect against errors in your forecasts. Specific policies should be established regarding the minimum level of inventory to maintain in each area, over and above forecasted demand, as a **safety stock**. Also, a policy is needed to set the minimum amount of cash that you believe will enable your firm to meet financial obligations, should sales revenue fall below the amount that has been forecasted.

Look Ahead, Now

Don't stop with a sales forecast for Year 3, Quarter 1. In our example, it was shown that sales can be expected to grow in Quarter 2 because of the seasonal factor, but the growth will be tempered somewhat by the projected decrease in real GDP. That is going to happen even if you don't plan an aggressive marketing program. Work out the numbers for the rest of the year so that your production department can plan to have enough production capacity on line to meet your needs. If an expansion in capacity will be required, the plans must be made right away because it takes time to expand (See Chapter 8).

Your company's production **could** be expanded quickly by about 20 percent if all production workers work overtime. Beyond that, even adding second-shift production requires a full quarter of production-worker training before anything can be produced. And investing in more capacity may take from one to three quarters of construction, depending on which investment alternative is chosen.

So plan ahead—now! Start by completing your sales forecast for each quarter of Year 3. Then make estimates of capacity requirements for the following year so that your operations department can get started.

Summary of Relationships

1. **Gross Domestic Product** in *The Business Policy Game* is patterned after actual indexes of economic growth. **Interest rates** and the **stock market index** usually are considered to be leading indicators related to changes in GDP.

2. **Future sales** may be forecast by use of a model that is illustrated with the sales forecast work sheets found in Appendix D. The work sheet also is available in a spreadsheet template on your Player's Program Disk in file FORECAST.WK1.

Future sales = Previous sales + Incremental sales

Incremental sales in this model can be described as a function of real gross domestic product (GDP), seasonal factors (S) and various marketing factors that have been described (M1, M2, ... Mn). These factors include price changes, advertising, sales salaries and commissions, number of salespeople and new model introductions of a firm and its competitors. Thus,

Incremental sales = f(GDP, S, M1, M2, ... Mn)

3. **Sales forecasts** should be made separately for each **market area**.

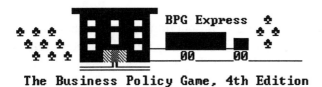
CHAPTER 7

PRODUCTION: PLANNING, SCHEDULING AND COSTS

Your firm's production department should begin the simulation by setting functional-level production goals and objectives and developing production strategy to accomplish these goals. Production goals should support the overall goals developed at the business level and should focus upon what production can contribute to achieving the business-level goals. The following business-level goal was used as an example in Chapter 4:

Maintain a rate of return on stockholders' end-of-Year 2 investment in your company's stock (goal) of at least 20 (hurdle) percent (index) through Year 7 (time).

Production goals and objectives that support this business-level goal might be:

Goal: Limit inventory storage costs (goal) to one (hurdle) percent (index) of sales (time implicit).

Objective: Maintain an inventory level (goal) at the end of each quarter (time) equal to four weeks (hurdle) of sales (index).

Goal: Maintain sufficient production capacity (goal) to meet the growth (hurdle) in customer demand (index) during management's tenure (time).

Objective: Increase production capacity (goal) by 30 (hurdle) percent (index) during Year 4 (time).

Other goals and objectives may focus upon production costs and capacity utilization.

Production strategy should be designed to enable your production department to attain its goals and objectives. The strategy should plan for the allocation of production resources to gain maximum efficiency while meeting market demand. The strategy for the inventory goal would focus upon production scheduling. The strategy for matching capacity with demand would involve all options for expansion and contraction of capacity. An effective production strategy should include **all** of the production variables which require resources.

The quarter to quarter tactical decisions which your production management must make are described below. These decisions should be considered in the light of your firm's sales forecast and guided by your production strategy and overall company policy. This chapter will provide suggestions for planning current and future production needs, discuss the scheduling of production for the current quarter and outline the costs associated with various production alternatives. Before we proceed, let's take a little time to discuss the actual production process that takes place within your plant(s). This should give you better insight into the production facilities your firm manages.

The Production Process

Your firm fabricates approximately half of the parts needed to manufacture its product and purchases the remaining parts. Thus, a production line consists of several fabricating machines plus an assembly line. The production line is balanced so that the fabricating machines are able to provide parts at the rate they are needed to meet the demands of the assembly line.

Your firm has contracted with a raw materials supplier and a parts vendor for all of its materials and parts. The contract calls for each supplier to deliver the materials and parts needed for one day's production run to your plant at least an hour prior to the beginning of the first shift each day. This provides sufficient time to ensure that the materials and parts are positioned at their required locations before the line begins to operate. The actual volume of materials and parts can be adjusted on a daily basis to compensate for variations in production due to breakdowns, illness and normal fluctuations in production volumes.

Past experience has shown that your suppliers are very reliable. You can also depend upon your line supervisors to make the needed day-to-day adjustments in materials and parts supplies. Thus, your production team can focus upon providing and scheduling sufficient production capacity to meet market demand. It also is responsible for product development and employee training.

Operations Planning and Scheduling

Existing Capacity

Your firm has six production lines available for use as you assume management responsibilities at the beginning of Year 3. Each of the lines is capable of producing 4,000 units during a forty-hour week. Thus, normal production per line is 52,000 units during a thirteen-week quarter.

With six lines operating at normal capacity, your plant will produce about 312,000 units during each quarter.

Actual production, however, may vary from this amount by up to 5 percent in Merica because of factors beyond your control. For example, if production machine down-time is greater than normal, your plant might produce as few as 296,000 units. Conversely, efficiency of your production workers could turn out to be very high in another quarter and the six lines might produce as many as 327,000 units. Experience has shown that production facilities in Sereno tend to have wider variances, with actual output more likely to be less than scheduled output. Variances may be as high as 15 percent.

While your current production capacity is somewhat fixed, you have a number of alternatives for adjusting capacity. A temporary reduction in your firm's production schedule may be arranged if you wish to lay off workers to idle one or more lines for the entire quarter. Workers laid off this quarter are furloughed for one quarter and are recalled on the first day of the next quarter unless you lay them off again. For a layoff lasting more than 13 weeks, it sometimes is more cost effective to deactivate a line. When a line is deactivated, workers are discharged and the machinery is secured, so that reactivation will require one quarter's advance notice to train new workers and prepare the machinery for active use. The costs associated with layoff and deactivation procedures are outlined below.

Production may be expanded by scheduling overtime work, by adding a second shift in your home area plant, by adding additional lines in an existing plant, by constructing additions to a plant, or by construction of new plants in other marketing areas. Overtime costs are described below, under "Production Costs," and the necessary procedures and cash outlays required for other forms of expansion of production facilities are described in Chapter 8.

With these various production alternatives in mind, and considering the costs associated with each alternative, the next step is to determine the strategy that your firm will use to produce sufficient units to meet your sales demand. Suggestions were made in Chapter 6 for completing a sales forecast. This forecast should serve as the basis for the production plans that you will make.

Level Versus Seasonal Production

There are two basic approaches to production planning for a product that has sharp seasonal fluctuations in its sales. One strategy is to plan production during each period of operations that will be approximately equal to the expected sales during that period. Because of higher seasonal demand in the second and fourth quarters, your firm could undertake heavy production schedules during those quarters each year, while idling some lines or otherwise reducing the amount of production during the first and third quarters.

This type of plan has the obvious advantage of enabling your firm to operate with a minimum investment in finished goods inventory. Storage costs could be held at relatively low levels, and the cost of funds necessary to finance inventory accumulations would be minimal. The disadvantage to such a plan is that production costs are likely to be considerably higher. Sharp seasonal fluctuations in production will require adding large numbers of workers to your labor force during the second and fourth quarters of each year and operating your production facilities at or above normal capacity during those quarters. Conversely, during the first and third quarters many of the workers would be temporarily laid off, and a significant portion of your production facilities would be standing idle.

In developing your firm's policies regarding production, you will wish to compare the costs and relative flexibility of seasonal production with a strategy that sometimes is called a level-production plan. A simplified version of the level-production plan would require you to estimate the total volume of expected sales during the coming year and divide that amount by four. Production during each quarter of simulated operation then should be equal to approximately one-fourth of expected annual sales. During the first and third quarters, your firm would produce more goods than are necessary to meet expected sales, and inventories would accumulate to meet the larger demands of the second and fourth quarters.

Obviously, inventory storage costs would be higher than with seasonal production, and more cash would be necessary to finance the inventory buildup. On the other hand, level production would enable you to maintain a stable work force and better utilize your production capacity. A projection of production costs, inventory storage requirements and the cost and availability of funds to finance those inventories will assist you in deciding which type of production plan will best meet the needs of your firm. You may decide to use a combination of both plans that would permit some seasonal variation of production but still involves some inventory buildup for the peak sales quarter.

Inventory Storage Costs

Each production plant (home and non-home area) has room to store 300,000 units of finished product. Thus, your firm begins Year 3 with storage space for 300,000 units in your home-area plant. If additional plants are built, they also will include storage for 300,000 units. It costs 10 cents per unit (or 60 centavos in Sereno) to store unsold goods in your plant(s) for a quarter. If the inventory exceeds the available storage space in a plant, your firm will rent space in a public warehouse in the same area to store the additional units of product. Units will **not** be shipped to other areas for storage. Public warehouse storage costs amount to 30 cents per unit of product (or Ps 1.80 in Sereno). Units in storage in the public warehouse will be sold prior to the units stored in your plant. All storage costs for a quarter are paid at the beginning of the following quarter.

Production Plan Work Sheets

Work sheets are provided in Appendix D for developing a production plan and estimating production costs. A spreadsheet template of the Production Plan Work Sheet also is available on the disk packaged with this manual in file PRODPLAN.WK1. These work sheets will assist your firm in planning your production requirements, scheduling the necessary production and estimating costs. If your sales forecasts indicate a need for expanding your production facilities, you also will find these work sheets extremely useful in planning the rate at which you should expand and the type of expansion that you should undertake. Investment alternatives for expansion of your plant are detailed in Chapter 8, along with the costs that are associated with each alternative.

Each work sheet has space for one quarter's operations, with a column for each area and for a consolidation of values. Thus, you may want to use a series of work sheets to forecast production requirements for at least a year. The spreadsheet template file on your disk contains four quarterly work sheets plus a consolidated yearly work sheet. As the competition progresses, the accuracy of your production forecast can be assessed and forecasts of future production requirements can be revised.

An example of the top section of a Production Plan Work Sheet is shown in Figure 7-1. The work sheet will assist you in determining the amount of production that must be scheduled for the quarter as well as the number of units each sales office should order. Our discussion will focus upon the Merica Area 1 column, which we will assume is for the home area, although the other columns will be referenced at times. Suppose that you have forecast sales in Merica Area 1 for the first quarter of Year 3 to be about 103,000 units, as illustrated in Figure 6-1. Your sales estimates should be entered (in thousands of units) on the first line of the Production Plan Work Sheet, as shown in Figure 7-1.

If your management has adopted a seasonal production strategy, you may wish to maintain a relatively small safety stock on hand, say 20 percent of expected sales. Adding this to your sales forecast will yield the total number of units needed for the quarter by area. The minimum number of units needed to meet your expected sales in Merica, Area 1, and still maintain your safety stock will be about 124,000 units:

$$103 + 21 = 124 \text{ units}$$

So enter 124 on the work sheet as Total Units Required.

We find from Appendix C that Merica Area 1 had 29,000 units of inventory on hand at the end of Year 2, Quarter 4, so enter 29 for Beginning Inventory.

Sales offices must place orders to obtain goods to sell in their areas. No orders, no goods! While a sales office has priority in obtaining goods from its local plant, all units produced and not specifically ordered by the sales office may be sold to affiliates. Thus, it is very dangerous for a sales office to rely upon the output of a plant in its area unless the output is committed by a sales office order. The size of the necessary sales office order is determined by subtracting Beginning Inventory from Total Units Required. In our example, the sales office order for Merica 1 would be 95,000 units.

$$124 - 29 = 95$$

Enter 95 under Sales Office Orders on the work sheet.

THE BUSINESS POLICY GAME PRODUCTION PLAN WORK SHEET					
World _1_ Company _1_ Year _3_ Quarter _1_	Consoli-dated	Merica Area 1	Merica Area 2	Merica Area 3	Sereno
OUTPUT, INVENTORY, AND SALES ANALYSIS (in thousands of units)					
Sales Forecast	318	103	75	75	65
Safety Stock	64	21	15	15	13
Total Units Required	382	124	90	90	78
Beginning Inventory	55	29	10	10	6
Sales Office Orders	327	95	80	80	72
Production Scheduled	328	328	0	0	0
Local Sales Office Purchases	95	95	0	0	0
Local Sales Office Shortage	232	0	80	80	72
Goods Available to Affiliates	233	233	0	0	0
Affiliate Sales Office Purchases	232	0	80	80	72
Sales to Affiliates	232	232	0	0	0
Goods Available for Sale	383	125	90	90	78
Sold to Customers	318	103	75	75	65
Sold to Liquidators					
Ending Inventory	65	22	15	15	13

FIGURE 7-1

Illustration of the Production Plan Work Sheet—Top Section

Production is scheduled in lumps of 52,000 units per line for a normal 40 hour week. If your only sales office was in Merica Area 1, your firm would need to schedule only two lines to meet the demand. The remaining four lines would have to be idled or deactivated. However, we will assume your firm has a sales office in each of the four market areas. If we further assume that Merica Area 2 and Merica Area 3 each requires 80,000 units and Sereno requires 72,000 units (if you believe these are accurate forecasts, I have a piece of the Brooklyn Bridge I would like to sell you), consolidated sales office orders would total 327,000 units or a little more than the normal capacity of six lines, producing 52,000 each for a total of 312,000 units. Thus, the additional 15,000 units will have to be produced using overtime. Six lines running 42 hours per week should produce 327,600 units. Rounding this to thousands of units, 328 is entered on the work sheet for Production Scheduled.

For a producing area, Local Sales Office Purchases from the plant are equal to the Sales Office Order as long as sufficient goods are produced to supply that amount. If production is less than the amount of the order, the difference should be recorded as a Local Sale Office Shortage. Then, with sufficient production, subtract the Local Sales Office Purchase (95,000) from the Production Scheduled (328,000) to find the Goods Available to Affiliates.

$$328 - 95 = 233$$

With 233,000 units available to supply all of the other sales offices, there is enough to fill all of the orders. In our example, the Affiliate Sales Office Purchases for the non-producing areas equal the Sales Office Orders. The Sales to Affiliates equals the Affiliate Sales Office Purchases, or 232,000 units:

$$80 + 80 + 72 = 232$$

When more than one plant is in operation, units are Sold to Affiliates according to a long-standing company policy. Goods available for shipment to affiliates are shipped from Sereno first, from domestic non-home areas second (in numerical order) and finally from the home area. The Sold to Affiliates entries would reflect this priority. If goods available for shipment are less than Sales Office Orders, shipments will be pro-rated according to the size of the orders.

In each area, Goods available for sale equals Beginning Inventory plus Production Scheduled plus Affiliate Sales Office Purchases minus Sales to Affiliates. Goods Sold to Customers equals either the sales forecast or Goods Available for Sale if it is less than the sales forecast. The ending inventory is equal to Goods Available for Sale minus Sold to Customers. Note how these values have been entered on the work sheet.

Plan your production requirements now for the rest of Year 3. Then plan an additional quarter as you complete each decision set. This will provide your firm with a running, four-quarter production plan that will allow time to expand your productive capacity when needed.

Scheduling

On each quarterly decision form, **all available production lines in each plant and for each shift must either be scheduled for production, idled or deactivated**. If a line is available for production but is not scheduled to produce, it must be idled (the employees will be laid off for the quarter) or deactivated. Unless all available lines are accounted for on the decision form, the computer program will reject your decision set with an error message requiring you to account for all available lines.

1. Schedule lines. Production lines scheduled for first-shift operation must be entered on the decision form for the market area in which they are located. Enter the number of production lines that are to be producing (not more than the maximum available) and the number of hours that are to be scheduled per week (from 40 to 48). Make sure your entry is for a market area (or

areas) in which you have a plant. If your entry is in the wrong area, the decision values will be rejected by the decision-entry program.

Limits:　　Lines:　　0 to maximum number of lines available
　　　　　　Hours:　　0, 40 to 48 (per week)

	Sales Office Orders (000s)	Production Schedule	
		Lines	Hours
Area 1	# 87	# 6	# 40
Area 2	# 75	#	#
Area 3	# 75	#	#
Sereno	# 75	#	#
2nd Shift		#	#

　　2. <u>Second shift</u>. Production on a second-shift line is possible only in a firm's home-area plant. Enter the number of second-shift lines that are to be producing (up to the maximum number of lines available) and the number of hours per line that are to be scheduled each week (from 40 to 48). As with the first shift, all available second-shift lines must either be scheduled for production, idled or deactivated.

IMPORTANT NOTE

Second-shift lines are not available and may not be scheduled until production workers have been trained to operate the lines. The training process is described in Chapter 8. Training of new second-shift workers requires one quarter before production may begin. **Advance planning is required, at least one quarter before you intend to begin production**. Thus, if you wish to begin production on one or more second-shift lines in Year 3, Quarter 2, you **must** make an entry for 2nd shift under New Lines for Year 3, Quarter 1.

Limits: Lines:　　　0 to maximum number of lines available
　　　　Hours　　　0, 40 to 48 (per week)

　　3. <u>Temporary Layoff</u>. Production lines that are available but not scheduled for production and have not been deactivated should be idled by a temporary layoff. A layoff is for one quarter. The lines are available and the workers may be recalled to resume production in the

following quarter. Enter the number of lines which you plan to leave idle on the decision form under Capacity Adjustment–Layoff. Make sure that all first-shift lines are accounted for and all second-shift lines are accounted for (scheduled, idled or deactivated). If you idle a first-shift line, a corresponding second-shift line must be idled or deactivated unless there remain at least as many active first-shift lines as second-shift lines. A second-shift line may not continue operating unless there is a corresponding line on the first shift. Check to make sure your entry is for the area in which you want to idle lines. Each idled line results in a charge of $52,000 per quarter (or Ps 312,000 in Sereno), subject to inflation. The amount will be reported as Temporary Layoff Costs in the Production Cost Analysis section of the Operating Information Report (Report D).

Limits: 0 to number of lines available

> **IMPORTANT NOTE**
> If your firm decides to operate its plant at less than normal capacity, lines that are not used **must** be idled or deactivated. Lines that have been idled are immediately available for production in the following quarter or they may be idled again at that time if you need to maintain reduced production levels.

	Sales Office Orders (000s)	Capacity Adjustment		
		Layoff	Deac-tivate	Reac-tivate
Area 1	# 87	#	#	#
Area 2	# 75	#	#	#
Area 3	# 75	#	#	#
Sereno	# 75	#	#	#
2nd Shift		#	#	#

    4. <u>Deactivate lines</u>. Any line that is available for production (both first and second-shift) may be deactivated and removed from production until such time as you choose to reactivate the line. Enter the number of lines that you desire to deactivate in the appropriate area on the decision form under Capacity Adjustment–Deactivate. Deactivated lines are not available the following quarter and may not be scheduled again for production until they have been reactivated (see paragraph 5 on the next page).

    Deactivated lines provide less flexibility because they may not be used for production again until they have been reactivated, which takes a full quarter of preparation. Deactivated lines incur a one-time cost of $100,000 (or Ps 600,000 in Sereno) when they are taken out of production. The deactivation cost of $100,000 for each second-shift and $100,000 for each first-shift line is charged under Other Expenses on the income statement. Remember, all costs are subject to increases due to inflation.

The only restriction on your ability to idle or deactivate production lines is that the number of second-shift lines may not exceed the number of producing lines on the regular shift. In other words, if first-shift lines are **idled**, any second-shift line utilizing the same equipment must be idled at the same time. If first-shift lines are **deactivated**, corresponding second-shift lines must be deactivated, too.

Limits: 0 to the number of lines available for production

5. <u>Reactivate lines</u>. First and second-shift production lines that have previously been deactivated may be reactivated and made available for production. Reactivation takes one quarter and requires an expenditure of $50,000 per line (or Ps 300,000 in Sereno) for training workers. This charge is reported under Training Expense on your income statement. These costs are subject to the inflation rate of the country. Lines that previously have been deactivated (and are available for reactivation) are reported in the Operating Information Report.

	Area 1	Area 2	Area 3	Sereno
Lines Available for Reactivation	2	0	0	0

Enter the number of lines to be reactivated under the appropriate area on the decision form. Lines may not be scheduled for production until the following quarter.

Limits: 0 to number of lines previously deactivated

Research and Development

At the close of Year 2, each firm in your world was spending approximately $70,000 per quarter on product research and development (R & D). Money spent on R & D funds a research team located at your firm's headquarters which is developing advanced designs of your current product. In commercial R & D applications such as yours, the amount of money spent in product development may have little relation to the results obtained in the short term. Rapidly increasing the budget for a research department probably involves bringing many new research people on line. Each of the new people will require space and time to get acquainted with the project at hand. It may involve significant expenditures in the short run without immediate payoffs (although later returns may turn out to be significant).

Another BPG simulated company with only modest immediate expansion may show similar immediate results, if any, though perhaps not with the same long-run expectations. This has to do with the law of diminishing returns when expenditures are rapidly increased. Much of the expenditure of the rapidly expanding company may have little immediate effect, but with the prospect of later payoffs. While the relationship between the amount of funds spent and the time required to develop a new product is unlikely to be linear, you can expect substantial continuous funding of Research & Development efforts ultimately to yield a stream of new models. Of course, after a certain point, additional funds will not lead to any appreciable decrease in the time it takes to develop a product.

The personnel working in your R & D department are highly skilled professionals. They are difficult to find and thus cannot easily be replaced once they leave the firm. Dramatic swings in the R & D budget from quarter to quarter will likely have a negative impact upon the morale of the department causing some of your best people to leave. If severe budget cuts are experienced, a new model which is close to release may be scrapped for lack of funds. Later increases in funds may restart the project; however, the time required to complete the project will be much longer than if the project had been carried through to completion originally. The additional time is due to the extra time required to replace personnel who were previously working on the project, as well as the time required to bring existing personnel who were working on the project back up to speed.

An effective research and development program is an essential element of a firm's success. Without such a program, your firm would have no new products to introduce into the market-place. Your product offering would become obsolete relative to that of your competitors and your sales would be expected to suffer severely.

R&D/Training	
(home currency)	
R&D	$ 72
Trng	$ 68

Operations and Production Employee Training

Training expenditures for operations and production employees are funded at the corporate headquarters. Your firm spends operating funds on three different types of employee training.

1. People are hired to replace salespeople who quit, retire, die or are promoted. Those new employees must be taught company policies and operating procedures. This type of training can be minimized by following practices that promote a stable work force. Training of salespeople is discussed in Chapter 5.

2. New production employees must be trained to operate expanded production facilities. This type of training is discussed in Chapter 8 under additional production lines.

3. Training that upgrades operations and production employee skills may qualify them for assignment to more complex jobs or for promotions. Training is provided to maintain employee competence levels and to introduce employees to new equipment and production processes. This type of training is discussed below. The amout of this training budget is a decision variable to be entered on the decision form.

The expenses for all three types of training are included in Total Training Expenses on your income statement.

Expenditures for ongoing training of production and operations employees should lead to lower production costs by enhancing employee skills and by improving manufacturing processes. Cost reduction becomes especially important when new products are developed, as new products tend to cost more to produce than do older products. There are significant advantages in being a low-cost producer in terms of profit margins and flexibility during price wars. The more money your firm spends on training, the more it can expect to save on production costs. However, the law of diminishing returns still applies.

Cost reductions from this type of training are reported in the Operating Information Report (page 2, Report E) as a savings level. The higher the savings level, the greater the savings. The amount spent for such training is included in Total Training Expense under Administrative and General Expense, along with other training costs (for new production and sales employees). The reported standard costs per unit include the cost savings which have been realized. These cost savings also are applied to any future models that your firm may decide to produce. Basic labor and material costs reported for new models include the cost savings.

An effective training program is an essential element of your firm's success. Many firms spend between 1 and 5 percent of their budget on training. Without such a program, your production processes are likely to become less efficient relative to your competitors. You almost would be guaranteed the dubious distinction of being the high-cost competitor. Your company would be doomed to failure! We urge you to support a strong, continuous training program.

Production Costs

Basic **standard unit costs** for Model 1, Quality 2 (your current model and quality) at the beginning of Year 3 are as follows:

	Merica	Sereno
Labor	$2.88	Ps 8.90
Materials	1.23	5.72
Maintenance	.25	1.50
Total	$4.36	Ps 16.12

Standard cost levels may be different for each model—usually being higher for a new model than for an existing model. Also, standard costs vary according to quality levels, with labor and materials costs for Quality 1 being 10 percent higher than for Quality 2. Costs for Quality 3 are 10 percent lower.

When a new model is reported in your Operating Information Report, its standard costs and savings level also will be reported. The costs are reported for each area in local currency. These are the costs that your firm would incur if it had a plant in that area. In this way, you can plan the availability of funds required to produce the new model if you should put it into production. For example, the availability of Model 2 with a savings level of 2 might be reported to you, as follows:

STANDARD COSTS PER UNIT				
for next quarter				
	Merica Area 1 $	Merica Area 2 $	Merica Area 3 $	Sereno Ps
Model 2 Quality 2 Labor Cost	2.64	2.64	2.64	8.15
Savings Level 2 Material Cost	1.37	1.37	1.37	6.37
Model 1 Quality 2 Labor Cost	2.46	2.46	2.46	7.59
Savings Level 2 Material Cost	1.23	1.23	1.23	5.72
Note: For Quality 1 add 10%. For Quality 3 subtract 10%.				

The costs reported are those for quality level 2. If you should choose, for example, to introduce Model 2 with a higher quality (level 1) then 10 percent should be added to the reported costs for Model 2, Quality 2. If you choose Quality 3, subtract 10 percent from the reported costs for Quality 2.

All production costs are subject to inflation and will escalate at a rate approximately equal to the rate of change in the Consumer Price Index (CPI) for the country. Remember that inflation rates differ by country. The effects of inflation are incorporated in the reported levels of standard costs for all models and these costs are those that will be in effect during the quarter following the report. The material and labor costs of interest to your firm are those in the country or countries in which you have production plants.

Operations and production employee training focuses upon reducing labor and material costs by increasing employee skill levels and maintaining employee identification with and commitment to your firm. Savings realized from training will be available to reduce basic cost levels below the level that otherwise would occur, **for any model**. For example, suppose that a training program has successfully reduced labor costs by another 20 cents per unit (or Ps 1.20 in Sereno) by achieving savings level 3. The basic standard costs for models number 1 and 2 in Merica would be $2.26 and $2.44, respectively, instead of those reported in the example above.

```
┌─────────────────────────────────────────────────────────────────────────┐
│                      STANDARD COSTS PER UNIT                              │
│                         for next quarter                                  │
│                                                                           │
│                                  Merica   Merica   Merica                 │
│                                  Area 1   Area 2   Area 3   Sereno        │
│                                    $        $        $        Ps          │
│                                                                           │
│   Model  2 Quality 2  Labor Cost    2.44     2.44     2.44     6.95       │
│   Savings Level  3    Material Cost 1.37     1.37     1.37     6.37       │
│                                                                           │
│   Model  1 Quality 2  Labor Cost    2.26     2.26     2.26     6.39       │
│   Savings Level  3    Material Cost 1.23     1.23     1.23     5.72       │
│                                                                           │
│   Note:   For Quality 1 add 10%.   For Quality 3 subtract 10%.           │
└─────────────────────────────────────────────────────────────────────────┘
```

The costs, of course, will rise in subsequent quarters to reflect the impact of inflation as shown by changes in the Consumer Price Index. Suppose that you continue this quarter producing Model 1, even though Model 2 is available. If the labor cost savings of 20 cents per unit were to be realized and the Consumer Price Index in both Merica and Sereno were to rise by another 2 percent (a very unlikely occurrence), the following report would be shown the next quarter in the Operating Information Report.

```
┌─────────────────────────────────────────────────────────────────────────┐
│                      STANDARD COSTS PER UNIT                              │
│                         for next quarter                                  │
│                                                                           │
│                                  Merica   Merica   Merica                 │
│                                  Area 1   Area 2   Area 3   Sereno        │
│                                    $        $        $        Ps          │
│                                                                           │
│   Model  2 Quality 2  Labor Cost    2.49     2.49     2.49     7.09       │
│   Savings Level  3    Material Cost 1.40     1.40     1.40     6.50       │
│                                                                           │
│   Model  1 Quality 2  Labor Cost    2.31     2.31     2.31     6.52       │
│   Savings Level  3    Material Cost 1.25     1.25     1.25     5.83       │
│                                                                           │
│   Note:   For Quality 1 add 10%.   For Quality 3 subtract 10%.           │
└─────────────────────────────────────────────────────────────────────────┘
```

To extend the example a little further, suppose that you then begin production of Model 2, Quality 2. In that quarter your firm develops a new model, model number 3, with labor and materials costs about 10 percent higher than for model number 2, and the Consumer Price Index rises by another 2 percent in Merica and 3 percent in Sereno. The following report would be included in the Operating Information Report for that quarter:

Note that costs for Model 2 are the same as in the previous quarter, except for an inflation adjustment. Model number 3 costs are more than for model number 2 but are lower than they would have been without the cost savings from training. Cost savings apply to all models that may be available or become available in the future.

```
┌─────────────────────────────────────────────────────────────────────┐
│                      STANDARD COSTS PER UNIT                          │
│                         for next quarter                             │
│                                                                       │
│                              Merica   Merica   Merica                 │
│                              Area 1   Area 2   Area 3    Sereno       │
│                                $        $        $         Ps         │
│                                                                       │
│  Model  3 Quality 2  Labor Cost    2.79     2.79     2.79     8.03    │
│  Savings Level  3    Material Cost 1.57     1.57     1.57     7.36    │
│                                                                       │
│  Model  2 Quality 2  Labor Cost    2.54     2.54     2.54     7.30    │
│  Savings Level  3    Material Cost 1.43     1.43     1.43     6.70    │
│                                                                       │
│  Note:   For Quality 1 add 10%.   For Quality 3 subtract 10%.         │
└─────────────────────────────────────────────────────────────────────┘
```

If subsequent models (numbers 4, 5, etc.) are developed without changing the model number being produced, only the costs of the three most recently developed models will be reported. Following development of model number 3 in the previous illustration, suppose that your management chooses not to introduce it but instead maintained full production of model number 2. Then, a few quarters later, your Research and Development Department reports model number 4 available. A few quarters after that, Model 5 is released while your firm continues to produce Model 2. The following quarter's costs for model numbers 3, 4 and 5 would be reported, but you would have to estimate the costs for model number 2, which would change proportionately to those of model number 3.

```
┌─────────────────────────────────────────────────────────────────────┐
│                          IMPORTANT NOTE                               │
│ Increases in costs for all models will be due to inflation, and       │
│ decreases would be due to successful training activities resulting    │
│ in labor or materials cost savings or, perhaps, both.                 │
└─────────────────────────────────────────────────────────────────────┘
```

Standard unit costs are based upon a forty-hour work week with output levels at normal capacity. Normal production is at a rate of 100 units per line per hour. Actual costs are calculated as indicated below and will be reported quarterly in the Operating Information Report. **All costs, except depreciation of existing plant and equipment, are subject to inflation adjustments**. An illustration of production costs is provided in Figure 7-2.

Production Cost Components

Your finance department will need estimates of the amounts of the various components of production cost in order to estimate cash flows and provide sufficient cash to cover these costs, along with other expenditures that will take place during the upcoming quarter. In addition, these estimates will be used in preparation of *pro forma* financial statements for the quarter. The lower section of the Production Plan Work Sheet will be useful in providing these estimates. This part of the Production Plan is illustrated in Figure 7-3.

	Consoli-dated M$000s	Merica Area 1 M$000s	Merica Area 2 M$000s	Merica Area 3 M$000s	Sereno Ps000s
PRODUCTION COST ANALYSIS					
Labor Cost	874	874	0	0	0
Materials Cost	374	374	0	0	0
Maintenance Cost	76	76	0	0	0
Shutdown Cost	0	0	0	0	0
Total Cash Expenditures	1324	1324	0	0	0
Equipment Depreciation	107	107	0	0	0
Plant Depreciation	26	26	0	0	0
Total Production Cost	1457	1457	0	0	0
Total Unit Production Cost	4.67	4.67	0.00	0.00	0

FIGURE 7-2
Reported Costs of Production
Quarterly Operating Information Report

1. Total **labor cost** per hour for straight-time production amounts to 100 times the basic cost level for model number 1 at the beginning of Year 3 for each production line ($288 or Ps 890 in Sereno). The union contract provides for a 10 percent premium for workers on a second-shift operation, or $317 per hour for model number 1 at the beginning of Year 3 (Ps 979 in Sereno). Overtime work (more than 40 hours per week) is paid at one and one-half times the normal rate, or $432 per hour in Merica for model number 1 during Year 3, Quarter 1. To comply with statutory requirements in Sereno, overtime labor costs (more than 40 hours per week) are paid at double time, twice the normal rate, in pesos (Ps 1780 in Year 3, Quarter 1). Contract restrictions make impractical any operations at less than forty hours per week or more than forty-eight hours per week.

An easy way to estimate labor cost is to multiply the cost per unit by the number of units to be produced during the quarter. For straight-time production, this involves using the reported standard labor costs. The cost of units to be produced on overtime or with second-shift operations needs further adjustment to provide for the premium pay on those shifts. Continuing our example using Merica currency, and using the reported costs from Appendix C, if your company is to schedule 6 lines of production at 42 hours per week (about 328,000 units), using the reported labor costs of $2.88 per unit for Model 1, total labor costs for the coming quarter would be estimated as:

$$
\begin{array}{lrcl}
\text{Straight time} & \$2.88 \times 312,000 & = & \$898,560 \\
\text{Overtime} & 4.32 \times 16,000 & = & \underline{69,120} \\
\text{Total} & & & \$967,680
\end{array}
$$

This value should be rounded to $968,000 and entered under Labor Cost, in thousands of dollars.

THE BUSINESS POLICY GAME PRODUCTION PLAN WORK SHEET					
World ___ Company ___ Year ____ Quarter _____	Consoli-dated	Merica Area 1	Merica Area 2	Merica Area 3	Sereno
TOTAL PRODUCTION COST ANALYSIS (total cost in thousands of dollars or pesos)					
Labor Cost	968				
Materials Cost	403				
Maintenance Cost	82				
Layoff Cost	0				
Total Cash Expenditures	1453				
Equipment Depreciation	107				
Plant Depreciation	26				
Total Production Cost	1586				
UNIT PRODUCTION COST ANALYSIS (cost per unit in dollars or pesos)					
Unit Labor Cost	2.95				
Unit Materials Cost	1.23				
Unit Maintenance Cost	.25				
Unit Layoff Cost	0				
Total Unit Cash Expenditures	4.43				
Unit Equipment Depreciation	.33				
Unit Plant Depreciation	.08				
Total Unit Production Cost	4.84				

FIGURE 7-3

Illustration of the Production Plan Work Sheet—Lower Section

2. **Materials cost** for raw materials used in the manufacturing process is equal to the basic cost level ($1.23 for model number 1 at the beginning of Year 3) for each unit of production. New models generally have higher materials costs. The cost to produce 328,000 units would be $402,948.

$$\$1.23 \times 328,000 = \$403,440$$

Rounded to thousands of dollars, enter 403 for Materials Cost on the work sheet.

3. **Maintenance cost** averages $25 per hour at the beginning of Year 3 for each production line that is operating, or $0.25 per unit. To produce 328,000 units would require

$$\$0.25 \text{ x } 328,000 = \$82,000$$

Round this to thousands of dollars, and enter 82 on the work sheet for Maintenance Cost.

4. **Layoff cost** is standby cost for lines that have been idled. At the end of Year 2, standby cost for idled lines amounts to $4,000 per line per week. If one line is idled for thirteen weeks, standby cost totals $52,000 and output is reduced by about 52,000 units.

Continuing our example, all six available lines are scheduled for production, so there will be no layoff cost.

5. **Total cash expenditures** is merely the sum of items 1 to 4 above. For our example, add the values and enter the total:

$$968 + 403 + 82 + 0 = 1,453$$

Dividing $1,453,000 by the 328,000 units to be produced gives a unit cost cash expenditure of $4.43. The value of the total cash expenditure should be reported to the finance department for inclusion in the Pro Forma Cash Flow Work Sheet for the coming quarter (see Chapter 10).

6. **Equipment is depreciated** on a straight-line basis over 7 years. That is, current-quarter depreciation charges are calculated as 1/28th (3.5714 percent) of the original book value of all equipment in place during the quarter. It should be noted that this is **not** the same as taking 1/28th of the value of net equipment on the balance sheet. Net equipment is the **depreciated** value of equipment in place rather than the original book value.

Six production lines were installed in the original 8-line plant in your home area in Year 1, Quarter 1, at a total cost of $3,000,000. Thus, the current equipment depreciation charges for our example are $107,142.

$$\$3,000,000 \text{ x } .035714 = \$107,142$$

Round the value and enter 107 on the work sheet for Equipment Depreciation. The dollar value of equipment depreciation charges will change when you add production lines, but the depreciation rate still will be the same. It should be noted that higher prices for new equipment result from inflation, and price levels will continue to rise in proportion to the change in the Consumer Price Index.

If your firm should decide to install one new line during Year 3, Quarter 2, increase the previously-estimated equipment depreciation charges by 1/28th of the cost of the new equipment for the line next quarter. The full amount of the payment will be capitalized and, therefore, must also be depreciated. If the inflation factor is a one percent increase from Year 3, Quarter 1, the additional amount for equipment depreciation for each new line would be about $18,000.

$$.035714 \times \$500,000 \times 1.01 = \$18,036$$

No new lines are planned for this quarter so our entry is 107.

7. **Plant depreciation** charges are computed and added to the cost of production. Buildings are depreciated on a straight-line basis over a period of 31.5 years in the simulated world, or at a rate of 0.7937 percent of their original book value for each quarter. The original plant in your home area was completed in Year 1, Quarter 1 at a total cost of $3,300,000. It is being depreciated over a 31.5-year period at a rate of 0.7937 percent per quarter. The dollar cost of depreciation thus is $26,192 (rounded to $26,000) per quarter.

If a **new plant** is constructed in another market area (see Chapter 8), the depreciation charges are handled in the following manner: At the end of each quarter of construction, payments made to the contractor are capitalized and depreciation charges are increased by 0.7937 percent of the amount of the payments made. If an eight-line plant is under construction in Merica, for example, quarterly payments of $1,100,000 (plus inflation) will be capitalized at the end of the quarter and depreciation charges will be increased by about $9,000 per quarter.

$$0.007937 \times \$1,100,000 = \$8,731$$

After three quarters of construction, when the plant is available for use, the total depreciation charges would consist of a little more than $52,000 per quarter—$26,000 on the preexisting plant and about $26,000 (plus inflation) on the new plant. Once the plant has been completed, depreciation charges do not change with inflation because they are based on original cost.

The same procedure is followed for computing depreciation charges on **additions** to existing plants. Two quarterly payments of $450,000 are capitalized and depreciation charges are increased by about $4,000 during each quarter of construction.

$$0.007937 \times \$450,000 = \$3,572$$

The only difference is that construction of new additions is completed in two quarters of simulated operations while new plant facilities require three quarters of construction before completion.

8. **Total Production Cost** is the sum of Total Cash Expenditures plus Equipment and Plant Depreciation. For our example,

$$1,453 + 107 + 26 = 1,586 \text{ (or \$4.84 per unit, see below)}$$

This amount should be reported to the finance department for inclusion in the *pro forma* Income Statement (See Chapter 10). It will form the basis for the estimate of cost of goods sold for next quarter.

These costs can be converted easily to a per unit basis by dividing each cost by the number of units produced during the quarter. For example, total production cost per unit is $4.84:

$$\$1,586,000 \div 328,000 = 4.84$$

Unit cost provides a common denominator which allows for comparison of costs across areas and quarters.

Cost Variance

Actual costs may vary somewhat from those shown above. While production normally is at a rate of 100 units per hour per line, or 4,000 units per week, this rate may not be realized. A seemingly random variation of as much as 5 percent in either direction may occur because of efficiencies or inefficiencies experienced in actual operation. Companies operating production facilities in Sereno have found wider variances in actual volume of production compared to scheduled volume, and hence wider variance in actual costs compared to scheduled costs. Experience has shown that actual production in Sereno is more likely to be less than the scheduled amount, and variances as wide as 15 percent have been noted.

Variations in output may be due to a number of factors. Absenteeism may be higher than normal, down-time of machinery more than expected, or raw material deliveries delayed. All of these factors would cause production levels to be somewhat lower than anticipated. Actual expenditures, therefore, would be slightly lower than those scheduled. Unit costs (total production costs divided by the number of units produced) would be somewhat higher because total labor and maintenance costs will remain at the same level while the number of units produced has declined. Alternatively, absenteeism and machinery down-time may be less than normal resulting in higher than normal levels of production. These variations are beyond the control of your management.

Operations of new plants in other areas will be subject to the same cost functions as those of the existing plant in the home area. A second shift is not possible outside of the home area, however, because of a shortage of supervisory personnel.

Illustration of Overtime Costs

Figure 7-4 illustrates the current quarterly costs of first-shift production at straight time and at various amounts of overtime in your existing home-area plant. The dollar costs are for one line operating for one quarter and are based on the standard unit costs for model number 1 at the beginning of Year 3. Strait-time labor costs are $2.88 per unit. Overtime unit costs are $4.32 per unit. Plant depreciation is based upon use of six operating lines, with the amount shown being one-sixth of $26,192. Equipment depreciation is one-sixth of $107,142.

	Hours Scheduled				
	40	42	44	46	48
Labor	$149,760	$160,992	$172,224	$183,456	$194,688
Materials	$63,960	$67,158	$70,356	$73,554	$76,752
Maintenance	$13,000	$13,650	$14,300	$14,950	$15,600
Equip't depreciation	$17,857	$17,857	$17,857	$17,857	$17,857
Plant depreciation	$4,365	$4,365	$4,365	$4,365	$4,365
Total cost	$248,942	$264,022	$279,102	$294,182	$309,262
Output (in units)	52,000	54,600	57,200	59,800	62,400
Unit cost	$4.79	$4.84	$4.88	$4.92	$4.96

FIGURE 7-4
First-Shift Production Cost Per Line

It should be noted that total unit production costs increase rapidly as the amount of over-time increases. Labor costs for all additional units produced after 40 hours per week are higher due to the overtime premium. The higher unit labor costs more than offset the fact that the fixed depreciation charges are averaged over the larger number of units produced. If labor costs were proportionately higher than depreciation charges, as they may be for some models, the unit cost differential between straight time and overtime would be even greater.

Summary of Relationships

1. **Basic unit costs**: reported standard costs include inflation-related cost increases as well as savings that may have been realized from successful training programs.

2. **Basic Labor cost, regular shift**, per hour:
    straight-time rate: 100 times basic labor cost
    Merica overtime rate: 150 times basic unit labor cost
    Sereno overtime rate: 200 times basic unit labor cost

3. **Labor cost, second shift**, per hour: same as straight-time rate + 10 percent premium

4. **Material cost per unit**: basic unit material cost as reported

5. **Maintenance cost**, per line:
    $25 per hour, or $0.25 per unit in Merica (subject to inflation)
    Ps 150 per hour, or Ps 1.50 per unit in Sereno

6. **Standby cost for an idle line**:
    $4,000 per line per week (Ps 24,000), or $52,000 per quarter (Ps 312,000)
    Output reduced by about 4,000 units per week, or 52,000 units per quarter

7. **Equipment depreciation charges:** calculated on a straight-line basis over 7 years, or 3.5714 percent of original book value each quarter

8. **Plant depreciation charges**: calculated on a straight-line basis over 31.5 years
    for existing plant: $26,000 per quarter
    for new plant or addition: 0.7937 percent of construction in place each quarter

9. **Deactivation cost**: one-time charge of $100,000 per line, (or Ps 600,000)
    applies both to first-shift lines and second-shift lines separately

10. **Inventory storage cost** amounts to 10 cents (or 60 centavos) per unit for the first 300,000 units, the maximum storage capacity of a plant. Beyond that, public warehouse space is used to store all inventory exceeding the 300,000 limit, at a cost of 30 cents (or Ps 1.80) per unit. A sales office not associated with a manufacturing plant in the same area uses a public warehouse to store all inventory. Quarterly storage costs are paid on the number of units in beginning inventory.

CHAPTER 8

PRODUCTION: CAPACITY CHANGES

Your management team will need to make an early decision regarding expansion of production capacity. All of the plants in your industry world have been operating fairly close to capacity. Sales in the industry have been increasing at a rate that soon will require additional facilities if the demand for your product is to be met. Questions that need to be answered before making an investment decision include:

1. "How much additional productive capacity will be required?"

2. "Which, if any, of the expansion options should our firm undertake?"

Your estimate of production requirements (see Chapter 7) should assist you in answering the first question. The answer should be to expand capacity enough to meet expected sales demand as long as the expansion contributes toward meeting the goals of your firm and contributes to its profitability. An answer to the second question requires an evaluation of the expansion options discussed in this chapter, a comparison of their costs and the time required to implement them. In addition, there must be sufficient cash available to finance the investments that your firm decides to undertake. Various investment options are described below in the order of the time required for their implementation.

In an inflationary economy, one expects prices generally to follow the level of price changes in the economy of a country. All construction, hiring and training costs outlined in this chapter are those in effect at the beginning of Year 3, as you assume management of the company. The costs in effect for subsequent quarters may be estimated by adjusting the Year 3, Quarter 1 costs using the Consumer Price Index (CPI) of the country for the most recent quarter prior to the one in which the expenditures will occur (prices are set based upon the previous quarter's cost of living reports). **All construction contracts include a provision for cost increases due to inflation** over the period of construction.

Investment Options

Overtime

Working your production crews overtime is the fastest way to expand production. Furthermore, it is the only way in which production can be expanded without a delay of at least one quarter. By scheduling overtime, it is possible to increase output by about 20 percent over the normal forty-hour week production level. Restrictions in the union contract make it impossible to schedule production for less than **forty hours** or for more than **forty-eight** hours per week.

Units produced while crews are working overtime are somewhat more expensive than those manufactured during the normal workweek. In Merica, production employees are paid time-and-a-half for overtime work. Unit labor costs thus are 50 percent more for goods produced when production lines are running overtime. To comply with host country laws, production employees in Sereno are paid double time resulting in a doubling of labor costs for overtime work. These extra labor costs are partially offset by depreciation charges being spread over a larger number of units of production. Overtime costs are described in Chapter 7.

Second Shift

A second shift of workers may be scheduled for existing first-shift production lines in your **home-area plant**. This will enable you to double production without any additional investment in plant facilities or equipment. Second-shift workers receive a 10 percent premium wage for working nights.

At the beginning of Year 3, it costs $100,000 and requires one quarter to hire and train workers to operate a second shift on a home-area production line. If you wish to schedule production for a second shift on one or more of your existing lines in Year 3, Quarter 2, you **must**, in Quarter 1, enter the number of lines desired under New Lines–2nd Shift on the decision form. During the first quarter of Year 3, workers will be hired and trained, with the costs appearing as Training Costs on your firm's Income Statement. The second shift will be available to begin production on the line(s) during the second quarter of Year 3. At that time it must be scheduled for production, idled with a temporary layoff or deactivated (See Chapter 7). A second shift may be added to all producing lines in the home-area plant. There is no provision in the model for second-shift operations in other plants.

To add second-shift lines, enter the number of lines on the decision form under New Lines–2nd Shift. The line(s) will be available for production during the **following** quarter.

Limits: 0 to number of 1st shift lines operating in home area

Additional Production Lines

The existing plant in your home area was built to house eight production lines. To date, only six lines have been built. Thus, there is space for two additional lines as indicated in the Operating Information Report (see Appendix C).

	Area 1	Area 2	Area 3	Sereno
Space Available for New Lines	2	0	0	0

New production lines have the same operating characteristics, costs and output capabilities as existing lines. **One quarter** is required to install the necessary equipment and to hire and train workers for new production lines. In order to have additional lines available for production during the third quarter of Year 3, it would be necessary to begin construction of those lines in Quarter 2.

A capital expenditure of $500,000 (or Ps 3,000,000 in Sereno) is required to purchase new equipment for each line that is added. In addition, it costs $100,000 (Ps 600,000) to hire and train new employees to work on each new production line. The capital expenditure and hiring and training costs are incurred during the quarter of construction. Your Cash Flow Analysis statement will show an expenditure for equipment of $500,000 (Ps 3,000,000) per line, and the Income Statement will show a training expense of $100,000 (Ps 600,000) per line, to cover hiring and training costs. These costs are subject to inflation.

Equipment is depreciated on a straight-line basis over seven years, with no salvage value. Quarterly depreciation charges equal 1/28th (3.5714 percent) of the original cost. New equipment expenditures are capitalized during the quarter in which the line(s) are constructed and depreciation charges also are levied. Thus, an expenditure of $500,000 for equipment for one line would increase equipment depreciation charges for the quarter by about $18,000.

$$0.035714 \times \$500,000 = \$17,857$$

The only limitation on the number of lines which can be under construction at one time is the availability of space in the plant. Your firm could increase its production capacity by one-third as early as Quarter 2 of Year 3 by adding lines 7 and 8 to your existing plant during Quarter 1. While operating costs of new lines are the same as for existing lines, unit production costs will be somewhat lower because plant depreciation charges will be spread over the larger number of units produced in the plant during the quarter.

To begin construction and train workers, enter the number of new lines to be added on the decision form. The entry should be made in the market area where a plant with additional space is located. After the construction has begun, no further entry is necessary until the lines are ready and available for production. Entries in subsequent quarters will result in starting **additional** new lines at that time (if space is available; otherwise the entries will be rejected by the decision-entry program). When ready for production, and not before, new lines must be scheduled for production, idled or deactivated.

Limits: 0 to number of lines for which space is available

	Sales Office Orders (000s)	Construction		
		New Lines	New Add'n	New Plant
Area 1	# 87	#	#	#
Area 2	# 75	#	#	#
Area 3	# 75	#	#	#
Sereno	# 75	#	#	#
2nd Shift		#	← ← ← ←	

Addition to Existing Plant

When the plant in your home area was built, sufficient land was reserved to permit the building of an addition on each of two sides of the plant. Each addition will provide space for two production lines and each represents an increase of 25 percent of the presently available space for production capacity. Your existing plant shell has room for eight lines. Adding two more will give you space to install a total of ten lines. **Two quarters** are required to complete construction of a new addition.

The installation of production lines in the addition may be started during the second quarter of addition construction so that the lines will be available for production as soon as the plant addition is completed. Construction may begin on only **one two-line addition** for any plant during any quarter. If desired, however, construction may be started on another addition in a subsequent quarter while the first is still under construction, provided that such construction will not cause the maximum plant capacity of twelve lines to be exceeded.

At the beginning of Year 3, construction of a new addition requires a capital expenditure of $900,000 (Ps 5,400,000), which must be paid to the contractor in two installments over the construction period. Construction contracts contain a provision for increasing installment payments by the rate of inflation during the contract period. Your Cash Flow Analysis Statement will show a capital expenditure of $450,000 (Ps 2,700,000) or more (remember inflation) during each quarter of construction. These amounts will be capitalized and depreciated at the same rate as the existing plant. Depreciation is on a straight-line basis over 31.5 years, with no salvage value. Quarterly depreciation charges amount to 0.7937 percent of the **original cost** of all construction in place at the end of each quarter. After completion, construction of one new two-line addition will cause depreciation charges to be increased by at least $7,143 (Ps 42,860) per quarter:

$$\$900,000 \times .007937 = \$7,143$$

To begin construction, enter "2"—the number of lines of capacity—under Construction–New Add'n on the decision form in the marketing area in which you wish to construct the new addition. After construction has begun, no further entries are necessary except to begin construction of the production lines so that the lines will be available for production when desired. New-line construction may be started during the second quarter of construction of the new addition, or any time thereafter.

Limits: 0 **or** 2 lines (to a maximum capacity of 12 lines)

Construction of a New Plant

The final option for expanding production capacity is to construct a new plant in another market area. Your company may locate a plant in any area you desire, provided that you do not already have a plant in that area. You may move into a competitor's home area or into Sereno. Plant construction requires **three quarters** to complete. A plant may be built with a capacity of either two, four, six, eight or ten lines. Additions may be built later to increase plant size to a maximum capacity of twelve lines. Construction costs for each plant size are shown below. Costs are those in effect at the beginning of Year 3, and are subject to inflationary changes. Depreciation is on a straight-line basis over 31.5 years, with no salvage value. Quarterly depreciation charges are calculated as 0.7937 percent of the original cost.

Capacity	--------Merica--------		----------Sereno----------	
	Cost	Quarterly	Cost	Quarterly
2 lines	$1,200,000	$400,000	Ps 7,200,000	Ps 2,400,000
4 lines	1,900,000	633,333	11,400,000	3,800,000
6 lines	2,600,000	866,666	15,600,000	5,200,000
8 lines	3,300,000	1,100,000	19,800,000	6,600,000
10 lines	4,000,000	1,333,333	24,000,000	8,000,000

Local governments in all of the market areas would like your firm to build a plant in their area to stimulate job growth. Sereno further requires your firm to reinvest 50 percent of net profits until a reserve equal to 50% of capital stock has been accumulated to encourage local investment. Likewise, Merica areas strongly encourage local investment to stimulate job growth. Local tax breaks and other benefits often are offered to attract a new plant.

Construction costs must be paid to the contractor in three installments during the construction period. Construction contracts contain a provision for increasing installment payments by the rate of inflation during the contract period. If an eight-line plant is being built, your Cash Flow Analysis will show a capital expenditure of at least $1,100,000 (Ps 6,600,000) during each quarter of construction, with the total expenditure amounting to $3,300,000 (Ps 19,800,000) or more. Construction payments are capitalized and subject to depreciation during the quarter in which they are paid.

Building a plant shell, by itself, will not permit you to produce any goods. In order for production to begin, **production lines** must be installed at a cost of at least $600,000 (Ps 3,600,000) each, including hiring and training costs for new workers. If you plan to schedule production as soon as the plant is finished, you **must** begin installation of production lines during the third quarter of plant construction. The plant and new lines will be installed and workers trained during that quarter. Any number of lines up to the full capacity of the plant may be installed. Space availability for new lines will be reported in the Operating Information Report as soon as construction may begin.

Operating costs and production capabilities for a new plant will be the same as those for the existing plant in your home area. Second-shift operations, however, are not feasible in non-home areas because of a shortage of supervisory personnel.

Your firm will realize transportation cost savings after completing a new manufacturing plant. A sales office that is located in an area with a plant stores its inventory within a partitioned area of the plant warehouse. Thus, no costs are incurred for shipments to the sales office in the area. Transportation costs for sales in that area only are due for shipments from the plant to customers in the same area at a rate of 10 cents (60 centavos) per unit. This results in a savings of 60 cents per unit for shipments to a domestic sales office and 90 cents per unit for shipments to Sereno. See Chapter 5 for information on transportation expenses.

To begin construction of a new plant, enter the number of lines of capacity that are desired (2, 4, 6, 8 or 10) in the market area in which the new plant is to be located. After construction has begun, no further entry is required except to begin construction of new lines prior to the start of production.

Limits: 0 in home area; 0, 2, 4, 6, 8 or 10 lines in other areas

Closing a Plant

If your firm has overbuilt its productive capacity, it may decide to close one of its plants. You may close a plant in any area by entering a negative value of one (-1) under plant construction for the area on the decision form. At the same time you must deactivate all production lines. All employees, including plant executives, will automatically be discharged. The plant will be sold at 90 percent of book value to a local developer. The book value includes any new additions which may have been built or still are under construction.

After deactivation, the equipment in the plant will be sold to an equipment supplier at 90 percent of book value. Both the developer and the equipment supplier will make payment during the quarter in which the plant is closed, so the proceeds can be used to meet expenses during the quarter.

Summary

<u>Investment Options</u>

1. **Overtime work** to 48 hours a week may increase production by about 20 percent. Labor costs for working more than 40 hours per week are 50 percent higher than normal in Merica and 100 percent higher in Sereno. Fixed costs are spread over more units. There is no delay in implementation.

2. A **second shift** may be added to lines in your home-area plant. Labor costs are 10 percent higher. There is a one-quarter delay while workers are hired and trained at a cost of $100,000. Second-shift production lines may be idled or deactivated the same as first shift lines.

3. **Additional production lines** may be added, space permitting, at a cost of $500,000 (Ps 3,000,000) each. Hiring and training of new workers costs $100,000 (Ps 600,000) per line. Construction requires one quarter. All costs of construction, hiring and training ($600,000 or Ps 3,600,000) are charged during the quarter of construction.

4. **Additions to existing plants** may be made so long as the maximum plant size of twelve lines capacity is not exceeded. Each addition has capacity for two production lines and costs $900,000 (Ps 5,400,000). Construction requires two quarters and costs are charged at the rate of $450,000 (Ps 2,700,000) per quarter, subject to inflation.

5. A **new plant** may be constructed in any marketing area where your company does not already have a plant. Construction requires three quarters to complete and one-third of the total cost must be paid during each quarter of construction, subject to inflation. Total and quarterly costs are:

Capacity	--------Merica--------		----------Sereno----------	
	Cost	Quarterly	Cost	Quarterly
2 lines	$1,200,000	$400,000	Ps 7,200,000	Ps 2,400,000
4 lines	1,900,000	633,333	11,400,000	3,800,000
6 lines	2,600,000	866,666	15,600,000	5,200,000
8 lines	3,300,000	1,100,000	19,800,000	6,600,000
10 lines	4,000,000	1,333,333	24,000,000	8,000,000

6. **Closing a plant**. An existing plant may be closed. If closed, all lines must be deactivated. Employees will be discharged. The plant and its equipment will be sold for 90 percent of book value.

7. **Training costs**, per line (subject to inflation):
    for newly constructed lines: $100,000 or Ps 600,000
    for new second-shift lines: $100,000 (home area only)
    for reactivated 1st and 2nd-shift lines: $50,000 or Ps 300,000

All costs shown are those in effect at the beginning of Year 3 and are subject to local inflationary increases in proportion to changes in the Consumer Price Index.

Plant Closure

Closing a plant involves shutting down operations, deactivating all lines and selling the building and equipment. Both the building and equipment are sold for 90 percent of book value. Proceeds of the sale are received during the quarter of sale.

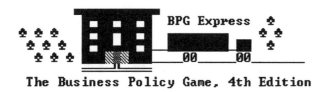
CHAPTER 9

FINANCE: STRATEGY AND CAPITAL BUDGETING

The management of your firm's financial affairs provides a major challenge for your team. You must coordinate the financial requirements of marketing, production, distribution and expansion decisions for your parent company as well as each of its subsidiaries. You must provide the cash to pay for company operations, to cover production expansion costs, to make interest payments on borrowed funds, to repay financial obligations promptly, to pay taxes when due and to make dividend payments to stockholders. In addition, your management should provide a sound capital structure, give assurance to creditors that your obligations will be met promptly, plan for and help to provide a reasonable level of profitability and assure a reasonable return to your stockholders. Measures of the success of your financial management include your stock price, your return on investment and your credit rating.

Prior to making specific financial decisions, your firm's financial managers should set financial (functional-level) goals and objectives and develop financial strategy to accomplish these goals (see Chapter 4 for a discussion of goal and objective setting and strategy development). Financial goals should support the overall goals developed at the business level. The financial goals should focus upon what finance can contribute to achieving the business-level goals. The following business-level goal was used as an example in Chapter 4:

Maintain a rate of return on stockholders' end-of-Year-2 investment in your company's stock (goal) of at least 20 (hurdle) percent (index) through Year 7 (time).

Supporting finance goals and objectives might be:

Goal: Develop a financial structure with a debt-to-equity ratio (goal) of 35 (hurdle) percent (index) by the end of Year 7 (time).

Objective: Increase the debt-to-equity ratio (goal) by 5 (hurdle) percentage points (index) during Year 3 (time).

Goal: Upgrade the firm's credit rating (goal) to Number (index) One (hurdle) by the beginning of Year 5 (time).

Objective: Maintain a $500,000 (hurdle & index) cash balance (goal) during each quarter of Year 3 (time).

Other goals and objectives may focus upon other financial ratios and your firm's financial structure.

     Financial strategy should be designed to enable your finance department to attain its goals and objectives. The strategy should plan for the allocation of financial resources to gain maximum efficiency while meeting market demand. The strategy for the debt-to-equity goal would focus upon the sources used for external funding. The strategy for upgrading the credit rating would involve maintaining sufficient cash reserves, a strong earnings growth and regular dividend payments. An effective finance strategy should include **all** of the finance variables used in managing resources.

     The quarter-to-quarter tactical decisions which your finance managers must make are described below. These decisions should be based upon your firm's sales forecast and production plan and the resulting need for resources. Decision making should be guided by your financial strategy and company policy.

     A considerable amount of planning is required prior to making financial decisions, as the impact of many financial decisions will extend over a considerable period of time. Tools which we encourage you to use in financial planning include the Capital Budget, Pro Forma Cash Flow Analysis, Pro Forma Income Statement and Pro Forma Balance Sheet. These tools will be described below along with a description of the items that will be reported in your financial statements. But first we will begin with a discussion of the financial decisions your firm will be making.

LYIT INFORMATION RESOURCE CENTRE

Finance Decisions

Financing and Investment Considerations

     Partly as a result of the limited availability and high cost of financing in Sereno, your company's board of directors has established a company-wide policy that all external financing be obtained by the parent company and all external investment of funds (certificates of deposit) be made by the parent company. The financing and investment decisions on the decision form apply only to the parent company.

However, funds must be managed for the parent company and all of its subsidiaries. Funds available in one subsidiary's bank accounts cannot be used to pay expenses of another subsidiary. If a subsidiary runs out of cash, the parent firm will provide cash by purchasing additional stock in the subsidiary. If the stock purchase cannot be met with the parent firm's existing cash, external financing may be necessary for the parent company. If financing is not arranged, the parent firm may incur an emergency loan even though it had sufficient cash to meet its own financial requirements in the home area. Other subsidiaries may have more cash than they need, but pesos in Sereno cannot be used to directly pay dollar obligations in a Merica subsidiary.

Two questions must be answered when planning cash requirements:

1. How much cash is available?
2. Where is the cash available?

Cash sometimes can be transferred from a subsidiary to the home office to pay for goods purchased from the home-area plant. Sale of goods to a subsidiary requires payment during the quarter of the sale. Part of the payment will help pay manufacturing costs. The 20 percent markup will help to cover administrative expenses in the area where the goods are manufactured. Cash also may be transferred by the subsidiary paying dividends to the parent company. But all profits of subsidiaries are not immediately available to the parent company. Dividend payments of subsidiaries are limited to 80 percent of net subsidiary profits until accumulated retained earnings in the subsidiary have been built up to 50 percent of the book value of capital stock. After that, 100 percent of retained earnings may automatically be paid as dividends to the parent firm, subject to the following restriction:

> Dividend payments may not reduce a subsidiary's cash balance below $100,000 (in Merican subsidiaries) or Ps 1,000,000 (in Sereno).

After retained earnings reach 50 percent of capital stock, dividends that are missed because of a cash shortage may be paid in subsequent quarters when more cash is available. This is company policy.

The construction of a new plant, plant addition or production lines will be financed by the area subsidiary to the extent that capital is available. However, if there is insufficient cash, the parent company will purchase enough stock in the subsidiary to cover the cash shortage. This will be handled automatically when you submit construction decisions for your subsidiary. Also, if you submit operating decisions for a subsidiary that require more working capital than the subsidiary has available, the parent company will cover the shortfall by purchasing stock in the subsidiary. In all cases, funds crossing national boundaries will be transferred at current exchange rates during the quarter when the transactions occur. If you anticipate that a subsidiary will require more cash than will be available at the home office, the parent company must plan for external financing by arranging bank loans, selling bonds or selling stock.

Bank Loan—Parent Company

Your corporate headquarters has established a $2.5 million line of credit with your local banker. You may draw against this line of credit by floating a 3-month bank loan to be repaid at the beginning of the following quarter. Interest is charged at the short-term rate that is available during that quarter to a company with your credit standing. Interest, amounting to one-fourth of the annual rate (because the loan is for 3 months) is paid **during** the quarter that the loan is outstanding. Your subsidiaries may not borrow external funds. Their cash needs are met by selling common stock to the parent corporation.

Because short-term loans are made for a period of only three months, your banker has agreed to deduct automatically the repayment amount from your bank account during the following quarter.

Bank loans are secured by inventory and receivables, and may not exceed 50 percent of the value of receivables plus inventory at the end of the previous quarter. Your line of credit requires an **annual cleanup**, so a loan request will be denied if your firm has had a loan outstanding during each of the past **three** consecutive quarters.

If sufficient funds are not provided to meet all obligations, including those of subsidiaries, an **emergency bank loan** will be provided at **five percentage points** above the normal interest rate. In addition, your banker and the bond credit analysts will review your credit standing. Emergency borrowing automatically will result in a reduction of your company's credit rating. If required, an emergency loan will be granted without making an entry on the decision form. As with standard bank loans, emergency loans are automatically repaid from your bank account on the first day of the following quarter. Interest is charged, at the premium rate, during the quarter when the loan is outstanding.

Finance (000s)	
Bank Loan	$
Bond Issue	$
Stock Issue	#
Dividends	$
Time CDs	$ *1000*

To execute a loan, enter the amount desired (in thousands of dollars) under Bank Loan on the decision form. If you decide to borrow $1,000,000, enter 1000. Do not include commas in your entry.

Maximum loan: 50 percent of receivables plus inventory
Maximum loan: 0 if a loan was outstanding in each of the previous three quarters
Limits: 0 to 2500 (in thousands of dollars)

Sale or Redemption of Bonds—Parent Company

1. Bond Issue. Your firm's long-term debt may be increased by issuing bonds in multiples of $1,000,000. New issues are callable ten-year secured bonds carrying the long-term rate of interest that will be available to a company with your credit rating during the quarter of issue. Bonds must be secured by plant and equipment and the value of existing bonds, new bonds to be issued plus bonds already outstanding, may not exceed 75 percent of net fixed assets at the end of the previous quarter. Furthermore, your investment banker will consider an issue too risky to underwrite if the existing bonds, plus new bonds to be issued, exceed 50 percent of total equity (consisting of the previous quarter's total equity plus the proceeds of new shares to be sold simultaneously with the bonds).

Subsidiaries may not borrow external funds, so a bond issue is not available to them.

Enter the amount of new bonds to be sold (in thousands of dollars) on the decision form under Bond Issue. If you decide to issue $4,000,000 worth of bonds, for example, enter 4000 on the decision form. Do not include commas in your entry.

Maximum issue: 50 percent of equity or 75 percent of net fixed assets, whichever is less

Limits: 0 to 9000 (in thousands of dollars), in million dollar lots

2. Bond redemption. Bonds that are outstanding may be called and redeemed in amounts that are multiples of $100,000 except that there is a restriction in the bond indenture that prohibits the redemption of more than $500,000 of the face amount of bonds in any one quarter. You will be required to pay a five percent call premium on all bonds that are called. If your firm has more than one bond issue outstanding, the bonds carrying the highest interest rate will be redeemed first. If bonds are to be redeemed, enter the face amount of the bonds for which redemption is desired (in thousands of dollars), preceded by a minus sign, under Bond Issue on the decision form. If you decide to redeem $500,000 worth of bonds, enter -500 on the decision form. The five percent call premium will be charged automatically and reported under Other Expense on the income statement.

Maximum redemption: Total amount of bonds outstanding (if less than $500,000)

Limits: -500 to 0 (in thousands of dollars) in hundred thousand dollar lots

Sale or Repurchase of Common Stock—Parent Company

1. Stock Issue. New shares of common stock of your parent company may be issued through an investment banker in multiples of 100,000 shares, provided that the new issue will be large enough to raise at least $1 million. The investment banker will make a firm offer at any time of a price that will be determined by the following formula:

$$\text{Issue price} = \frac{\text{(shares outstanding)} \times \text{(latest market price)}}{\text{(shares outstanding)} + \text{(shares to be issued)}}$$

If your firm's credit rating is 2, the calculated value is the issue price. If your firm's credit rating is 3, subtract 10 percent of the formula value from the issue price. If your credit rating is 1, add 10 percent.

Enter the number of new shares to be issued (in thousands of shares) on the decision form under Stock Issue. If your firm decides to issue 4,000,000 shares of stock, enter 4000 on the decision form. Do not include commas in your entry.

Minimum issue: Enough shares to raise $1 million
Limits: 0 to 9000 (in thousands of shares) in 100,000 share blocks

2. Stock Repurchase. Shares of your firm's common stock may be repurchased by placing a purchase order with the firm's stockbroker. The shares will be purchased at a price that is **10 percent above the market price** reported at the end of the previous quarter. Stock is repurchased by entering the number of shares to be repurchased, preceded by a minus sign, in the Stock Issue section of the decision form. Repurchase must be made in multiples of 100,000 shares. If your firm decides to repurchase 500,000 shares of stock during the current quarter, enter -500 on the decision form. Your corporate charter requires that there be at least 3 million shares outstanding, so repurchases are limited to an amount that would leave at least 3 million shares after the repurchase. Shares may not be repurchased if the transaction would result in a negative balance of Accumulated Earnings on the balance sheet.

Maximum repurchase: number of shares outstanding minus 3 million
                                          0 if Accumulated Earnings are negative

Limits: -500 to 0   (in thousands of shares)

Sale of Common Stock—Subsidiaries

Each of your subsidiaries is 100-percent owned by the parent corporation. Under company policy, the subsidiaries will not raise external funds, and a funds shortage is met by the parent company's purchase of additional shares in the subsidiary. When the subsidiary has insufficient cash available to meet its operating and capital investment requirements, stock will be sold automatically to the parent corporation. No entry is required on the decision form.

Dividends—Parent Company

Cash dividends may be paid to stockholders; but a restrictive bond covenant provides that the dividends paid in any quarter, taken together with dividends paid in the previous three quarters, may not exceed the total amount of earnings in the previous four quarters of operations. Thus, if total earnings in the previous four quarters amounted to $200,000 and dividends already paid in the previous three quarters amounted to $190,000, the maximum dividend that could be paid in the current quarter would be $10,000. Dividends may not be declared if the accumulated retained earnings account on the balance sheet has a negative balance.

Enter the amount of cash dividends to be paid (in thousands of dollars) under Dividends on the decision form. If your firm decided to declare the permissible amount of $10,000 in dividends in the above example, you would enter 10 on the decision form.

Maximum: Net income last 4 quarters minus dividends last 3 quarters

Maximum: 0 if retained earnings are negative

Limits: 0 to 9999 (in thousands of dollars)

Dividends—Subsidiaries

Earnings repatriated from your subsidiaries are treated as dividends from the subsidiaries. As the subsidiaries are 100-percent owned by the parent company, all repatriated profits from Sereno, as well as dividends from your domestic subsidiaries, are paid to your parent company. Subsidiary dividends are not included on the decision form, but are calculated as follows.

Your foreign subsidiary, Sereno, operates under governmental regulations controlling the repatriation of company profits. The subsidiary may pay dividends to its parent company equal to the entire amount of current quarter after-tax profits with the following restrictions:

1. Twenty percent of the profits must be set aside in an equity reserve (part of accumulated earnings) until the reserve has accumulated to an amount at least equal to 50 percent of capital stock.

2. Dividends may only be paid if, after payment, there will be a minimum cash balance of one million pesos in local currency (held in local banks).

Your company's board of directors has established a uniform policy for all subsidiaries, both foreign and domestic. Thus, these same rules apply to Merican subsidiaries. The minimum cash balance requirement at Merican banks under this policy is $100,000. Only 80 percent of a subsidiary's profits will be paid to the parent company until the balance of the accumulated earnings account is at least 50 percent of the book value of the subsidiary's capital stock. After the accumulated earnings account reaches 50 percent, dividends that are missed because of insufficient funds (including the minimum cash balance requirement) will be paid later if cash balances rise.

Certificates of Deposit—Parent Company

Three-month time Certificates of Deposit (CDs) may be purchased in multiples of one hundred thousand dollars. Purchases may be made at the beginning of any quarter. CDs mature at the beginning of the next quarter, three months later. Interest will be earned on deposits at the rate reported in the Quarterly Industry Report for 3-month time CDs. The reported rate is the rate quoted by your bank for any CD investments to be made in the following quarter. Interest will be credited to your account on the last day of the quarter in which the deposit is made, with quarterly interest calculated at one-fourth of the annual rate.

IMPORTANT NOTE

While interest is credited on the last day of the quarter that the deposit is made and may be used to meet expenses of the quarter, the funds from the deposit itself are not available until the next day—the first day of the subsequent quarter. Thus, if your firm should need emergency cash during the quarter in which the funds are invested in CDs, the funds will not be available to meet the need.

To purchase time CDs, enter the amount of the purchase, in thousands of dollars, on the decision form under Time CDs. If your firm decides to purchase $400,000 worth of CDs, enter 400 on the decision form. Do not include commas in your entry. Repayment of the CDs as well as crediting your account with earned interest will be done automatically by the bank.

Limits: 0 to 9900 (in thousands of dollars), in hundred thousand dollar lots

Investment Analysis

One of the most critical strategic decisions your firm must make is how to adjust production capacity to meet the forecasted demand for your product. The expenditures required for expansion of production facilities are very large relative to those required to implement most operating decisions. A decision to build a new plant with six lines of capacity requires a total expenditure of at least $6,200,000 (Ps 37,200,000), including construction of production lines and training of new workers. This amount is almost two-thirds of the total equity invested in your firm at the beginning of Year 3. Such a decision has been referred to by some as a "you bet your company" decision. The commitment is for a long period of time and the effect of such a decision will continue to influence the profitability of your firm for the rest of the simulation.

Nevertheless, when sales projections exceed your firm's productive capacity, most firms make plans to increase capacity. There are several methods to do so. A second shift may be added in the home area, new lines may be added to existing plants if space is available, new additions may be added to existing plants if space is available and new plants may be built. The method of expansion has both financial and production ramifications. We are concerned here with the financial dimension of the investment.

Several methods of evaluating investment alternatives have been suggested by different authors or used by business managers. We suggest that you review a standard textbook on financial management to help you choose the most appropriate method for your firm. Select the method which most closely meets the needs of your firm and proceed with the analysis.

Flexibility and Risk

Certain attributes of investment proposals are difficult, sometimes impossible, to quantify. Their impact is often difficult to assess. However, they must be considered in the decision-making process as factors that will affect the success of the investment decision. For *The Business Policy Game*, these factors include flexibility and risk. Some of the investment options provide more flexibility than others. The construction of an addition with new lines for your home-area plant provides the option of adding a second shift with relative ease. Should the production capacity of your first-shift operations turn out to be insufficient to meet demand, the capacity of your expansion can be quickly doubled (in one quarter) by adding a second shift. Construction of a new plant, on the other hand, will provide only the production capacity of the installed first-shift lines. A second shift is not available outside of your home area. The flexibility of each investment proposal must be weighed against the relative costs and estimated returns from the proposal.

There are risks associated with your sales forecast and the resulting accuracy of your estimated future returns. If your sales forecast turns out to be too high, your estimate of returns from a given investment proposal probably also will be too high. Profits from the new investments thus, may turn out to be less than anticipated. On the other hand, if your estimates are too low, you may not provide sufficient production capacity to meet your actual needs. Your profits will suffer because of lost sales that you might otherwise have made.

Capital Budgeting

Provisions for Adequate Funds

Your expansion plans are not complete until you have completed a capital budget for the required funding! Plans must be made so that sufficient funds will be available to meet your expenditure requirements, if any, for new plant and equipment. There may be times, also, when your firm wants to undertake a new project, but it may not be able to raise sufficient capital to fund the project. Procedures for raising funds by borrowing and by selling stock were discussed earlier in this chapter, along with penalties that will be incurred if you fail to provide sufficient funds to meet your needs.

For expansion of manufacturing capacity to take place, funds must be provided to pay for the construction of buildings, installation of equipment and training of workers. The Capital Budget Work Sheets shown in Figure 9-2 have been developed to assist you in planning for funding of expansion projects. Copies of this form are provided in Appendix D. A spreadsheet template of the form also is available in file CAPBUD.WK1 on the Player's Program Disk that came with this manual. Before using the spreadsheet template, read Appendix B which contains instructions for using the templates.

Capital Expenditures

We will use the Capital Budget Work Sheet to illustrate a planned production expansion. We recommend that you complete work sheets for each of the next four quarters if an expenditure is planned. (Shouldn't you always be planning at least one year ahead?) Then update your plan with each new quarter and add work sheets as required. Following this scheme, you will always have one year's expenditures planned in advance. The forms are easy to complete and help your firm keep track of its funds requirements and planned sources. This reduces unpleasant surprises.

The first step in completing a work sheet is to identify your market areas. The first area on the work sheet is designated as your home area. The second and third areas are blank and should be labeled with the other two Merica areas. (The first screen in the Capital Budget spreadsheet template has two cells for the area labels. The labels will automatically appear on the remaining work sheets.) The fourth area is labeled Sereno. Next, fill in the World, Company, Year and Quarter numbers as well as the projected exchange rate in Sereno.

You will recall that production capacity can be expanded in three ways: building a plant, building a plant addition or adding first or second-shift lines in a plant where space is available. Multiple projects can be entered on a work sheet; for example, you may decide to build a plant in one area and build an addition or add production lines if space is available in another area. In the capital expenditures section of the work sheet, enter the number of lines which your firm has decided to fund under the type(s) of expansion you are planning. Enter the costs that will be incurred during the quarter for the project(s). The sum of each column represents the total funds required for each area during the quarter. Calculate the consolidated cost by summing across columns. Be sure to translate Sereno pesos to dollars when calculating the sum. Otherwise, your total will be in peso-dollars, a denomination which your friendly banker will have difficulty understanding. You may wish to use the exchange rate forecast data shown on your Quarterly Industry Report to estimate exchange rates for translation of pesos during consolidation of financial statements.

The Capital Budget Work Sheets in Figure 9-2 show a four-line plant planned for Sereno. In this example, your management team has decided that it wants two new lines in Sereno to begin producing in the second quarter of Year 4 and two more lines in the fourth quarter. Investment expenditures for the new 4-line plant, equipment and training will extend over five quarters of Years 3 and 4. Each work sheet covers one quarter so it is necessary to use four work sheet forms (see Figures 9-2a, 9-2b, 9-2c and 9-2d). There is no need to complete a work sheet for Year 4, Quarter 2. Except for the small loan repayment required in that quarter, no entries are required.

The amount and timing of funds requirements for the project are shown in Figure 9-1. The cost of building a four-line plant in Sereno at Year 3, Quarter 1 prices is Ps 11,400,000, paid over the 3-quarter construction period at approximately Ps 3,800,000 per quarter. The plant is planned for Sereno, so we must factor in Sereno inflation rates. The Sereno CPI is indexed to 100 in Year 2, Quarter 4. If the Sereno CPI for Year 3, Quarter 2 is projected at 106, the plant cost for Year 3, Quarter 3 would be Ps 4,028,000:

$$Ps\ 3,800,000 \times (106 \div 100) = Ps\ 4,028,000$$

Remember, prices are based upon the most recently completed quarter's CPI, as the current quarter's CPI is unknown until the quarter is over. The cost for the fourth quarter would be about Ps 4,142,000 if the CPI is growing at about 3 percentage points per quarter, making it 109 for Quarter 3. A CPI of 112 for Quarter 4 would raise plant costs to Ps 4,256,000 for the first quarter of Year 4.

Equipment costs for two new lines in Year 4, Quarter 1 also would rise because of inflation to about Ps 6,720,000 from Ps 6,000,000 in Year 3, Quarter 1. Likewise, training costs would rise to Ps 1,344,000 from Ps 1,200,000 (Ps 600,000 per line). Finally, a projected CPI of 118 for Quarter 2 would boost equipment costs for Quarter 3 to Ps 7,080,000 and training costs to Ps 1,416,000. Total capital expenditures required by the project would be Ps 8,170,000 in Year 3 and Ps 20,816,000 in Year 4. See Figure 9-1 for a summary of the required investment.

Amounts in Thousands of Pesos	Year 3				Year 4			
	Q1	Q2	Q3	Q4	Q1	Q2	Q3	Q4
Investment:								
New Plant	0	0	4,028	4,142	4,256	0	0	0
Equipment	0	0	0	0	6,720	0	7,080	0
Training	0	0	0	0	1,344	0	1,416	0
Totals	0	0	4,028	4,142	12,320	0	8,496	0
Annual Totals		8,170				20,816		

FIGURE 9-1
Amount and Timing of Investment Costs
4-Line Plant Expansion in Sereno

These values have been entered in the top half of the work sheets of Figure 9-2, with the values in the Consolidated column being calculated by dividing those in the Sereno column by the projected exchange rate for each quarter. This translates peso values to dollars. Then they would be added to the values (if there were any) in the columns for the parent company and the two Merica subsidiaries.

Sources of Funds

You may be able to fund part of your expansion project internally from quarterly earnings. This works only if operations generate sufficient cash that is not required for other purposes. Cash may be available from quarterly earnings within the market area in which the expansion is taking place (Sereno in our example) and from your parent company. Home-area cash includes cash flows from operations and funds which have been paid to the parent as dividends from other subsidiaries.

Because of the project's size, your firm probably will have to fund a substantial portion of the capital budget from external sources by selling bonds and/or common stock. Company policy states that only your parent firm can obtain external funding. Any funding from external sources will have to be passed through to subsidiaries, as needed, by additional purchases of subsidiary stock. This transaction will be taken care of internally. Thus, you only need to determine the source and amount of external funding required. The proportion of funds obtained from each source is a matter for your management to decide. You need to consider the cost of funds from the various sources and the risks involved in utilizing financial leverage through borrowing. The minimum size requirement of new bond and stock issues may affect your decision, too.

Bond analysts and your banker will expect you to fund a substantial portion of the project with equity, through retention of earnings or by selling common stock. Your investment bankers have indicated that they only will underwrite a new bond issue if the new issue does not boost your bond to equity ratio above 50 percent. Thus, total bonds outstanding (new issue plus existing bonds) must not exceed 50 percent of total equity (existing equity plus any new stock issue). You may want to limit the risks of financial leverage by borrowing a smaller proportion of your funds requirements than the maximum amount that is permitted by your investment bankers.

The lower half of the Capital Budget Work Sheet has space to specify the mix of funds you plan to use to finance your expansion. The exact proportions of the mix become less firm as you project further into the future. Some adjustments may be needed after the cash budget is completed each quarter.

Begin planning for funding by estimating the approximate amount of **cash** that you expect to be available each quarter from internal sources and enter that in the Quarterly Earnings sections of the work sheet. Remember that available cash from other non-home areas is transferred to your home area each quarter and may be available for the parent company to use in providing funds elsewhere. Cash from operations in Sereno and in your home area that is not required for other uses may be available to fund capital investments. Any shortfall will have to be made up by short-term borrowing or by the sale of stock or bonds. Bonds provide attractive financing during periods of relatively low interest rates and stock is attractive during periods of relatively high market prices. A temporary bank loan may be used as long as the terms of your line of credit are not violated (See the "Bank Loan—Parent Company" section on page 127).

THE BUSINESS POLICY GAME CAPITAL BUDGET WORK SHEET							
World _1_ Company _1_ Year __3_ Quarter __3__				Consolidated M$000s	Home Area M$000s	Merica Area_2_ M$000s	Merica Area_3_ M$000s	Sereno Ps 000s

CAPITAL EXPENDITURES (enter number of lines and cost by area):

	M1	M2	M3	S		Exchange Rate → →		6.03
Plant				4	668				4028
Addition									
Lines									
Total Expenditures					668				4028

SOURCES OF FUNDS:

	Consolidated	Home Area	Merica Area_2_	Merica Area_3_	Sereno
Quarterly Earnings	100	50			300
Stock Sold to Parent	-----	-618			3728
Sale of Bonds			-----	-----	-----
Sale of Common Stock			-----	-----	-----
Short-Term Bank Loan	568	568	-----	-----	-----
Total Sources	668	0			4028
Less Loan Repayment			-----	-----	-----
Total Available Sources	668	0			4028
Surplus/Deficit	0	0			0

Copyright © 1995 by Richard V. Cotter and David J. Fritzsche

Figure 9-2a
Capital Budget Work Sheet Illustration (Year 3, Quarter 3)

THE BUSINESS POLICY GAME CAPITAL BUDGET WORK SHEET					

World _1_ Company _1_ Year __3_ Quarter __4__					Consoli- dated M$000s	Home Area M$000s	Merica Area_2_ M$000s	Merica Area_3_ M$000s	Sereno Ps 000s

CAPITAL EXPENDITURES (enter number of lines and cost by area):

	M1	M2	M3	S	Exchange Rate → →				6.09
Plant				4	680				4142
Addition									
Lines									
Total Expenditures					680				4142

SOURCES OF FUNDS:

	Consoli- dated	Home Area	Merica Area_2_	Merica Area_3_	Sereno
Quarterly Earnings	99	50			300
Stock Sold to Parent	- - - - -	-631			3842
Sale of Bonds			- - - - -	- - - - -	- - - - -
Sale of Common Stock			- - - - -	- - - - -	- - - - -
Short-Term Bank Loan	1149	1149	- - - - -	- - - - -	- - - - -
Total Sources	1248	568			4142
Less Loan Repayment	568	568	- - - - -	- - - - -	- - - - -
Total Available Sources	680	0			4142
Surplus/Deficit	0	0			0

Copyright © 1995 by Richard V. Cotter and David J. Fritzsche

Figure 9-2b
Capital Budget Work Sheet Illustration (Year 3, Quarter 4)

THE BUSINESS POLICY GAME
CAPITAL BUDGET WORK SHEET

World _1_ Company _1_ Year __4_ Quarter __1__					Consoli-dated M$000s	Home Area M$000s	Merica Area_2_ M$000s	Merica Area_3_ M$000s	Sereno Ps 000s

CAPITAL EXPENDITURES (enter number of lines and cost by area):

	M1	M2	M3	S		Exchange Rate → →			6.22
Plant				4	684				4256
Addition									
Lines				2	1296				8064
Total Expenditures					1980				12320

SOURCES OF FUNDS:

	Consolidated	Home Area	Merica Area_2_	Merica Area_3_	Sereno
Quarterly Earnings	98	50			300
Stock Sold to Parent	- - - - -	-1932			12020
Sale of Bonds			- - - - -	- - - - -	- - - - -
Sale of Common Stock	3000	3000	- - - - -	- - - - -	- - - - -
Short-Term Bank Loan	31	31	- - - - -	- - - - -	- - - - -
Total Sources	3129	1149			12320
Less Loan Repayment	1149	1149	- - - - -	- - - - -	- - - - -
Total Available Sources	1980	0			12320
Surplus/Deficit	0	0			0

Copyright © 1995 by Richard V. Cotter and David J. Fritzsche

Figure 9-2c
Capital Budget Work Sheet Illustration (Year 4, Quarter 1)

THE BUSINESS POLICY GAME
CAPITAL BUDGET WORK SHEET

World _1_ Company _1_ Year __4_ Quarter __3__					Consoli- dated M$000s	Home Area M$000s	Merica Area_2_ M$000s	Merica Area_3_ M$000s	Sereno Ps 000s

CAPITAL EXPENDITURES (enter number of lines and cost by area):

	M1	M2	M3	S			Exchange Rate → →		6.27
Plant									
Addition									
Lines				2	1355				8496
Total Expenditures					1355				8496

SOURCES OF FUNDS:

	Consoli-dated	Home Area	Merica Area_2	Merica Area_3	Sereno
Quarterly Earnings	98	50			300
Stock Sold to Parent	- - - - -	-1307			8196
Sale of Bonds	1000	1000	- - - - -	- - - - -	- - - - -
Sale of Common Stock			- - - - -	- - - - -	- - - - -
Short-Term Bank Loan	257	257	- - - - -	- - - - -	- - - - -
Total Sources	1355	0			8496
Less Loan Repayment	0		- - - - -	- - - - -	- - - - -
Total Available Sources	1355	0			8496
Surplus/Deficit	0	0			0

Copyright © 1995 by Richard V. Cotter and David J. Fritzsche

Figure 9-2d
Capital Budget Work Sheet Illustration (Year 4, Quarter 3)

A loan in this context sometimes is called a bridge loan because it provides a bridge between the time when funds are needed and the sometimes longer time required to sell stock or bonds. Also, minimum issue size for longer-term securities may make a bridge loan particularly attractive if all of the funds are not needed at once.

Getting back to our example, suppose your firm has planned to allocate Ps 300,000 cash for the project each quarter from quarterly earnings in Sereno, with the balance to be funded by the parent corporation. We have entered the following peso values in the Sereno column to show sources of funds:

```
Sources of funds:
                        Year 3                      Year 4

              Q2      Q3      Q4      Q1      Q2      Q3      Q4

Quarterly Earnings      300     300     300             300
Stock Sold to Parent    3728    3842    12020           8196
```

For the parent company to purchase stock in the Sereno subsidiary will require the following dollar amounts, calculated by dividing the peso shortage in Sereno by the projected exchange rates. The amount of dollar funds that must be transferred is shown as the cost of the stock, in thousands of dollars.

```
                        Year 3                      Year 4

              Q2      Q3      Q4      Q1      Q2      Q3      Q4

Projected exch. rate    6.03    6.09    6.22            6.27
Dollar cost of stock    618     631     1932            1307
```

The dollar costs have been entered as negative numbers in the Home Area columns of Figure 9-2. Amounts that are expected to be received by the Sereno subsidiary are expected to be paid out by the parent company. As intra-company transactions, they offset each other and the consolidated value is 0.

If the parent company can allocate $50,000 in cash from each quarter's earnings, the amounts shown in the table on the next page will require external financing.

The last two quarters of Year 3 require investment expenditures of $668,000 (Ps 4,028,000) and $680,000 (Ps 4,142,000) respectively. Note that these values reflect Sereno's inflation rate and the projected current exchange rates. Because each balance beyond the $100,000 earnings retained in cash each quarter is too small to justify a new issue of bonds or stock, we used a short-term bridge loan for the balance of $568,000 for the third quarter, and need to cover the $581,000 for the fourth quarter. Because the bank loan must be repaid each quarter, the fourth quarter's loan must include enough to repay the amount borrowed during the third quarter plus the external funds required for the construction during the fourth quarter. Thus, the total loan requirement for the fourth quarter is $1,149,000.

$$\$568,000 + \$581,000 = \$1,149,000$$

During the first quarter of Year 4, the initial construction will be completed. At that time, a stock offering will be made to pay off the loans and provide funds for the final quarter of construction.

Amounts in Thousands of Dollars	Year 3			Year 4			
	Q2	Q3	Q4	Q1	Q2	Q3	Q4
Financing required		618	631	1932		1307	
Less cash from earnings		50	50	50		50	
External financing		568	581	1882		1257	

The loan amounts have been entered under Short-Term Bank Loan for the home area in Quarter 3 and Quarter 4. The Sources of Funds have been consolidated. Each column has been totaled. Total Sources equal Total Expenditures for those quarters.

To summarize the planned external financing, we decided to use bank loans as a bridge until the final quarter of plant construction when a stock issue will be floated to capitalize the expansion project. A stock issue of $3,000,000 in Year 4, Quarter 1 is used to pay off the $1,149,000 loan, as well as to meet most of the construction payment for the quarter. However, we still will be short $31,000 after applying the cash from internal sources. We have decided to take out another short-term loan with the intention of paying it off with earnings from Year 4, Quarter 2 as no construction expenses will be incurred during that quarter.

> **IMPORTANT NOTE**
> The number of shares to be issued for the stock flotation and the exact amount to be raised from the issue cannot be determined until the selling price of the stock is known at the end of the quarter prior to the issue (see "Sale or Repurchase of Common Stock--Parent Company" earlier in this chapter).

During the third quarter of Year 4, $1,257,000 of external financing is required to fund the additional two new lines in Sereno and a $1 million bond issue is planned. The remaining $257,000 will be obtained by taking out another short-term loan. Short-term loans again are available since no loan was taken in the second quarter—that is, the bank loan was cleaned up.

After all the sources of funds have been entered, add the columns to obtain Total Sources. Then subtract any loan repayments to obtain Total Available Sources of funds. Subtract Total Expenditures from Total Available Sources to obtain the Surplus/Deficit balance. In our example, there are no surpluses or deficits because we have planned to cover exactly the amounts needed to fund the capital investments.

Suppose that instead of taking out a short-term loan in Year 3, Quarter 3, we chose to plan for a stock issue in that quarter. Because the minimum size of a stock issue is $1 million, there would be a surplus in that quarter. Surpluses may be invested by the parent company in CDs. Deficits indicate that additional financing (or lower expenditures) must occur to avoid cashing out.

Finally, calculate the consolidated entries by summing across the four areas. Pesos should be translated to dollars using the projected exchange rate for each quarter. Then the Sereno values (after translation) are added to the dollar balances in the three Merica areas. This consolidation is automatically done for you when you use the spreadsheet template. The Sale of Bonds, Sale of Common Stock and Short-Term Bank Loan home-area values from the work sheet for each quarter may be transferred to the financial section of your decision form. Don't forget to include decision-form entries for any additional funding requirements from your Pro Forma Cash Flow Work Sheet, discussed in Chapter 10.

Summary

Financial Decisions

1. Three-month **Certificates of Deposit** may be purchased in multiples of $100,000, to a maximum amount of $9,900,000. Interest is earned at the rate reported in the previous quarter's Industry Report. Interest is paid during the quarter in which the investment is made. The principal is not available until the following quarter.

2. Secured **bank loans** are available under a $2,500,000 line of credit subject to a maximum limit of 50 percent of accounts receivable plus inventories and to a one-quarter annual cleanup requirement in 4 consecutive quarters. Loans are issued at the short-term rate of interest available during the quarter of issue. They must be repaid in three months. Emergency loans, required because of insufficient cash on hand, are charged a penalty rate of interest (five percent above the current rate) and result in a lower credit rating.

3. Secured **bonds** with a face value of $2 million are outstanding at the end of Year 3. The bonds mature in ten years, carry a coupon rate of 10 percent and are callable with a five percent call premium. New bonds may be issued with a ten-year maturity at the long-term rate of interest available during the quarter of issue. They, too, are callable with a five percent call premium. Bonds may only be issued if the resulting ratio of bonds to equity will be less than 50 percent. They will be secured by plant and equipment and must result in a ratio of bonds to net fixed assets of less than 75 percent. Bonds are sold in multiples of $1 million. Outstanding bonds may be called (repurchased) in multiples of $100,000, to a maximum of $500,000 in any quarter. The call premium is paid during the quarter of repurchase.

4. **Dividends** may be declared in any quarter, subject to the restriction that current dividends plus dividends paid during the previous three quarters should not exceed earnings in the previous four quarters. Dividends may not be paid if the payment would result in a negative balance in the Accumulated Earnings account.

5. **Common stock** may be issued at a price to be determined by a formula shown in the text. At the beginning of the simulation, 6 million shares are outstanding. New issues are sold in multiples of 100,000 shares, with a minimum-sized issue being enough shares to raise at least $1 million. Stock that is outstanding may be repurchased at a price 10 percent above the stock price reported at the end of the previous quarter. Repurchases are in multiples of 100,000 shares, to a maximum of 500,000 shares in any quarter. A repurchase is permitted only if the resulting number of shares outstanding will be at least 3 million with positive Accumulated Earnings.

Investment Analysis

Proposals for new investments to expand production capacity should be evaluated using an acceptable method of evaluating investment alternatives. Flexibility and risk of the proposals should be included in the evaluation.

Capital Budget

Work sheets are provided to assist in the preparation of a capital budget. Expansion projects to be undertaken should be listed, funds requirements should be scheduled and plans should be made for obtaining the required funds.

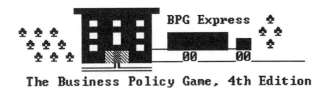

CHAPTER 10

FINANCE: FINANCIAL PLANNING

This chapter will help you understand the financial statement reports: Consolidated Income Statement (Report A), Consolidated Cash Flow Analysis (Report B) and Consolidated Balance Sheet (Report C) . As you read the chapter, we encourage you to look at copies of the Year 2, Quarter 4 reports which you will find in Appendix C. This can be especially helpful in understanding the linkages among the subsidiary and parent company financial statements and the process of consolidating financial statements. Consolidated statements are expressed in dollars, the currency of your parent company located in Merica. The Sereno subsidiary's financial statements are expressed in pesos, the currency of Sereno. The peso values must be translated to dollars before they can be consolidated with the financial statements of the parent company and its Merican subsidiaries. Intra-company transactions offset each other in consolidation to show a net consolidated balance of zero for the accounts that report these transactions.

All financial statement values, except those for equity accounts on the balance sheet, are translated at current exchange rates. Equity accounts on the balance sheet are translated at historical rates—those that were used in the original transactions. As a result, the consolidated balance sheet will not balance if there have been changes in exchange rates over time. The difference between translated total assets and translated liabilities plus equity accounts is adjusted in the Cumulative Translation Adjustment account so that the consolidated balance sheet will balance.

Profit Planning and the Income Statement

The management of each firm is judged, in part, by its profit performance. All of your decisions should be weighed in terms of their effect on your firm's net income. While profit is not the only criterion of successful management, or even necessarily the major one, poor profit performance is a sure sign of management failure.

The preparation of a *pro forma* income statement is one way to estimate and plan for your profit position in the future. We recommend that your management team establish a policy of preparing *pro forma* income statements for each of the next four quarters. Then prepare a new statement (four quarters ahead) after each quarter of play so that you will always have a full year of *pro forma* statements available. This will enable you to estimate the impact which your firm's decisions will have on profits before the decisions are actually implemented. This should reduce unpleasant surprises. A Pro Forma Income Statement Work Sheet (shown in Figure 10-1) has been provided for this purpose. Extra copies are available in Appendix D and a spreadsheet template of the work sheet is included in file FINANCE.WK1 on the Player's Program Disk packaged with this manual. The categories on the work sheet match those in the quarterly Consolidated Income Statement (Report A). See Appendix C for an example. Appendix B includes suggestions for using spreadsheet templates in your decision support system.

If the projected income on your Pro Forma Income Statement is less than desired, you may want to alter part of your firm's planned decision set to bring it in line. When you receive the reports for the quarter, we suggest that you compare the actual results of operations with your *pro forma* statements. An analysis of the differences between forecasted and actual results will help sharpen your forecasting skills and will provide a control mechanism for your management team.

The following discussion will help you complete your *pro forma* statements. They can be a little tricky when consolidating operations across countries. The format has been designed so that you can complete a *pro forma* statement for each market area by quarter. Each work sheet represents one quarter's operation. Column one of the work sheet contains the entry labels. Column two contains consolidated entries. The third column is for your firm's home area data. Columns four and five are for your firm's other two Merica market areas. Column six is for Sereno data. First, we will set up the work sheet by labeling the two unlabeled market areas and entering the World, Company, Year and Quarter numbers. Then we will continue with the illustration that started with a sales forecast in Chapter 6.

Our discussion will focus on transactions for your home area. We recommend that you verify the work sheet entries for all areas and for the consolidated column.

Sales and Cost of Goods Sold

Gross Revenue from Sales has three sources. Revenue is received from customers, from affiliates (the parent company and subsidiaries may purchase manufactured goods from each other) and from liquidators. Your firm consists of a parent corporation in your home area and three subsidiaries. Two subsidiaries are in other Merica areas and one is in the Latin American country of Sereno.

1. Net Sales to Customers. Copy the Expected Sales Revenue values for each market area from your Sales Forecast Work Sheet, Figure 6-1. (You **did** complete the Sales Forecast Work Sheet?) We have entered these estimates, in thousands of dollars (or pesos) as $1009 in the

home area, $735 each in Areas 2 and 3 and Ps 4745 in Sereno. The consolidated column is calculated by summing the sales for the four market areas. Sereno sales must be translated from pesos to dollars prior to consolidation.

Translation is accomplished by dividing sales in pesos by the projected peso exchange rate for the quarter. We suggest that you use the exchange rate forecast value found in your Quarterly Industry Report for the quarter you are planning. The exchange rate for Year 3, Quarter 1 is forecasted to be 6.00.

$$\$ \text{ Sales} = \text{Ps Sales} \div \text{Ps Exchange Rate}$$

$$\text{Ps } 4,745,000 \div 6.00 = \$790,833$$

Then, adding the dollar values for all areas yields the Consolidated Net Sales to Customers. Rounding all values to thousands of dollars results in:

$$\$1,009 + \$735 + \$735 + \$791 = \$3,270$$

2. Net Sales to Affiliates. Your parent firm, located in your home area, has three subsidiaries. One subsidiary is located in each of your non-home domestic market areas and a subsidiary is located in the Latin American country of Sereno. Each market area has a sales office which is responsible for managing the sales force and the product inventory in the area. If there is no plant in the area, the local sales office must buy its product from an affiliate, your parent firm or any subsidiary with a production plant. If there is a plant in the area and it is unable to fill the local sales office order completely, the shortage will be filled by affiliates if goods are available. Note that local sales offices are given priority in shipment allocations when there is a manufacturing plant in the same area. Sales to affiliates are recorded in local currency (currency of the country in which the plant making the product is located) at cost plus 20 percent to cover handling and administrative costs. Sales to affiliates are internal transactions and offset each other when the financial statements are consolidated.

The Production Plan Work Sheet (illustrated in Chapter 7) shows Affiliate Sales Office Purchases of 232,000 units. We first multiply the number of units by the unit production cost shown on the Production Plan Work Sheet ($4.84). Then we multiply the result by 1.2 to add the 20 percent markup for administrative and handling costs. Finally, we round the result and enter it on the work sheet as 1347.

$$232,000 \times 4.84 \times 1.2 = 1,347,456$$

3. Net Sales to Liquidators. When a new model is introduced, any units of the old model which have not been sold by the end of the first quarter of production of the new model are sold to a liquidator. The same liquidator will purchase any remaining inventory in the area if you decide to close your sales office. The liquidator has agreed to buy your old models at a price equal to the book value of inventory. This will be your production cost, or for goods purchased from affiliates, the purchase cost.

THE BUSINESS POLICY GAME PRO FORMA INCOME STATEMENT (000s)					
World _1_　Company _1_ Year __3_　Quarter __1__	Consoli- dated	Home Area	Merica Area_2_	Merica Area_3_	Sereno
Net Sales: to Customers	3270	1009	735	735	4745
to Affiliates (cost + 20%)	-------	1347	0	0	0
to Liquidators (at cost)	0	0	0	0	0
Total Sales	3270	2356	735	735	4745
Beginning Inventory	281	135	·56	56	202
Goods Manufactured	1586	1586	0	0	0
Purchases from Affiliates	-------	0	465	465	2509
Goods Available for Sale	1867	1721	521	521	2711
Ending Inventory	355	106	87	87	453
Cost of Goods Sold	1512	1615	434	434	2258
Less Value Added Tax	79	-------	-------	-------	474
Gross Profit	1679	741	301	301	2013
Advertising Expense	150	48	42	42	110
Sales Salaries	119	37	31	31	121
Sales Commissions	61	22	16	16	41
General Selling Expense	395	106	93	93	615
Transportation Expense	193	10	56	56	428
Sales Office Depreciation	12	3	3	3	19
Other Selling Expense	0	0	0	0	0
Total Selling Expense	930	226	241	241	1334
Research & Development	74	74	-------	-------	-------
Total Training Expense	70	70	0	0	0
Storage Expense	11	3	3	3	11
Executive Compensation	150	75	25	25	150
Loan Interest	0	0	-------	-------	-------
Bond Interest	50	50	-------	-------	-------
Other Expense	0	0	0	0	0
Total Admin. and Gen. Expense	355	272	28	28	161
Total Operating Expense	1285	498	269	269	1495
Operating Profit	394	243	32	32	518
CD Interest	0	0	-------	-------	-------
Capital Gain (Loss)	0	0	0	0	0
Net Profit (Loss) Before Tax	394	243	332	32	518
Less Income Tax	154	96	12	12	202
Net Profit (Loss) After Tax	240	147	20	20	316
Dividends from Subsidiaries	-------	82	-------	-------	-------
Dividends to Parent	-------	-------	20	20	253
Dividends to Shareholders	209	209	-------	-------	-------
Added to Retained Earnings	31	20	0	0	63

Figure 10-1
Illustration of Pro Forma Income Statement Work Sheet

If you plan to produce a new model and your sales forecast and production plan project that one or more of your market areas will have an inventory of the old model at the end of the quarter, make this calculation: multiply the number of unsold units of the old model by the value per unit of Beginning Inventory (see paragraph 5, below) to arrive at the value of sales to liquidators for the area. If a sales office is closed, the unsold goods will be sold to the liquidator and the same calculation should be made. All sales are made in local currency. In our example, no sales office will be closed and the model produced last quarter will be the one produced this quarter, so there will be no Sales to Liquidators.

4. <u>Total Sales</u>. Calculate total sales by adding the three categories of sales in each column. Consolidated Total Sales will not equal the sum of the area Total Sales because Sales to Affiliates, which are intra-company transactions, are included in area sales but are offset against Purchases from Affiliates when consolidating sales. To reconcile Total Sales, deduct the value of Sales to Affiliates from the sum of the Total Sales for the individual areas. This apparent double counting will be taken care of below when we consolidate values for Gross Profit.

5. <u>Beginning Inventory</u>. The value of Beginning Inventory is taken directly from the ending inventory shown on last quarter's balance sheet (see Appendix C) or from the previous quarter's work sheet. The Beginning Inventory for your home area is $135,000.

6. <u>Goods Manufactured</u>. This cost can be taken directly from the Total Production Cost entries on the Production Plan Work Sheet (see Figure 7-3). Currently, production is taking place only in your home area. The cost shown is 1586 which should be entered on the work sheet.

7. <u>Purchases from Affiliates</u>. Any sales office operating in an area which does not have a manufacturing plant must buy the products it sells from an affiliate. This may be the parent or any subsidiary with a production plant. If there is a plant in the same area with the sales office, but the plant is unable to supply the total needs of the sales office, additional units of product may be bought, if available, from affiliates.

The Production Plan Work Sheet shows the number of units each affiliate sales office plans to purchase. A shipment's cost can be determined by multiplying the number of units purchased from a plant by the Total Production Cost per unit shown on the Production Plan Work Sheet and then adding the 20 percent markup.

Since we have only one plant located in the home area, the other three areas will purchase goods from that plant. Sales office orders shown on the Production Plan Work Sheet (Fig. 7-1) are 80,000 units each for Merica areas 2 and 3 and 72,000 units for Sereno. Sufficient capacity is available so that all orders will be filled. The purchase costs are calculated by multiplying the unit production cost from the Production Plan Work Sheet by the number of units purchased and adding the 20 percent markup. The cost is rounded to thousands and entered as $465 for the two Merica areas and Ps 2509 for Sereno.

Merica 2 & 3:	$80,000 x $4.84 x 1.2 = $464,640
Sereno:	$72,000 x $4.84 x 1.2 x 6.00 = Ps 2,509,056

8. <u>Goods Available for Sale</u>. For each area, Goods Available for Sale consists of the value of Beginning Inventory plus Goods Manufactured plus Purchases from Affiliates. Because goods purchased from affiliates are offset against goods sold to affiliates, the consolidated cost of goods available is less than the sum of the individual sales offices' cost of goods available for sale. The difference is the amount of Purchases from Affiliates. The manufacturing cost of those goods is included in the cost of Goods Available for Sale in the area where they are manufactured. The 20 percent markup is a way to allocate some of the administrative costs to the purchasing unit. Therefore, to consolidate the cost of Goods Available for Sale, subtract the sum of all Purchases from Affiliates (equal to the sum of all Sales to Affiliates) from the sum of individual area cost of Goods Available.

	Cost	Less Purchases	Consolidated Cost
Area 1	$1721		$1721
Area 2	$ 521	$465	$ 56
Area 3	$ 521	$465	$ 56
Sereno	Ps 2711 ÷ 6	Ps 2509 ÷ 6	$ 34
Totals	$3215	$1348	$1867

You may encounter a small rounding error as a result of translating the values of individual accounts separately and then translating the rounded totals to add to the totals from other areas. We will enter 1867 in the consolidated column, resulting from adding the consolidated totals:

Beginning Inventory	$ 281
Goods Manufactured	$1586
Goods Available	$1867

9. <u>Ending Inventory</u>. Inventories are valued on a first-in, first-out (FIFO) basis. Thus, goods held in inventory will be sold before newly manufactured or purchased goods. You may estimate the value of **Ending Inventory** for each area as follows:

a. Add the number of **units** you expect to produce or purchase during the coming quarter to the number of **units** in inventory at the beginning of the quarter to obtain the number of **units** available for sale. Subtract the number of units you expect to sell to affiliates and to customers during the quarter from the number of units available for sale to determine the number of units in your anticipated ending inventory. This number should be available by area from the Production Plan Work Sheet (Figure 7-1). Continuing our example, it is 22,000 for your home area.

b. Note the current Total Unit Production Cost for the area, from your Production Plan Work Sheet (Figure 7-3). For your home area, it is $4.84.

c. Multiply the number of units in **ending** inventory by the unit production cost. For goods purchased, use the unit purchase cost, equal to unit production cost plus 20 percent. If the number of units in inventory at the **beginning** of the quarter is **less than expected** sales (that is, all units from the beginning inventory will be sold), the result will be the value of ending inventory.

$$\$22,000 \times \$4.84 = \$106,480$$

For our example, 106 is the value to enter for Ending Inventory.

d. If the number of units in beginning inventory **exceeds expected sales**, a different calculation will have to be made. Because all of the units to be sold would have been produced or purchased in the previous quarter, some of the units in this quarter's ending inventory also will have been produced or purchased in the previous quarter and some in the current quarter. The value of the beginning inventory should be divided by the number of units in stock to estimate the unit cost of goods on hand when the quarter started. Then multiply the unit cost of beginning inventory by the number of units you expect to sell to determine the cost of units from beginning inventory which will be sold. Subtract this value from your estimate of the cost of Goods Available for Sale to provide an estimate of the value of your ending inventory.

10. <u>Cost of Goods Sold (COGS)</u>. Subtract the Ending Inventory value from the Goods Available for Sale value to obtain the Cost of Goods Sold for each area. For your home area, this will be:

$$\$1,721 - \$106 = \$1,615$$

As with Goods Available for Sale, the consolidated value of Cost of Goods Sold excludes the value of Purchases from Affiliates.

	Area COGS	Less Purchases	Consolidated COGS
Area 1	$1615		$1615
Area 2	$ 434	$465	$ -31
Area 3	$ 434	$465	$ -31
Sereno	Ps 2258 ÷ 6	Ps 2509 ÷ 6	$ -42
Totals	$2859	$1348	$1511

The negative values for the subsidiaries in the Consolidated Cost of Goods Sold column are because they don't plan to sell all of the goods they will purchase. Some were returned to inventory and will be charged to Cost of Goods Sold when they are sold in a later quarter.

11. <u>Less Value Added Tax</u>. Value added tax is levied on all domestic sales made in Sereno at the rate of 10 percent of the sales price. Thus, the tax is Ps 474,000.

$$\text{Ps } 4{,}745 \times .1 = \text{Ps } 474$$

Note that Value Added Tax is deducted from gross receipts for income tax purposes and thus is deducted from sales before gross profit is calculated.

Gross Profit

When income is consolidated for your firm, Sales to Affiliates and Purchases from Affiliates are offset against each other and net to zero. Your Gross Profit on sales is calculated by subtracting the Cost of Goods Sold from the value of Gross Sales. In the case of Sereno, the Valued Added Tax also is subtracted. For the home area:

$$\$2{,}354 - \$1{,}615 = \$739$$

The consolidated value should equal the sum of the area values after translating the Sereno value to dollars.

$$\$741 + \$301 + \$301 + (\text{Ps } 2{,}013 \div 6) = \$1{,}679$$

It is wise to check occasionally for consistency. A comparison of this value with the Gross Profit reported for Year 2, Quarter 4 shows that it is somewhat lower than last quarter. This is to be expected, because sales are expected to be lower (mostly due to the seasonal effect) and production costs are expected to be slightly higher (because of inflation).

Selling Expense

You may want to refer to Chapter 5 for a detailed discussion of selling expenses and how they are calculated.

1. <u>Advertising</u>. Enter the total amount you plan to spend on advertising for each market area. In developing the sales forecast shown in Figure 6-1, we assumed an increase in advertising expenditures of five percent. Advertising expense in Year 2, Quarter 4 in your home area was $46,000 (see Appendix C) so an increase of 5 percent would total $48,300 (rounded to thousands of dollars)

$$1.05 \times \$46{,}000 = \$48{,}300$$

Areas 2, 3 and Sereno also are increased by 5 percent.

2. <u>Sales Salaries</u>. Multiply the salary you plan to pay the sales force by the number of salespeople you plan to employ and enter the result. Your company had 12 salespeople in your home area in Year 2, Quarter 4. If you expect to keep the same salary level as last quarter ($3,000 for each salesperson), and nobody quits, then total sales salaries will be $36,000.

$$12 \text{ x } \$3,000 = \$36,000$$

However, this would result in a real salary decrease due to inflation. We will adjust the salary upward to keep salaries at a constant level of purchasing power. The CPI increased nearly 3 percent last quarter. Thus, we will increase salaries by 3 percent for this quarter for a total of $37,000.

$$\$36,000 \text{ x } 1.03 = \$37,080$$

Areas 2 and 3 salaries also are increased by 3 percent. Sereno salaries will be up 4 percent.

3. <u>Sales Commissions</u>. Multiply the sales commission you plan to pay per unit by the number of units you expect to sell and enter the result. If you keep present commissions at 20 cents per unit, you are again decreasing real compensation due to inflation effects. We will increase commissions by 5 percent to 21 cents per unit. Sales of 103,000 units will require paying $21,630 rounded to $22,000.

$$103,000 \text{ x } \$0.21 = \$21,630$$

Areas 2, 3 and Sereno also are increased in a similar manner.

4. <u>General Selling Expense</u>. Multiply the number of salespeople you plan to employ by $4,000 (the semi-variable portion of general selling expenses). Multiply 20¢ (the variable portion of general selling expenses) by the number of units you expect to sell. Add the above two products to $37,500 (the fixed portion of general selling expenses for each sales office). For our example, this will total about $106,100 in the home area, rounded to $106,000.

$$(12 \text{ x } \$4,000) + (\$0.20 \text{ x } 103,000) + \$37,500 = \$106,100$$

Similar calculations are made for areas 2 and 3. The calculation for Sereno, in pesos, is

$$(13 \text{ x Ps } 24,000) + (\text{Ps } 1.20 \text{ x } 65,000) + \text{Ps } 225,000 = \text{Ps } 615,000$$

5. <u>Transportation Expense</u>. The transportation expense depends upon the location and destination of product shipments. See Chapter 5 for a discussion of these expenses. As there is a plant in your home area, transportation costs for the area are limited to 10 cents per unit shipped to customers. Other areas will have to pay shipping costs from your home area to the area sales office plus shipping costs from the sales office to the customer. With forecasted sales of 103,000 units, transportation costs are estimated at $10,300 (103,000 x .1) rounded to $10,000.

Transportation costs to or from Sereno are invoiced in dollars, so the Sereno subsidiary must convert pesos at the projected exchange rate. Costs within Sereno are invoiced in pesos.

The transportation expense calculation for each area is:

	Sales Office Purchases	Sales to Customers	Transportation Expense
Area 1	0	$.10 x 103	$10
Area 2	$.60 x 80	$.10 x 75	$56
Area 3	$.60 x 80	$.10 x 75	$56
Sereno	$.90 x 6 x 72	Ps .60 x 65	Ps 428

6. <u>Sales Office Depreciation</u>. Each market area and Sereno have a sales office. The original cost of a sales office completed in Year 1, Quarter 1 was $400,000 (or the peso equivalent at that time). Depreciation charges are calculated on a straight-line basis over 31.5 years with no salvage value. This amounts to 0.7937 percent of the original cost each quarter.

Depreciation for each existing domestic sales office is $3,000 per quarter ($3,175 rounded.) The depreciation for the Sereno office is the peso equivalent of $3,000 at the exchange rate in effect at the end of Year 1, Quarter 1 when the office was built.

$$\$400,000 \times .007937 = \$3,175$$

Note that if you were to close a sales office and then later decide to open a new office in the area, the depreciation rate would be based upon the cost of the new sales office in the quarter when it was acquired. That would be $400,000 inflated by the prior quarter's CPI.

7. <u>Other Selling Expense</u>. This line is used to record selling expenses that are not recorded elsewhere.

8. <u>Total Selling Expense</u>. The sum of advertising, sales salaries, sales commissions, general selling expense, transportation expense and other selling expense is entered here. For our example, the amount for the home area totals $226,000.

$$\$48 + \$37 + \$22 + \$106 + \$10 + \$3 + \$0 = \$226$$

Advertising expenditures, sales salaries and commission rates are subject to your management's direct control and may be changed during any quarter. General selling expense, transportation expense and other selling expense are only indirectly under your control. A successful marketing plan that results in increased sales, for example, will also increase general selling expense and transportation expense. Training new members of the sales force will increase total training expense. All expenses should be expected to increase at least at a rate to keep up with inflation.

Administrative and General Expense

1. Research and Development (parent company only). Enter the total amount you plan to spend for Research and Development. We will adjust R & D spending upward by 3 percent to keep up with inflation. Thus, R & D for the quarter will total $74,000

$$\$72,000 \times 1.03 = \$74,160$$

2. Total Training Expense. The cost of training new salespeople, training employees when adding production lines and ongoing training of production and operations workers is reported under Total Training Expense. Training new salespeople costs $5,000 per person. Training workers for a new production line costs $100,000 per line. Ongoing training of production workers is an expense item totally under your discretion. You may spend as little or as much as your management desires. Last quarter, ongoing training of production workers amounted to $68,000. Our example assumes no new lines or new salespeople for this quarter. We will increase the ongoing training by the rate of inflation, or 3 percent. Thus, total training expense will be $70,000

$$\$68,000 \times 1.03 = \$70,040$$

3. Storage Expense. Storage Expense is computed for inventories on hand at the end of the previous quarter. It costs 10 cents (60 centavos) per unit for the first 300,000 units stored in any marketing area that contains a production plant. Units in excess of 300,000 must be stored in a public warehouse at a cost of 30 cents (Ps 1.80) per unit. Units stored in areas without a manufacturing plant are kept in a public warehouse. Last quarter, 29,000 units were stored in the plant warehouse in your home area. That would cost $3,000. ($2,900 rounded)

$$29,000 \times .1 = 2,900$$

4. Executive Compensation. Quarterly compensation for executives at the beginning of Year 3, Quarter 1 are:

	Merica	Sereno
Each plant	$50,000	Ps 300,000
Sales office	$25,000	Ps 150,000

For the current quarter, your home area has a plant and a sales office. Thus, executive compensation for your home area will be $75,000. Compensation in other areas includes only amounts for sales office executives.

5. Loan Interest (parent company only). This is the interest to be paid on any short-term bank loans. Bank loans normally are charged the short-term interest rate available to a company with your credit rating. Interest is paid during the quarter that the loan is obtained. You can

estimate it as one-fourth of the annual interest rate multiplied by the size of any bank loan that you plan to take out during the coming quarter.

Inasmuch as you have not yet completed your Pro Forma Cash Flow Work Sheet, the amount of any bank loan that would be required to meet operating expenses is not yet known. If you decide to take out a bank loan, return to the Pro Forma Income Statement and add the additional interest expense here.

6. <u>Bond Interest</u> (parent company only). You can estimate bond interest by calculating the interest payment for one quarter on new bonds sold during the current quarter and add the result to the quarterly interest payment for bonds outstanding at the end of the previous quarter. Bond interest payments are based upon interest rates in effect during the quarter that the bonds are issued. Interest payments on new bonds may be computed at a quarterly rate equal to one-fourth of the annual interest rate in effect during the quarter of issue. Interest payments on the bonds that were outstanding at the beginning of Year 3 are computed at the rate of 2.5 percent of the face value each quarter (10 percent per year).

$$\$2,000,000 \times 0.025 = \$50,000$$

If bonds are repurchased, subtract the amount of interest that would have been paid on those bonds. When bonds are repurchased, those with the highest interest rate will be repurchased first.

For our example, no bond sale or repurchase is contemplated, so bond interest would continue at the rate of $50,000 per quarter.

7. <u>Other Expense</u>. This category covers expenses that are not included elsewhere. The entry represents the total of these expenses. Examples of items that may be included as other expense are:

a. A deactivation charge of $100,000 per line is assessed if your firm should deactivate any of your production lines (see Chapter 7).

b. A call premium of five percent of the face value is charged on any bonds that may be repurchased (see Chapter 9).

c. Moving expenses for salespeople of $5,000 (Ps 30,000) each (see Chapter 5).

d. Severance pay for salespeople of $5,000 (Ps 30,000) each (see Chapter 5).

As no Other Expense is anticipated, a 0 has been entered in the work sheet for the example.

8. <u>Total Administrative and General Expense</u>. This is the sum of items 1 through 7. For our example, the total for the home area is $272,000:

$$\$74 + \$70 + \$3 + \$75 + \$0 + \$50 + \$0 = \$272$$

Total Operating Expense

Total Operating Expense is the sum of Total Selling Expense and Total Administration and General Expense. For our example, this is $498,000 in the home area.

$$\$226 + \$272 = \$498$$

Operating Profit

Operating profit is calculated by subtracting Total Operating Expense from Gross Profit. For our example, the amount is $243,000.

$$\$741 - \$498 = \$243$$

Other Income

1. <u>CD Interest</u> (parent company only). Income from interest on CD investments is calculated as one-fourth of the annual CD interest rate, reported in the previous quarter's Quarterly Industry Report. The rate reported, shown in Appendix C, is 9.50 percent. If you were, for example, to re-invest the $100,000 that your predecessors invested last quarter, you would earn about $2,375 (rounded to $2,000), reported as CD Interest.

$$(0.0950 \times 100,000) / 4 = \$2,375$$

For now, 0 is entered here. Until the cash flow analysis is completed, it will not be known if there will be surplus cash to invest. This entry can be completed later if you decide to invest surplus cash in certificates of deposit.

2. <u>Capital Gain (Loss)</u> (parent company only). Capital losses are realized when you sell a capital asset for less than book value. In *The Business Policy Game*, the sale of a plant or a sales office results in a capital loss. Your firm will receive 90 percent of the book value of the building and equipment. Thus, you should record a capital loss of 10 percent of the book value of the asset. In our example, no capital assets are being sold, so there will be no Capital Gain (Loss).

Profits, Taxes and Dividends

　　1.　Net Profit Before Tax.　Net profit before tax can be estimated by adding CD Interest and Capital Gain (Loss), if any, to Operating Profit.　With no CD investment or sale of capital assets, enter the same amount as for Operating Profit.　For our example, this is $243,000 in the home area.

　　2.　Income Tax.　Income tax is assessed against net profit at a rate of 39 percent for both Merica and Sereno.　The income tax assessments for the subsidiaries are calculated by multiplying the net profit before tax by the tax rate:

```
Area 2        $32 x .39 =    $12
Area 3        $32 x .39 =    $12
Sereno     Ps 518 x .39 = Ps 202
```

The parent company is taxed on the consolidated net income before tax, less a credit for income taxes paid by the subsidiaries:

```
Consolidated taxes are      $394 x .39 = $154

Tax credit for subsidiary payments:

Area 2:              $12
Area 3:              $12
Sereno:  Ps 202 ÷ 6 = $34

   Total Credit                   $58

   Net parent company tax         $96
```

　　No taxes are assessed on an operating loss.　The tax laws in the simulation do not permit a tax-loss carry-back, even for previous quarters in the current calendar year.　The entire loss is carried forward to be applied against future profits prior to tax assessment.　The amount of the loss carry-forward does not appear on the balance sheet.

　　If a subsidiary has a loss instead of a profit, the subsidiary pays no tax in that quarter.　The amount of the tax loss carry-forward is deducted from future profits before assessing taxes.　The loss reduces consolidated income so that the parent company's tax bill will be less in the quarter of the loss than it would be without the subsidiary loss.　If the subsidiary later earns a profit (but pays less tax because of the previous loss) the parent's assessment will reflect the full amount of the consolidated income before tax.　Therefore, a loss in a subsidiary may cause the parent's effective tax rate on home-area income to vary from the 39 percent used in the calculation.

　　3.　Net Profit After Tax.　Total the Income Tax amounts and subtract them from Net Profit Before Tax to calculate Net Profit After Tax.　For our example, Net Profit After Tax in the home area is $147,000:

$$\$243 - \$96 = \$147$$

In each country there are other business taxes that are not explicitly shown, but which are included in the operating costs of your firm. You can assume that all taxes are paid promptly and, thus, the tax people will not pay you an unexpected visit.

Dividends

Dividends to Shareholders are paid by the parent company. Dividends to Parent are paid by subsidiaries (these are not recorded on the decision form, but paid automatically when the funds are eligible to be transferred). When the financial statements are consolidated, the Dividends from Subsidiaries and Dividends to Parent net to zero (subject to small rounding errors).

    1.   Dividends to Parent (subsidiaries only). Profits paid to the parent company by a subsidiary are recorded as Dividends from Subsidiaries. When profits are paid by the Sereno subsidiary, they are converted from pesos to dollars at the current exchange rate.

Your foreign subsidiary, Sereno, operates under governmental regulations controlling the repatriation of company profits. The subsidiary may pay dividends to its parent company equal to the entire amount of current-quarter after-tax profits with the following restrictions:

        a. Twenty percent of the profits must be set aside in an equity reserve (part of Accumulated Earnings) until the reserve has accumulated to an amount at least **equal to 50 percent of capital stock**.

        b. Dividends may only be paid if, after payment, there will be a minimum cash balance of one million pesos (held in Sereno banks).

Your company's board of directors has established a uniform policy for all subsidiaries, both foreign and domestic. Thus, these same rules apply to Merican subsidiaries, too. The minimum cash balance requirement at Merican banks under this policy is $100,000. Only 80 percent of a subsidiary's profits will be paid to the parent company until the balance of the Accumulated Earnings account is at least 50 percent of the book value of the subsidiary's Capital Stock. After the Accumulated Earnings account reaches 50 percent, dividends that may be missed because of insufficient funds (including the minimum cash balance requirement) will be paid later if cash balances rise.

The subsidiaries in Merica, Areas 2 and 3, have met the equity reserve requirement. Capital Stock amounts to $753,000 and Accumulated Earnings amount to $373,000. The Sereno subsidiary still is building the reserve with a Capital Stock of Ps 5,762,000 and accumulated earnings of Ps 2,540,000. It is still Ps 341,000 short of the 50 percent requirement.

$$.50 \times Ps\ 5,762 = Ps\ 2,881$$

$$Ps\ 2,881 - Ps\ 2,540 = Ps\ 341$$

Thus, the entire net profit of Merica Areas 2 and 3, $20,000 each, will be paid to the parent firm. Only 80 percent of Sereno's net profit, Ps 253,000, will be paid to the parent.

    2. <u>Dividends from Subsidiaries</u> (parent company only). Sum the Dividends to Parent entries to arrive total dividends received by the parent. In our example, the Dividends from Subsidiaries total $82,000

$$\$20 + \$20 + (Ps\ 253 \div 6) = \$82$$

    3. <u>Dividends to Shareholders</u> (parent company only). Next, enter the amount of dividends that you expect to pay to shareholders during the quarter. Your stockholders expect regular dividend payments, even though none have been paid during the last two years. You need to establish a dividend policy as part of your finance strategy. You may, for example, decide to pay out 30 percent of net profits after taxes to stockholders. If this is your policy, you may wish to pay dividends of about $209,000, or about 30 percent of the previous quarter's consolidated profits (Year 2, Quarter 4 consolidated profits are shown in Appendix C).

$$\$698 \times 0.30 = \$209$$

$209,000 has been entered in the work sheet of Figure 10-1. The payment amounts to about 3.5 cents per share on the 6 million shares outstanding.

Added to Retained Earnings

    To the parent company's Net Profit After Tax, add the Dividends from Subsidiaries and subtract the amount of Dividends to Shareholders that you expect to pay during the quarter. Enter the result in Added to Retained Earnings. See below for treatment of this amount on the balance sheet. For our example, the amount to enter for the parent company's Added to Retained Earnings is $20,000.

$$\$147 + \$82 - \$209 = \$20$$

    Then, complete the Consolidated column. Dividends from Subsidiaries and Dividends to Parent net to zero as intra-company transactions. Consolidated Dividends to Shareholders equals the same as the parent company's amount for Dividends to Shareholders.

Cash Budgeting and the Cash Flow Statement

Your management team should keep enough cash on hand to meet all of your financial obligations promptly. We suggest that you plan to maintain a cash balance large enough to meet unexpected cash requirements and to provide a buffer in case your cash receipts are lower than anticipated or your expenditures turn out to be higher. If your firm does not have enough cash to meet your obligations during a quarter, you must take out an emergency bank loan. Your banker has agreed to provide an automatic loan to meet such short-term crises by supplying funds at an interest rate that is 5 percentage points higher than the short-term interest rate currently available to your firm. (After all, we can't let your firm go bankrupt!) If your firm's short-term rate is 10 percent, for example, the rate for an emergency bank loan will be 15 percent.

Running out of cash puts you technically in default of your financial obligations. Creditors will lose confidence in your firm, and your credit rating will be lowered. The lower credit rating will increase the cost of future borrowing and will reduce the proceeds from the future sale of common stock.

To reduce the risk of running out of cash and incurring an emergency loan, we suggest that you prepare a Pro Forma Cash Flow Work Sheet prior to finalizing the decision set for each quarter. A work sheet is provided for this purpose (illustrated in Figure 10-2, with extra copies provided in Appendix D). A spreadsheet template of the Pro Forma Cash Flow Work Sheet is included in file FINANCE.WK1 on the Player's Program Disk which came with this manual.

The categories on the work sheet match those on the quarterly Consolidated Cash Flow Analysis (Report B). See Appendix C for an example. Operating cash flow consists of cash receipts and payments directly associated with the operations of your company. Investment cash flow consists of cash receipts from investments and cash payments for new investments. Financing cash flow includes cash receipts and payments directly related to financing activities. These categories enable you to pinpoint problem areas more easily. The values shown in the work sheet of Figure 10-2 continue the example shown above from the Pro Forma Income Statement of Figure 10-1.

The Pro Forma Cash Flow Work Sheet is a way to budget your cash requirements. The work sheet should be used both as a planning tool and as a control device. The budget will help you plan your cash requirements so that surplus funds can be invested or external financing can be arranged if needed. After the quarter is completed, you should analyze the differences between estimated and actual receipts and expenditures in order to perfect your forecasting techniques. In addition, the analysis will help you spot areas in which future expenditures should be adjusted.

Pro Forma Cash Flow Work Sheet

Operating Receipts

  Sales in *The Business Policy Game* are made on credit. The accounts receivable balance carried over from the previous quarter will be collected during the current quarter. In Merica, one-half of each quarter's sales revenue will be collected by the end of the quarter. In Sereno, 40 percent of sales are collected in each quarter. For both countries, the uncollected portion will be shown on the balance sheet as accounts receivable and carried over for collection during the next quarter. All customers in *The Business Policy Game* are honorable and solvent, and thus no pro-vision for bad debts is required.

  1. Collect from Last Quarter Sales. Enter the accounts receivable value from last quar-ter's balance sheet (this would be the Pro Forma Balance Sheet if you are budgeting for more than one quarter) on the Collect from Last Quarter Sales line for each area. For your home area, this value is $605,000, taken from the Year 2, Quarter 4 balance sheet (see Appendix C).

  2. Collect from Current Quarter Sales. For each Merica area, enter one-half of the ex-pected sales revenue for the current quarter on the Collect from Current Quarter Sales line. For Sereno use 40 percent of the expected sales revenue. Expected sales values may be taken directly from the Pro Forma Income Statement of Figure 10-1. For your home area the value of current-quarter sales to be collected is about $505,000.

$$\$1,009,000 \times 0.5 = \$504,500$$

  3. Net Sales to Affiliates. This entry is the total value of goods shipped to the sales offices in the other three areas from current production at the plant. All shipments to other sales offices are invoiced at cost plus 20 percent to cover handling and administrative costs. This value can be taken directly from the entry on the Pro Forma Income Statement. For our example, the amount for the home area is $1,347,000. This amount will be consolidated with amounts Pur-chased from Affiliates by the subsidiaries as intra-company transactions, netting to zero.

  4. Net Sales to Liquidators. Sales to liquidators result from two different types of events. Units of an old model which are not sold during the quarter prior to the introduction of a new model are sold to a liquidator. When a sales office is closed, any remaining inventory of product also is sold to a liquidator. Your firm has a contract with a liquidator in each area to purchase any number of units of your product at your cost. This consists of the total production cost plus the 20 percent markup for purchases from affiliates. The amount can be estimated by finding the value per unit of beginning inventory and multiplying it by the number of units expected to be sold to the liquidator. It does not include the cost of shipping. This entry can be taken directly from the entry on the Pro Forma Income Statement. It is 0 for our example, as neither type of event is planned.

THE BUSINESS POLICY GAME PRO FORMA CASH FLOW WORK SHEET					
World _1_ Company _1_ Year _3_ Quarter _1_	Consoli- dated	Home Area	Merica Area_2_	Merica Area_3_	Sereno
Operating Receipts:					
Collect from Last Quarter Sales	2505	605	545	545	4860
Collect from Current Quarter Sales	1557	505	368	368	1898
Net Sales to Affiliates	-------	1347	0	0	0
Sales to Liquidators	0	0	0	0	0
Operating Expenditures:					
Production Cost	1453	1453	0	0	0
Purchases from Affiliates	-------	0	465	465	2509
Operating Expense	1223	445	266	266	1476
Taxes Paid	233	96	12	12	676
Net Operating Cash Flow	1153	463	170	170	2097
Investment Receipts:					
CD Interest	0	0	-------	-------	-------
CDs Matured	1000	1000	-------	-------	-------
Subsidiary Dividends Received	-------	82	-------	-------	-------
Fixed Assets Sold	0	0	0	0	0
Investment Expenditures:					
CDs Purchased	0	0	-------	-------	-------
New Equipment	0	0	0	0	0
Sales Office Investment	0	0	0	0	0
Plant Investment	0	0	0	0	0
Subsidiary Stock Purchased	-------	0	-------	-------	-------
Net Investment Cash Flow	1000	1082	0	0	0
Financing Receipts:					
Loans from Bank	0	0	-------	-------	-------
Stock Sold to Parent	-------	-------	0	0	0
Bond Sale	0	0	-------	-------	-------
Stock Sale	0	0	-------	-------	-------
Financing Expenditures:					
Interest Paid	50	50	-------	-------	-------
Dividends to Shareholders	209	209	-------	-------	-------
Dividends to Parent	-------	-------	20	20	253
Bank Loans Repaid	0	0	-------	-------	-------
Bonds Repurchased	0	0	-------	-------	-------
Stock Repurchased	0	0	-------	-------	-------
Net Financing Cash Flow	-259	-259	-20	-20	-253
Beginning Cash Balance	1814	1367	140	140	1000
Net Cash Flow for Quarter	1893	1286	150	150	1844
Cash Balance End of Quarter	3707	2653	290	290	2844
Required Loan (+ interest)	0	0	-------	-------	-------

FIGURE 10-2 - Illustration of Pro Forma Cash Flow Work Sheet

Operating Expenditures

    1. Production Cost. See Chapter 7 for information on estimating production costs. Production costs are entered for each area that has a plant. Total production costs entered on this line of your Pro Forma Cash Flow Work Sheet should **exclude depreciation** charges as no cash is required for depreciation. The value for cash expenditures on production for the Pro Forma Cash Flow Work Sheet may be copied from the Total Cash Expenditure line of your Production Plan Work Sheet (See Figure 7-3). For our example, the amount in the home area is $1,453,000.

    2. Purchases from Affiliates. Purchases from Affiliates reflect the payment for units of product that are purchased directly from the parent firm or another subsidiary. When financial statements are consolidated, Net Sales to Affiliates and Purchases from Affiliates net to zero. The value can be taken directly from the entry on the Pro Forma Income Statement (see Figure 10-1).

    3. Operating Expense. This entry consists of the cash operating expenditures that are shown on the Pro Forma Income Statement. It can easily be estimated by subtracting Sales Office Depreciation (a non-cash expense), Loan Interest and Bond Interest (both are financing expenses and are included later under Financing Expenditures) from Total Operating Expense on the Pro Forma Income Statement work sheet (see Figure 10-1). The result of this calculation for your home area is $445,000:

Total Operating Expense	$498
Less Sales Office Depreciation	3
Less Loan Interest	0
Less Bond Interest	50
Cash Operating Expense	$445

    4. Taxes Paid. Taxes are paid separately each quarter by each subsidiary. Sereno taxes include both the income and value added taxes and are paid to the Sereno government in pesos. The tax values may be taken directly from the entries on the Pro Forma Income Statement (see Figure 10-1). For Sereno, the taxes include:

Value Added Tax	Ps 474
Income Tax	202
Taxes Paid	Ps 676

Net Operating Cash Flow

    Net Operating Cash Flow for each column of the work sheet is the sum of Operating Receipts minus the sum of Operating Expenditures. The home-area value for our example is $464,000.

$$(\$\ 605 + 505 + 1{,}347 + 0) - (\$1{,}453 + \$0 + \$445 + \$96) = \$463$$

Investment Receipts (parent company only)

1. <u>CD Interest</u>. The amount of interest may be copied from the CD Interest line of the Pro Forma Income Statement. It is the amount that you expect to earn from funds invested in CDs for the current quarter (see Chapter 9). For our example, because we did not yet estimate surplus cash, the value is 0.

2. <u>CDs Matured</u>. Enter the dollar amount of Time Certificates of Deposit that will mature during the quarter. This is the amount that your firm invested last quarter, and may be copied from the last quarter's Balance Sheet (see Appendix C). The amount for our example is the Time Certificates of Deposit balance from the Year 2, Quarter 4 Balance Sheet, $1,000,000 (see Appendix C).

3. <u>Subsidiary Dividends Received</u>. Dividends from subsidiaries are the portion of profits paid by a subsidiary to the parent firm. Dividends paid by the Sereno subsidiary are converted to dollars at the current exchange rate. This is the sum of the dividends paid by each of the three subsidiaries to the parent. The value can be obtained directly from the entry on the Pro Forma Income Statement (Figure 10-1). For our example, this is $82,000.

4. <u>Fixed Assets Sold</u>. When a plant or a sales office is closed, the building is sold for 90 percent of book value (see Chapter 8). The cash received from the sale is recorded on this line. No closings are planned for the current quarter, and thus the entry is 0.

Investment Expenditures

1. <u>CDs Purchased</u> (parent company only). If you know that you will have surplus cash for the quarter, you may invest it in time certificates of deposit (see Chapter 9). For our example, we will enter 0 on this line. When the work sheet has been completed, it may be appropriate to come back to make an entry here.

2. <u>New Equipment</u>. If installation of new lines is planned for any area, enter the amount of the payment for equipment. (Training costs are part of Operating Expenses.) This amount may be copied from your Capital Budget Work Sheet (Figure 9-2). As we are not planning to add any new lines during the next quarter, the entry is 0.

3. <u>Sales Office Investment</u>. If you previously closed a sales office in an area and decide to reenter the area, you will have to build a new sales office (see Chapter 5 for details). If you began the simulation selling in less than four market areas and are permitted to enter new areas, you will have to build a new sales office when entering an area. In either case, it takes one quarter to build a new sales office at a cost of $400,000 at the beginning of Year 3. Enter the amount on this line for the area in which the office will be built. In our example, your firm has sales offices in all four areas, so the entry is 0.

4. Plant Investment. Enter the quarterly payment required for new plant and new addition construction. The calculation of these amounts is described in Chapter 8. The values may be copied from your Capital Budget Work Sheet (Figure 9-2). No construction is planned for this quarter, so our entries are 0.

5. Subsidiary Stock Purchased (parent company only). Subsidiary Stock Purchased is the investment, if any, that the parent firm plans to make in subsidiaries during the current period. Additional funding of subsidiary capital investments and operating expenditures is accomplished by purchasing stock in the subsidiary. This account and Stock Sold to Parent (below) are used to provide funds for cash deficits in a subsidiary. Normally, you should leave this line blank until after completing the work sheet. If any subsidiaries end up with a cash deficit, enter the amount of the deficit under Stock Sold to Parent and Subsidiary Stock Purchased. No financing appears to be required this quarter.

Net Investment Cash Flow

Net Investment Cash Flow is the sum of investment receipts minus the sum of investment expenditures. For our example, the work sheet values total $1,083,000 in the home area.

$$(\$0 + \$1,000 + \$82 + 0) - (\$0 + \$0 + \$0 + \$0 + 0) = \$1,082$$

Subsidiary Dividends Received and Subsidiary Stock Purchased are excluded from the consolidated total because they are offset against Dividends to Parent and Stock Sold to Parent as intracompany transactions.

Financing Receipts

1. Loans from Bank (parent company only). In estimating operating funds requirements, it is suggested that you leave the loan line blank until you have computed the expected cash available from other sources and have compared this amount with your expected cash requirements. The amount of a bank loan, if needed, can then be calculated by subtracting the expected cash requirements, including the desired minimum cash balance, from the amount of cash expected to be available from other sources. If your estimates are reasonably accurate, the result should be the approximate amount of cash that you need to borrow in order to meet your obligations. No loans are planned for this quarter. Thus, the entry is 0.

2. Stock Sold to Parent (subsidiaries only). A subsidiary finances cash deficits by selling stock to the parent firm. Normally, you should leave this line blank until completing the work sheet. If any subsidiaries end up with a cash deficit, enter the amount of the deficit under Stock Sold to Parent and Subsidiary Stock Purchased. When quarterly financial statements are consolidated, Stock Purchased in Subsidiaries and Stock Sold to Parent should net to zero (subject to small rounding errors). No financing appears to be required this quarter, so the entries are 0.

3. <u>Bond Sale</u> (parent company only). During Year 0, your firm issued $2,000,000 in 10 year bonds at an interest rate of 10 percent. Additional bonds, secured by plant and equipment, may be issued with a ten-year maturity date (See Chapter 9). Enter the face value of any bonds you plan to sell (in thousands of dollars). For our example, sale of bonds is not contemplated for this quarter, so the value is 0.

4. <u>Stock Sale</u> (parent company only). Your firm has 6,000,000 shares of no-par-value common stock outstanding at the beginning of Year 3 (See Chapter 9 for details of a new issue). Enter the expected proceeds of a stock sale. Proceeds may be estimated by multiplying the issue price by the number of shares you plan to issue. For our example, a sale of stock is not contemplated this quarter, so enter 0.

Financing Expenditures

1. <u>Interest Paid</u> (parent company only). Interest paid on bank loans and on bonds is recorded here. The amounts can be obtained from the Pro Forma Income Statement (Figure 10-1). In our example, they sum to $50,000.

$$\$0 + \$50 = \$50$$

2. <u>Dividends to Shareholders</u> (parent company only). Dividends are payable in the quarter in which they are declared. Enter here the amount of dividends that you plan to pay. Copy the value from the Pro Forma Income Statement (Figure 10-1). For our example, the amount is $209,000.

3. <u>Dividends to Parent</u> (subsidiaries only). Dividends to Parent are profits transferred by a subsidiary to the parent firm. Payments made by the Sereno subsidiary are converted to dollars at the current exchange rate. When financial statements are consolidated, Dividends to Parent and Subsidiary Dividends Received net to zero (subject to small rounding errors). These values may be taken directly from the Pro Forma Income Statement (Figure 10-1).

4. <u>Bank Loans Repaid</u> (parent company only). Enter the amount of any bank loan outstanding at the end of the previous quarter (which must be paid back in the current quarter). For our example, no bank loan was outstanding in Year 2, Quarter 4. The amount can be taken from the previous quarter's balance sheet (see Appendix C).

5. <u>Bonds Repurchased</u> (parent company only). Outstanding bonds may be repurchased with payment of a five percent call premium (See Chapter 9). Enter the principal amount of bonds to be repurchased. The call premium should be entered under Other Expense on the Pro Forma Income Statement and carried in the Pro Forma Cash Flow Work Sheet as part of Operating Expense. For our example, no bond repurchase is contemplated for Year 3, Quarter 1, so the amount is 0.

6. Stock Repurchased (parent company only). Repurchases are in 100,000-share blocks, with a maximum repurchase in any quarter of 500,000 shares (See Chapter 9). Enter the dollar value of expected stock repurchase (in thousands). Multiply the number of shares to be repurchased by the repurchase price. For our example, no share repurchase is contemplated for Year 3, Quarter 1, so the amount is 0.

Net Financing Cash Flow

Net Financing Cash Flow is the sum of Financing Receipts less the sum of Financing Expenditures. For our example, the amount for the home area is -$259,000.

$$(\$0 + \$0 + \$0) - (\$50 + \$209 + \$0 + \$0 + \$0) = -\$259$$

Dividends to Parent are excluded from the consolidated total because they offset Subsidiary Dividends Received (under Investment Receipts, above), as intra-company transactions. Stock Sold to Parent is consolidated with Subsidiary Stock Purchased (under Investment Expenditures, above).

Cash Flow Summary

1. Beginning Cash Balance. Enter the amount of cash on hand at the end of the previous quarter, as shown on the balance sheet. For our example, this is $1,367,000 in the home area (See Appendix C). This is a rather large cash balance and, unfortunately, it earns no interest. Your predecessors might have done well to have put another $1 million in time CDs in order to earn more interest.

2. Net Cash Flow for Quarter. The estimated net cash flow for the quarter should be calculated here. It is the sum of Net Operating Cash Flow plus Net Investment Cash Flow plus Net Financing Cash Flow. For our example, the amount is $1,286,000 in the home area.

$$\$463 + \$1,082 + (-\$259) = \$1,286$$

3. Cash Balance End of Quarter. The expected ending cash balance is the sum of Beginning Cash Balance plus Net Cash Flow for the Quarter. This calculation will help you decide whether you need additional financing or will have a cash surplus in the coming quarter. If the expected ending cash balance is lower than your minimum cash target, additional funds should be obtained from some source. If the difference shows considerably more cash available than your target, you may want to invest the excess funds in three-month time certificates of deposit, to pay additional dividends or use some of the cash to expand marketing activities or production capacity.

For our example, the expected ending cash balance in the home area is $2,653,000.

$$\$1,367 + \$1,286 = \$2,653$$

If the balance should be negative and a loan is required, you will need to borrow enough to cover the negative balance plus enough to restore your safety stock of cash. The loan will increase your interest charges for the quarter and change your tax liability. Because bank loans are discounted (the interest is taken off before you receive the cash), you should borrow enough to cover the interest, too. If you are not eligible for a loan (See Chapter 9), then other financing should be arranged or expenditures reduced.

At this point, you need to consider whether you may wish to revise your financial plans for Year 3, Quarter 1. There is obviously more cash than you will need for the quarter. You might invest some of it in time CDs. Be sure not to cut yourself too short, though. Keep a large enough cash buffer to be sure that all contingencies are covered. If you run out of cash, time CDs will not be available, and you may be forced to take out an emergency loan.

The Balance Sheet

Your Pro Forma Balance Sheet (See Figure 10-3) can be estimated using values from the balance sheet at the end of the previous quarter, the Pro Forma Cash Flow Work Sheet (Figure 10-2) and the Pro Forma Income Statement (Figure 10-1). The Pro Forma Balance Sheet will provide an estimate of the value of each of your balance sheet accounts at the end of the quarter. You may use the Pro Forma Balance Sheet in lieu of a cash flow analysis, if desired, to determine whether a bank loan will be necessary. To do so, estimate the value of all other balance sheet accounts and "plug" the cash balance to make the balance sheet balance. The plug value will register as a cash deficit or surplus, and can be shifted to a loan account or CD investment.

A *pro forma* balance sheet also provides a useful vehicle for estimating funds requirements over a longer period of time. We have provided a Pro Forma Balance Sheet work sheet (shown in Figure 10-3) for your use, with extra copies available in Appendix D. A spreadsheet template also is available on the Player's Program Disk packaged with this manual. It is included in file FINANCE.WK1. The values shown in Figure 10-3 continue the example that was used for the Pro Forma Income Statement and Pro Forma Cash Flow Work Sheet.

Current Assets

1. Cash Balance. This can be copied directly from the ending cash balance on the last line of the Pro Forma Cash Flow Work Sheet (Figure 10-2). For our example, this value for the home area is $2,653,000.

Alternatively, if you are using the Pro Forma Balance Sheet to estimate the funds requirements for future periods, enter the desired minimum cash balance—the amount that you intend to have on hand at the end of the period. Then, when you have finished estimating all of the other accounts, force the balance sheet to balance by using surplus cash to purchase time CDs or borrowing to make up a deficit.

2. Time Certificates of Deposit (parent company only). This entry may be copied directly from the entry in the Pro Forma Cash Flow Work Sheet (Figure 10-2). For our example, above, we did not anticipate investing in CDs, but after looking at the large cash balance that seems to be available, you may change your mind about this.

3. Accounts Receivable. Accounts receivable at the end of any quarter is equal to one-half of the expected sales for that quarter for Merica and 60 percent of expected sales for Sereno. In the cash flow work sheet, we estimated the half of Year 3, Quarter 1 sales that would be collected in the same quarter to be $505,000. The other half, obviously also $505,000, would remain on the books as accounts receivable. Actually, we have rounded both values upward which increases receipts by $1,000 ($1,009,000 ÷ 2 = $504,500). *Pro forma* statements are based on estimates, though, and small rounding errors should not change our conclusions very much.

4. Inventory. Inventory on hand at the end of the period can be copied directly from the Pro Forma Income Statement (Figure 10-1), where it was estimated in order to calculate the estimated cost of goods sold. For our example, the amount is $106,000 in the home area.

5. Total Current Assets. This is the sum of Cash Balance, Time Certificates of Deposit, Accounts Receivable and Inventory. For our example, the amount is $3,266,000 for the home area.

$$\$2,653 + \$0 + \$505 + \$106 = \$3,264$$

Fixed Assets

1. Net Sales Office. This entry is equal to the value of the sales office at the end of last quarter minus depreciation charges. The amount of depreciation can be taken directly from the Pro Forma Income Statement (Figure 10-1) and subtracted from the net sales office balance on the previous quarter's balance sheet (See Appendix C). For the home office in our example, the new value is $373,000.

$$\$376 - \$3 = \$373$$

2. Net Manufacturing Plant. This is equal to the value of the plant in an area at the end of the previous quarter plus capital investments during the current period minus depreciation charges. If a plant is sold, the amount would be reduced to 0 in that area. The plant depreciation charges can be taken directly from the Production Plan Work Sheet (Figure 7-3). It is $26,000. The book value of net plant was shown to be $3,092,000 on the balance sheet for Year 2, Quarter 4 (See Appendix C). No new plant investment is planned for this quarter. Thus, the current book value of net plant would be $3,066,000.

$$\$3,092 + 0 - \$26 = \$3,066$$

See Chapter 7 for a discussion of plant depreciation.

THE BUSINESS POLICY GAME PRO FORMA BALANCE SHEET (000s)					
World _1_ Company _1_ Year _3_ Quarter _1_	Consoli- dated	Home Area	Merica Area_2_	Merica Area_3_	Sereno
ASSETS:					
Cash Balance	3707	2653	290	290	2844
Time Certificates of Deposit	0	0	-------	-------	-------
Accounts Receivable	1716	505	368	368	2847
Inventory	355	106	87	87	453
Total Current Assets	5778	3264	745	745	6144
Net Sales Office	1489	373	373	373	2221
Net Manufacturing Plant	3066	3066	0	0	0
Net Manufacturing Equipment	2037	2037	0	0	0
Equity in Subsidiaries	-------	3634	-------	-------	-------
Total Fixed Assets	6592	9110	373	373	2221
Total Assets	12370	12374	1118	1118	8365
LIABILITIES AND EQUITY:					
Bank Loans	0	0	-------	-------	-------
Total Current Liabilities	0	0	-------	-------	-------
Bonds Outstanding	2000	2000	-------	-------	-------
Total Liabilities	2000	2000	0	0	0
Capital Stock	7500	7500	745	745	5762
Accumulated Earnings	2873	2873	373	373	2603
Cumulative Translation Adjustment	-3	-------	-------	-------	-------
Total Equity	10370	10373	1118	1118	8365
Total Liabilities and Equity	12370	12373	1118	1118	8365

FIGURE 10-3
Illustration of the Pro Forma Balance Sheet

3. <u>Net Manufacturing Equipment</u>. Manufacturing equipment is equal to the value of Net Manufacturing Equipment at the end of the previous period plus planned capital expenditures for new equipment during the current period minus equipment depreciation charges. If a plant is sold, the amount would be reduced to zero in that area.

The book value of net equipment was $2,144,000 at the beginning of Year 3, Quarter 1, as shown on the Year 2, Quarter 4 balance sheet (see Appendix C). No equipment purchases are contemplated for this quarter. Equipment depreciation charges of $107,000 can be taken directly from the Production Plan Work Sheet (Figure 7-3). For our example, the book value of equipment will be $2,037,000.

$$\$2,144 - \$107 = \$2,037$$

4. <u>Equity in Subsidiaries</u> (parent company only). The investment made by the parent firm in subsidiaries is carried as an asset, Equity in Subsidiaries. As earnings are retained in a subsidiary, they also increase the book value of the parent's Equity in Subsidiaries. Such amounts from the Sereno subsidiary are translated at the rate in effect during the quarter in which the earnings were retained. The translation to dollars when consolidating Sereno equity accounts uses the rate in effect at the time the investment was made (historical rate). The subsidiary equity accounts are consolidated with the parent's asset account, Equity in Subsidiaries, and should net to 0.

Begin the calculation of this entry with the Equity in Subsidiaries value from last quarter's balance sheet. Then add any subsidiary stock purchased this quarter (shown on the Pro Forma Cash Flow Work Sheet). Finally, add the current retained earnings of each subsidiary from the Pro Forma Income Statement.

In our example, no additional stock will be purchased in subsidiaries. The value of the investment in Equity in Subsidiaries for Year 2, Quarter 4 was $3,624,000 (See Appendix C). Sereno Accumulated Earnings are expected to increase by Ps 63,000 while Accumulated Earnings for the two Merica areas will not change (See Figure 10-1). Translating new Sereno retained earnings to dollars yields $10,500, rounded to $11,000.

$$\text{Ps } 63,000 \div 6 = \$10,500$$

No stock purchases are contemplated this quarter (Figure 10-2). Adding the Sereno earnings retention to last quarter's Equity in Subsidiaries gives a new value of $3,635,000.

$$\$3,624 + \$0 + \$11 = \$3,635$$

5. <u>Total Fixed Assets</u>. Total Fixed Assets is the sum of Net Sales Office, Net Manufacturing Plant, Net Manufacturing Equipment and Equity in Subsidiaries. In our example, the amount is $9,110,000.

$$\$373 + \$3,066 + \$2,037 + \$3,635 = \$9,111$$

In consolidation of fixed assets, exclude the value of Equity in Subsidiaries, as it is offset against the sum of values of Total Equity for all subsidiaries. Consolidated Total Fixed Assets can be estimated by adding Total Fixed Assets for each area and subtracting Equity in Subsidiaries ($3,635 in our example):

$$\$9,111 + \$373 + \$373 + (\text{Ps } 2,221 \div 6) - 3635 = \$6,592$$

6. Total Assets. Total Assets is the sum of Total Current Assets and Total Fixed Assets. For our example, the amount is $12,375 in the home area.

$$\$3,264 + \$9,111 = \$12,375$$

To consolidate Total Assets, exclude the values of Equity in Subsidiaries, as was done with Total Fixed Assets:

$$\$12,375 + \$1,118 + \$1,118 + (\text{Ps } 8,365 \div 6) - \$3,635 = \$12,370$$

Liabilities and Equity

1. Bank Loan (parent company only). The loan is equal to the amount that you plan to borrow during the quarter. In preparing the Pro Forma Cash Flow Work Sheet (Figure 10-2), we determined that a loan was not needed for this quarter, and thus the entry is 0.

If the Pro Forma Balance Sheet is being used to estimate funds requirements, we suggest that this category be left blank until the other amounts have been calculated. The bank loan can be utilized as a "plug" figure to make total assets equal total liabilities plus equity. The plug figure will indicate the additional funds that your firm requires during the coming quarter.

2. Total Current Liabilities (parent company only). Total Current Liabilities consists only of bank loans. For our example, the amount is 0.

3. Bonds Outstanding (parent company only). Bonds Outstanding is estimated by adding the amount of bonds outstanding at the end of the previous quarter plus or minus any new bonds you plan to issue or redeem in the current quarter. Long-term debt in *The Business Policy Game* is limited to bonds. As no new issue or repurchase is contemplated in our example, the amount is the same as was reported on the Year 2, Quarter 4 balance sheet, or $2,000,000 (See Appendix C).

$$\$2,000 + \$0 - \$0 = \$2,000$$

4. Total Liabilities (parent company only). Total Liabilities is the sum of Total Current Liabilities plus Bonds Outstanding. For our example, the amount is $2,000,000.

$$\$0 + \$2,000 = \$2,000$$

5. Capital Stock. Capital stock is equal to the cumulative value of cash received by your company for the sale of common stock. Your firm's common stock has no par value. Thus, if your firm plans to issue common stock, the expected net proceeds of the issue should be added to the value of Capital Stock at the end of the previous period.

If your parent company should repurchase some common stock, a portion of the value of the repurchased stock is attributed to the contribution to this account when the stock was first sold. Therefore, it is deducted from Capital Stock when the stock is repurchased. An estimate of the deduction can be made:

  a. Divide the amount of the parent's Capital Stock account (from the previous quarter) by the number of outstanding shares (See the Quarterly Industry Report, Appendix C) to get the average book value per share. If you planned to repurchase stock in Year 3, Quarter 1, this calculation would be:

$$\$7,500,000 \div 6,000,000 \text{ shares} = \$1.25 \text{ per share}$$

  b. Multiply the book value per share by the number of shares to be repurchased. This is the amount to subtract from the Capital Stock Account. If you planned to repurchase 100,000 shares, then the estimate is;

$$100,000 \text{ shares x } \$1.25 = \$125,000$$

This would reduce your Capital Stock account to $7,375,000:

$$\$7,500,000 - \$125,000 = \$7,375,000$$

  c. Then, subtract the **balance** of the amount of the repurchase from the Accumulated Earnings account (see paragraph 6e on the next page). The amount of the repurchase would be estimated by multiplying the number of shares to be repurchased by an amount equal to 110 percent of the latest reported market price (See the Quarterly Industry report, Appendix C).

$$100,000 \text{ shares x } \$4.37 \text{ x } 1.10 = \$480,700 \text{ (rounded to } \$481,000)$$

Subtracting the $125,000 deducted from the Capital Stock account leaves $356,000 to deduct from the Accumulated Earnings account, below.

$$\$481,000 - \$125,000 = \$356,000$$

For our example, the value of the Capital Stock account is the same as Year 2, Quarter 4, or $7,500,000 (see the balance sheet in Appendix C).

The equity accounts of the subsidiaries are consolidated with the parent's asset account, Equity in Subsidiaries and net to 0. Therefore, the consolidated equity accounts are equal to the equity accounts of the parent company.

6. <u>Accumulated Earnings</u>. These are earnings which have not been paid out in dividends, but reinvested in the firm. Subsidiary earnings which have not been paid in dividends are added to **both** the book value of the parent's Equity in Subsidiaries account (an asset) and the parent's Accumulated Earnings (an equity account) to reflect the increased value of the investment in the subsidiary.

To calculate the amount of the Accumulated Earnings account, start with the accumulated earnings from the previous quarter's balance sheet. Then, using values from the Pro Forma Income Statement (Figure 10-1):

    a. Add Net Profit After Tax (Figure 10-1).

    b. For the parent, add Dividends from Subsidiaries (Figure 10-1).

    c. Subtract dividends paid, whether to parent or stockholders (Figure 10-1).

    d. Add to the parent's Accumulated Earnings the amount of the subsidiaries' current Added To Retained Earnings (Figure 10-1).

    e. Subtract that part of any stock repurchase that is not allocated to the common stock account (see paragraph 5c, above).

For our example, the following values are used to calculate an estimate of accumulated earnings for the parent company and all subsidiaries.

	Area 1 $	Area 2 $	Area 3 $	Sereno Ps
Prev. Accumulated Earnings	2842	373	373	2540
Net Profit After Tax	+ 147	+ 20	+ 20	+ 316
Dividends from Subs.	+ 82			
Dividends to Parent		- 20	- 20	- 253
Dividends to Stockholders	- 209			
Subs' Retained Earnings	+ 11			
Stock Repurchase Amount	0			
Total Accum. Earnings	2873	373	373	2603

The consolidated value of Accumulated Earnings is equal to that of the parent because the equity accounts of the subsidiaries are consolidated with the parent's asset account, Equity in Subsidiaries, as intra-company transactions.

7. Cumulative Translation Adjustment. Because Sereno asset and liability accounts are translated at current exchange rates and equity accounts are translated at historical rates, the consolidated balance sheet will not balance if there have been any exchange rate changes. The Cumulative Translation Adjustment reflects any gain or loss in equity accounts because of exchange rate changes.

For *pro forma* statements, the expected balance of this account can be estimated as equal to consolidated assets minus consolidated liabilities minus consolidated Total Equity. It is a balancing account, to make the translated consolidated balance sheet balance. For our example, the value is - $3,000, reflecting an unrealized loss due to exchange rate changes to date (and, perhaps, the existence of rounding errors in our calculations).

```
Consolidated Total Assets              $12,370
Less Consolidated Total Liabilities     -2000

Equity should equal this balance       $10,370

Less Consolidated Capital Stock          7,500
Less Consolidated Accum. Earnings        2,873

Cumulative Translation Adjustment      $    -3
```

A quick check to see if your figure is reasonable is to translate Sereno Total Equity at a historical rate and then at the current rate. The difference between the two values should be close to the cumulative translation account entry. For example:

```
Current rate     Ps 8,365 ÷ 6.00 = $1,394.2
Historical rate  Ps 8,365 ÷ 5.98 = $1,398.8

Difference                          - 4.6
```

The difference between our estimated value and -4.6 is small, and likely due to the use of only one historical rate. Actual transactions occurred at more than one rate. Rounding errors over several previous quarters may contribute to part of the difference. The small difference should not cause you any problem. If you get a large difference, and exchange rate changes have been small, you probably have an error someplace.

8. Total Equity. Total equity is the sum of Capital Stock and Accumulated Earnings. In consolidation, the subsidiary's Total Equity is offset against the parent's asset account, Equity in Subsidiaries. For foreign subsidiaries, equity accounts are the only accounts that are translated at historical exchange rates (those that were in effect at the time of original transactions). All others are translated by calculating their dollar value each quarter at current exchange rates. In our example, total equity is equal to $10,373,000 in the home area:

$$\$7,500 + \$2873 = \$10,373$$

Consolidated Total Equity is $10,370:

$$\$7,500 + \$2,873 - \$3 = \$10,370$$

9. <u>Total Liabilities & Equity</u>. Adding Total Liabilities and Total Equity for the parent company gives $12,373,000 for our example.

$$\$2,000 + \$10,373 = 12,373$$

And Total Assets is approximately equal to Total Liabilities and Equity. It should be noted that if you should use different methods of estimation for some of the balance sheet items than for others, as we did, you might not show exact equality for both sides of the balance sheet. Also, because of several different estimation calculations, it is easy for a rounding error to occur. *Pro forma* statements are not accounting records, keeping track of every penny. They are estimates. If they don't always balance exactly, you will not be in trouble with your CPA. If this imbalance offends your sense of order, you may force a balance by adding (or subtracting) the difference to the expected cash balance. Then Total Assets will be equal to Total Liabilities plus Total Equity.

On the other hand, if the difference is large, you probably have made an error. You may have failed to consider something from one of your estimated statements that was considered on another. Check back over your figures to see what may have been omitted. And always check your *pro forma* statements against the printed reports that you receive at the end of the quarter. In this way you will find that errors made at the beginning of the quarter will stand out. Your estimating skills can be improved by checking up on their accuracy. But if you are in doubt, be sure to leave a big enough cash balance to take care of funds requirements that you may have overlooked! Don't get caught short on cash and be forced to take out an emergency loan.

If you are using the Pro Forma Balance Sheet to estimate funds requirements, the difference between total assets and total liabilities plus equity (assuming that you have estimated correctly) would indicate either surplus funds or additional funds requirements. If assets are greater than liabilities plus net worth, then additional cash would be required to finance the assets. If assets are less, then surplus cash would be available, and the difference can be added to the cash account or used to purchase CDs.

We suggest that a *pro forma* statement be made for the end of each of the next five years. This will enable you to project your long-term funds requirements and permit you to plan for the sale of common stock and bonds as additional funding becomes necessary. Alternatively, more funds may be generated internally than are needed to meet your estimated obligations. In that case, you may want to plan for investment in CDs, for increased dividend payments to stockholders, or to consider other alternative uses for the funds.

Summary

Pro Forma Income Statement

Work sheets are provided for the preparation of Pro Forma Income Statements. Calculations of various items are summarized in the text.

1. **Sales revenues** consist of sales to customers, to affiliates and to liquidators. Revenues were estimated from the sales forecast developed in Chapter 6 and the Production Plan Work Sheet (Figure 7-1).

2. **Goods Available for Sale** were estimated by adding beginning inventory (last period's ending inventory) to total production cost plus purchases from affiliates (both from Figure 7-1).

3. **Inventory** is valued on a first-in first-out basis. The value of ending inventory was estimated and subtracted from goods available for sale to estimate the cost of goods sold.

4. **Gross Profit** consists of total sales minus cost of goods sold minus value added tax. Purchases from and sales to affiliates are consolidated with each other as intra-company transactions.

5. **Selling Expense** includes advertising, sales salaries, commissions, general selling expense, transportation expense, sales office depreciation and other selling expense. Calculation of values for these accounts is described in Chapter 5.

6. **Research and Development** expense is a decision variable, under the control of your management.

7. **Training Expense** includes the cost of training new salespeople, training employees when adding production lines and ongoing training of production and operations employees.

8. **Storage** expense is computed on the number of units on hand at the beginning of the quarter.

9. **Executive Compensation** depends on the number of manufacturing plants and sales offices.

10. **Loan Interest** is paid quarterly on any bank loans outstanding. The amount of interest is determined by the current short-term rate of interest available to a company with your credit standing. The quarterly rate is one-fourth of the annual rate.

11. **Bond Interest** is paid quarterly on all outstanding bonds at the long-term rate of interest for a firm with your credit rating at the time the bonds were issued. The quarterly rate is one-fourth of the annual rate.

12. **Other Expense** is a category for expenses that are not separately stated, including moving expenses, severance pay, deactivation charges and call premiums for repurchased bonds.

13. **Operating Profit** is Gross Profit less Total Operating Expense.

14. **Other Income** consists of CD interest and capital gain or loss, if any.

15. **Income Tax** is assessed at a rate of 39 percent of net profit. A loss-carry-forward provision permits losses to be offset against future profits for tax assessment.

Pro Forma Cash Flow Work Sheet

A cash flow analysis should be prepared (work sheets are provided) to determine expected receipts and cash outlays for each quarter of operation. This will assist your management in providing sufficient funds to meet its obligations when due.

1. **Operating Receipts**. Receipts on customer accounts in any quarter will equal one-half of current-quarter sales in Merica and 40 percent in Sereno, plus the balance of accounts receivable from the end of the previous quarter. Sales to Affiliates are consolidated as intra-company transactions. Sales to Liquidators include obsolete-model goods held in inventory after introduction of a new model and unsold goods when a sales office is closed.

2. **Operating Expenditures** consist of Production Cost, Purchases from Affiliates, Operating Expense and Taxes Paid. Taxes include the income tax in all areas plus value added taxes in Sereno. Depreciation charges are excluded because they do not require a cash outlay. Bond and loan interest are extracted from Operating Expenditures and included under Financing Expenditures.

3. **Investment Receipts** consist of CD interest, maturing CDs, dividend payments received from subsidiaries and proceeds from the sale of fixed assets.

4. **Investment Expenditures** consist of CDs purchased, capital expenditures on plant and equipment, capital expenditures on a new sales office and purchases of stock in subsidiaries.

5. **Financing Receipts** consist of bank loans, bonds sold, common stock sold and, for subsidiaries, the proceeds of stock sold to the parent corporation.

6. **Financing Expenditures** consist of the amount of dividends paid to stockholders and, for subsidiaries, dividends paid to the parent company, loans repaid, bonds repurchased and stock repurchased.

7. **Beginning cash balance** equals the previous quarter's ending cash balance.

8. **Ending cash balance** equals beginning cash balance plus the net cash flow for the quarter.

Pro Forma Balance Sheet

Work sheets are provided for the preparation of a Pro Forma Balance Sheet. Amounts for this work sheet are estimated using values from the balance sheet at the end of the previous quarter, the Pro Forma Cash Flow Work Sheet and the Pro Forma Income Statement.

1. The **Cash Balance** is taken from the Pro Forma Cash Flow Work Sheet.

2. **Time Certificates of Deposit** are taken from the Pro Forma Cash Flow Work Sheet.

3. **Accounts Receivable** are taken from the Pro Forma Cash Flow Work Sheet, as the value of sales that is not collected by the end of the quarter.

4. **Inventory** is taken from the Pro Forma Income Statement.

5. **Net Sales Office** is calculated by subtracting sales office depreciation from the previous quarter's value for Net Sales Office. If a sales office is closed, the value is reduced to 0.

6. **Net Manufacturing Plant** is the value of net plant at the end of the previous quarter, plus capital investments during the current quarter, less depreciation charges. If the plant is closed, the value is reduced to 0.

7. **Net Manufacturing Equipment** is equal to the value of net equipment at the end of the previous quarter, plus planned capital expenditures, less depreciation charges. If the plant is closed, the value is reduced to 0.

8. **Equity in Subsidiaries** represents the value of the parent company's investment in the stock of the subsidiaries.

9. **Bank Loan** is taken from the Pro Forma Cash Flow Work Sheet.

10. **Bonds Outstanding** equal previous bonds outstanding, plus newly issued bonds, less bonds repurchased.

11. **Capital Stock** equals previous capital stock, plus newly issued common stock, less an allocation for repurchased stock.

12. **Accumulated Earnings** equal previous retained earnings, plus current additions to retained earnings, less proceeds of stock repurchase that are not allocated to the Capital Stock account.

13. **Cumulative Translation Adjustment** is a balancing item to make the consolidated balance sheet balance. It is required because foreign assets and liabilities are translated to the consolidated balance sheet at current-quarter exchange rates, while equity accounts are translated at historical rates.

14. **Exchange Rates**. It is important to distinguish between current and historical exchange rates when consolidating Sereno accounts. Current exchange rates are those in effect during the current quarter. Historical exchange rates are those in effect during previous quarters.

   a. Current exchange rates are used for all translations of peso accounts on the income statement and the cash flow statement. On the balance sheet, peso assets and liabilities are translated at current rates.

   b. Historical rates are used to translate peso values of equity accounts from the Sereno subsidiary. Because the consolidated value of assets minus liabilities will not equal the total of equity accounts if there have been changes in exchange rates, the difference is calculated as the Cumulative Translation Adjustment. This makes the consolidated balance sheet balance.

The Business Policy Game, 4th Edition

APPENDIX A

INSTALLING AND USING THE BPG COMPUTER PROGRAM

IBM and Compatible Users
(Macintosh Users: Skip to Page 191)

If you enter your decision set and save it on a floppy disk, your team will use the Player's Program Disk packaged with this manual and a formatted blank Decision/Data Disk.

Installing Player's Programs

A Player's Program Disk is included with this Player's Manual. Place it in your floppy disk drive and change the DOS prompt to the same drive. Type

    A: <enter> (or B: <enter>)

Then run the BPGSETUP program. Type

    BPGSETUP   <enter>

The program will prompt you for the installation path (C:\BPG is suggested) and let you choose options for partial installation if you desire to install the Decision Support System (DSS) templates separately.

IMPORTANT NOTE
Please be sure to look for a file named README on the distribution disk. It will include any information that became available after this manual was prepared. To read the contents of the file on your screen, type README from the DOS prompt for your Player's Program Disk.

Special Instructions for Floppy-Disk Users

Each team should create a Decision/Data Disk which is a formatted, empty disk with the following label:

```
Company c, World w
Company Name
BUSINESS POLICY GAME
Decision/Data Disk
```

where c is your Company number and w is your World number.

Submit the disk to your simulation administrator. Your administrator will transfer the data files necessary for you to print reports and enter your first decision set after the simulation has been run for the historical quarter Year 2, Quarter 4. Files transferred to your disk will include a decision file, a file of historical data required for the decision-entry program, and a full set of reports for Year 2, Quarter 4 (similar to those in Appendix C). The files are specific for your particular simulated company. As each team will have its own separate disk, it is important to know your company and world numbers in order to obtain the correct disk. The simulation administrator will tell you how to retrieve your disk after the files have been transferred.

A word about disk etiquette. Handle the disk carefully. Do not touch the surface. Do not bend it or spill coffee or other liquids on it. Do not play Frisbee with it. Treat the disk as you would a good friend, gently and carefully.

When entering data using a floppy disk, first place the disk in the disk drive. **Never place a disk in a drive which is spinning**. Be very careful not to touch the surface of the disk which is inside the cover you are holding. Take special care not to bend it. Gently slide the disk into the disk drive with the label side up.

Running *The Business Policy Game* Program

First, be sure that the DOS prompt showing on your monitor is for the disk drive and directory where *The Business Policy Game* player's programs were installed. If you are running the programs from a floppy disk, the DOS prompt may be

    A:>

If you are running from a hard disk or local area network, the prompt may also show a directory path, like

    C:\BPG>

If you are not sure of the correct directory, see your simulation administrator.

To run the BPG computer program, type BPG. The program will load from the disk and the opening window with the main menu will appear.

The main menu bar offers five options, listed across the top of the screen:

> New Decisions
> Chg Decisions
> Reports
> Setup
> Quit

Use the right or left arrow keys to highlight your choice and press <ENTER>, or simply press the first letter of your choice. Each choice is described in detail below.

1. **Setup**. First, press "S" to choose Setup. The drop-down menu offers three choices:

> Enter Data Path
> Color Monitor
> Monochrome Monitor

It is **very important** that you set the path to the files on your Decision/Data Disk (or the directory on your LAN, although the LAN path is likely to have been set for you). You **must** make this choice before you use the BPG program so that the program will be able to access your decision and report files. Your **first task** is to do this. Press "E" for Enter Data Path. The following window will appear to enable you to confirm the default path or set a new one.

```
┌─────────────────────────────────────────────────────────────────────┐
│                       SET PATH DESIGNATIONS                           │
│  Please enter the complete path for DECISION, REPORT and other data   │
│  files. The path will be used by BPG to find report files and to save │
│  decision files that must be transferred to the simulation            │
│  administrator.                                                        │
│                                                                       │
│     Example:  A:  (or B:)              (Use with floppy disk drives.)  │
│                                                                       │
│     Example:  C:\BPG4\DATA             (Use when saving data to a hard │
│                                         disk or a local area network   │
│                                                                       │
│                                                                       │
│  Enter path for DECISION and REPORT files:                            │
│                                                                       │
│            A:_____                 │
│                                                                       │
│                                                                       │
│                                                                       │
│                      Press <F10> to Continue                          │
└─────────────────────────────────────────────────────────────────────┘
```

For a floppy disk drive, designate:

> A: (or B:)

If the data will be in a directory instead of on a floppy disk, designate that directory, in a form similar to:

> C:\BPG4\DATA

If the simulation administrator asks you to enter your decisions to a local area network, the decision and data files may be included in the same directory where you install program files and spreadsheet templates.

If you have a monochrome monitor or LCD screen, you may find it easier to read the screens if you press "M" from the Setup Menu to choose Monochrome Monitor. This will change the default screen colors, making them easier to read. Pressing "C" to choose Color Monitor will change them back.

Each of the other menu items are described below. Your next task will be to examine the reports for Year 2, Quarter 4. Therefore, you might want to skip down to the "Reports" section, below.

2. **New Decisions**. To enter your first set of decisions, press "N," at the main menu for NEW DECISIONS. The data entry screen which will appear is in a format similar to that of the decision forms in this manual. The default entries on the screen are values from your decision set for the previous quarter. For your first set of decisions, Year 3, Quarter 1, the default values should be the same as those shown on the sample decision form, Figure 2-1. They are the same ones that were used to generate the reports for Year 2, Quarter 4 (see Appendix C).

Decision values are entered by moving the cursor to one of the variable fields on the screen and entering the new value for that variable. Move the cursor to the next field by pressing <ENTER> or move it back one field by pressing the <up-arrow> key. Other cursor-movement keys may be used to move around the input screen. They are as follows:

<ENTER>	Forward one field
<Down-arrow>	Forward one field
<Up-arrow>	Back one field
<Tab>	Forward one column
<Shft-tab>	Backward one column
<Page down>	Move to lower half of screen
<Page up>	Move to upper half of screen
<END>	Move to last field
<HOME>	Move to first field
<ESC>	Return to the main menu without saving values

If you should enter a value outside of the range permitted by the rules of the game, an error message will appear in the middle of the screen, suggesting the range of values that you may enter. If you have a question about the range of values for a particular decision variable, move the cursor to the numeric field for that variable and press the <F1> function key for context-sensitive help. A help screen will be superimposed on the input screen with information about that variable. As an example, the help screen for the Price variable is shown here. Press <ESC> to restore the decision-input screen.

```
                     Help:
PRICE
Amount to be charged for your product.
Enter dollars and cents for Areas
1, 2 and 3.  Enter pesos for Sereno.
If no sales office, value must be 0.
Maximum Change: Areas 1,2,3: 30 Percent
Maximum Change: Sereno:      40 Percent
LIMITS:  0.00 to 99.99 (areas 1, 2, 3)
         0 to 99999    (Sereno)
                    Press ESC to return
```

When you have finished entering your set of decisions, carefully check the values on the screen against the values on your decision form to make sure that you have entered all of the values and that they are correct. Each value that has been changed from the default value will be highlighted. While you may have been called a "good kid," you do not want to become the team goat for entering an incorrect decision which causes your firm to lose thousands of dollars.

After you are satisfied that your firm's decision set has been entered correctly, press the **<F10> function key**. There will be a short pause while all values from the screen are checked for conformation to the rules of the game. If any values fall outside of the permitted ranges you will be returned to the decision-entry screen with the cursor located in the field in question. A message at the middle of the screen will identify the problem. Additional help can be obtained by pressing the <F1> function key.

If all values pass the test, a menu will drop from the top bar with three choices:

```
Press Y to Save Decisions
Press N to Return to Menu without Saving
Press D to Return to Decision Input Screen
```

Press "Y" to save the decision. If you decide to return to the menu screen without saving the decision, press "N." If you would like to stay with the data entry screen (as you would if you pressed <F10> by mistake), press "D." Pressing "Y" or "N" will return you to the main menu screen. If you return to the menu without saving values, don't forget to run the program again, later, to enter your decision set.

Good luck! May your decisions be wise and your entries be error free. But just in case you discover, too late, that you have entered incorrect values, or in case you change your mind about some of the decisions that you have entered, read the next section.

3. **Change Decisions**. You may review or change your current-quarter decision set as many times as you like **prior** to the time designated by your administrator to run the simulation. **After the simulation has been run, it is too late**—you will have to live with the decision that was entered. This option is available **only** if you already have entered a set of decisions for the current quarter. If no decisions have been entered previously, you will receive an error message. In this case, try the first option from the menu, New Decisions.

After selecting the Change Decisions option, the data entry screen will appear. Instead of the previous quarter's decision set, the set that was previously entered for this quarter will be the default. You may change any of the variable values shown on the screen by moving the cursor to the variable field and entering the new value. Cursor-movement keys are the same as those shown above under "New Decisions."

After you are satisfied that your firm's decision set has been entered correctly, press the **<F10> function key**. There will be a short pause while all values from the screen are checked for conformation to the rules of the game. If any values fall outside of the permitted ranges, you will be returned to the decision-entry screen with the cursor located in the field in question. A message at the middle of the screen will identify the problem. Additional help can be obtained by pressing the <F1> function key.

If all values pass the test, a menu will drop from the top bar with three choices:

```
Press Y to Save Decisions
Press N to Return to Menu without Saving
Press D to Return to Decision Input Screen
```

Press "Y" to save the decision. If you decide to return to the menu screen without saving the decision, press "N." If you would like to stay with the data entry screen (as you would if you pressed <F10> by mistake), press "D." Pressing "Y" or "N" will return you to the main menu screen. If you return to the menu without saving values, don't forget to run the program again, later, to enter your decision set.

```
┌─────────────────────────────────────────────────────────────┐
│                      IMPORTANT NOTE                          │
│ A word of caution is in order.  It is possible to overwrite a new decision file on │
│ your disk with old data.  When you choose New Decisions from the main menu, │
│ the default values on the decision screen are from the previous quarter.  If you │
│ have previously entered new decision values for the current quarter, they may │
│ be retrieved as default values only when you select Change Decisions.  If you │
│ wish to review them later, but mistakenly select New Decisions, you may have │
│ a problem. The default values on the screen will not be the ones that you previ- │
│ ously entered but rather the values that were used for the past quarter.  Press │
│ <ESC>, return to the main menu and start over.  Otherwise, you may inadver- │
│ tently clobber your previously-entered decision file.  If, without changing any de- │
│ fault values, you press <F10> and SAVE the default values, last quarter's deci- │
│ sion values will be overwritten to your current-quarter's decision file.  Any previ- │
│ ously-entered values will be overwritten and lost forever.  Be Careful! │
└─────────────────────────────────────────────────────────────┘
```

4. **Reports**.   After setting the data path, you will be ready to view or print your initial set of reports showing historical data for Years 1 and 2 and your company's position at the end of Year 2, Quarter 4. Initially, and after the simulation has been run each quarter, your report files may be returned on your decision/data disk (or placed in your directory on a LAN). To view or print the reports, or to use the graph utility, select this option. Sample reports for Year 2, Quarter 4 may be found in Appendix C, or you may be asked to view or print copies from your disk. If your printed copies are different from those in the appendix, you should rely on the newly printed copies.

When you pull down the Reports menu, you have three options:

```
View
Print
Graph
```

a. **View**. You may use *The Business Policy Game* Report Viewer to view any of the reports that have been placed on your data disk or directory. Choose View, and the BPG Report Viewer and Notepad window will replace the main menu. Press <Alt>, then "R" for the Reports menu and choose from the list of reports that are available on your disk. You may print a displayed report directly from the File menu. Try the Help menu for instructions regarding use of the BPG Report Viewer and Notepad. To return to the main menu, press <Alt>, then "F" for File and "E" for Exit.

b. **Print**. Reports also may be printed directly without viewing them first. Choose Print to see the menu for printing company reports. Choose which reports you wish to print by entering "Y" for Yes or "N" for No for each category. Indicate

```
┌──────────────────────────────────────────┐
│          PRINT COMPANY REPORTS           │
│ Enter choices. Press <F10> to continue:  │
│                                          │
│   Print Company Reports (Y/N)?      Y    │
│   Print Industry Report (Y/N)?      Y    │
│   Supplementary Reports (Y/N)?      N    │
│   How many copies?                  1    │
│                                          │
│     Be sure that printer is on and       │
│       set to the top of the page         │
└──────────────────────────────────────────┘
```

the desired number of copies. Then press <F10> to continue. Your printer must be on-line and the paper should be positioned to start printing at the top of the page. When all reports have been printed, you will be returned to the main menu.

c. **Graph**. You may use the Graph utility to examine your team's performance over time. It also may be used to compare your team's performance with that of other teams in your world. Performance of each simulated firm is shown as a separate line on a graph. You have a choice of creating graphs using quarterly data or annual data. Quarterly data provide more detail. Annual data provide a clearer picture of trends in your world.

Select Graph to open a new window for the BPG Graph Utility. The utility has it's own menu with three choices:

```
File
Data
Graph
```

You will pull down the Graph menu to select which graphs to view. Before choosing Graph, however, it is important to make two kinds of choices. First, pull down the **Data menu** to select quarterly or annual data. This choice will remain in effect until you change it or exit the graph utility.

The BPG graph utility can print graphs to many graphic printers. You will be able to print better graphs from an HP LaserJet compatible printer than from a dot-matrix printer. Some printers print better images than others. When you pull down the **File** menu and choose **Print**, you have three choices:

```
HP LaserJet compatible
Epson/IBM dot matrix compatible
Do not print graphs
```

If you wish to print a graph, you **must** specify your choice of printers **before** you make your graph selection. If you should forget, it is easy to try again. After you have made the choice, you may continue to select different graphs and your choice will remain in effect until you change it or exit the graph utility.

If you prefer to save the graphics image to a .PCX file instead of printing, pull down the **File** menu and choose **Save**. The graph or graphs that you select following this choice will be saved to a file that can be viewed or printed from many graphics programs and Windows-based word processors. The file that you save will have a descriptive name with an extension of .PCX, as:

```
ASSETS.PCX
BOND-EQU.PCX
DIVSHARE.PCX
```

It will be saved to your previously-entered data path.

After these choices are completed, pull down the utility's Graph menu to select a graph. You may choose one of fourteen different variables to be graphed. For each variable that you pick, a line graph will be displayed, with performance of each company in your industry world represented by a separate line.

1. Assets (total)
2. Bonds/equity
3. Dividends/share
4. Earnings/share
5. Equity
6. Market share
7. Net income
8. Net income/equity
9. Net income/sales
10. Production cost (unit)
11. ROI (investor's)
12. Sales (dollars)
13. Selling costs (unit)
14. Stock price

Select one of the variables and a line graph of the variable that you have chosen will appear.

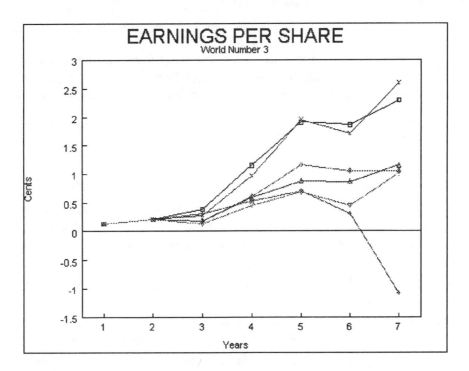

The graph will include either quarterly or annual data according to your previous choice from the Data menu. When you have finished viewing the graph, press any key. If you have made Print or Save selections, the graph will be printed and/or saved before returning you to the menu of the graph utility. You may pull down the Graph menu again to select additional variables to be graphed. If you wish, you may select the other data set (quarterly or annual) and continue to view graphs. When you have finished, pull down the **File** menu and select **Exit** to return to *The Business Policy Game* main menu bar.

　　　　5. **Quit**. Select this option when you want to end your current session with the computer. Two choices will appear superimposed over the menu screen

> ```
> Press N to Return to the Menu
> Press Y to Quit
> ```

Press "Y" to end the session. Press "N" to return to the main menu.

More Floppy-Disk User Instructions

　　　　After you have received the message that your current session has ended, and the disk drive has stopped spinning (the disk light is off), carefully remove the Decision/Data Disk. **Do not remove the disk until the disk drive has stopped spinning. The contents of a disk can be destroyed if you remove it while the drive is running.**

　　　　Return the disk to the security of your firm's records area. Arrange for its delivery of the disk to the administrator prior to the simulation run!

> **IMPORTANT NOTE**
> Your firm is responsible for providing the administrator with a disk containing the current quarter's decision set **prior** to the simulation run time. Failure to do so will result in the previous quarter's decision set being used for the missing current set.

Past Quarter's Reports

　　　　Each quarter, the old report files on your Decision/Data Disk will be updated with the current quarter's reports. That means that the reports from the previous quarter will be gone forever! If you would like to keep copies of the files, create a storage disk or make a separate directory on your hard disk and copy the files to that location. You may use a separate storage disk for each quarter. Alternatively, you may decide to rename the report files after you copy them to the storage disk so that you do not overwrite the files the following quarter when you copy that quarter's files to the disk. One renaming scheme might be to change the existing extension (that identifies your company and world) to an extension that identifies the year and quarter of the reports. **A word of caution**: **Please do not rename any files on your Decision/Data Disk**. The administrator's program that processes the simulation may not be able to find some of the files when it needs them.

　　　　The report files are in text (ASCII) format. Thus, you can read them with most any text editor or word processor. If files have been moved or renamed, you can read them with the BPG Report Viewer by pulling down the File menu and choosing Open.

Macintosh Users

If you enter your decision set and save it on a floppy disk, your team will use the Player's Program Disk packaged with this manual plus a formatted blank Decision/Data Disk.

Installing Player's Programs

1. Put the Player's Program Disk that came with this manual in a floppy drive and double click on the disk icon. Locate the file named BPG.sea and double click on it. When the opening window appears, click Continue. Select the location on the hard disk where you want to install the player's folder. Then click Save. The files in BPG.sea will be copied to the hard disk and unstuffed. When the installation is complete, a dialog box will notify you that the installation was successful.

2. The installed player's folder will be named BPG4.

> **IMPORTANT NOTE**
> Please be sure to look for a file named README on the distribution disk. It will include any information that became available after this manual was prepared. To read the contents of the file on your screen, type README from the DOS prompt for your Player's Program Disk.

Special Instructions for Floppy Disk Users

Each team should create a Decision/Data Disk which is a formatted, empty disk with the following label:

```
Company c, World w
Company Name
BUSINESS POLICY GAME
Decision/Data Disk
```

Then name the disk BPGcw where c is your Company number and w is your World number. For example, if your firm is Company 2 in World 1, you would name the disk BPG21. The Decision/Data Disk must be given this name so the simulation program will recognize it when reading your decision file and writing your reports.

Submit the disk to your simulation administrator. Your administrator will transfer the data files necessary for you to print reports and enter your first decision set after the simulation has been run for the historical quarter Year 2, Quarter 4. Files transferred to your disk will include a decision file, a file of historical data required for the decision-entry program, and a full set of reports for Year 2, Quarter 4 (similar to those in Appendix C). The files are specific for your particular simulated company. As each team will have its own separate disk, it is important to know your company and world numbers in order to obtain the correct disk. The simulation administrator will tell you how to retrieve your disk after the files have been transferred.

A word about disk etiquette. Handle the disk carefully. Do not spill coffee or other liquids on it. Do not play Frisbee with it. Treat the disk as you would a good friend, gently and carefully.

When entering data using a floppy disk, first put the disk in the disk drive. Grasp the disk, holding it with your fingers on the label end. Be very careful not to touch the surface of the disk which is inside the plastic cover you are holding. Gently slide the disk into the disk drive with the label side up. The drive will take control of the disk after it is pushed about halfway into the drive.

If the computer is off, turn it on and wait until the desktop appears prior to inserting your disk in a floppy drive.

Running *The Business Policy Game* Program

The disk icon for the drive containing your Decision/Data Disk (when using floppy disks for data entry) or your folder (when decisions are to be saved on a Local Area Network or LAN) should be named BPGcw, where:

> c = your company number
> w = your world number.

Thus, if your firm is Company 3 in World 2, your Decision/Data Disk (or folder) should be named BPG32.

Double click on the BPG4 disk icon or folder (where your Player's Program Disk was installed) to open the disk or folder. Find the application file named

    BPG

Double click on this file and the opening window will appear.

The menu bar displays four menus, listed across the top of the window:

    File
    Edit
    Setup
    Help

Click on a menu to pull it down. Then move the cursor to your choice and release the mouse key. Or you may hold down the command key and press the letter associated with your choice. Your **first task** is to set the path to your data files.

    1. <u>Setup</u>. (Click on Setup and select Path.)

        Path

It is **very important** that you set the path to the files on your Decision/Data Disk (or the directory on your LAN although the LAN path is likely to have been set for you). You **must** make this choice before you use the BPG program so that the program will be able to access your decision and report files. The following window will appear to enable you to confirm the default path or to set a new one.

```
            SET PATH DESIGNATIONS

Please enter the complete path for DECISION, REPORT, and
other data files.  The path will be used by BPG to find
report files and to save decision files that must be
transferred to the simulation administrator.

   EXAMPLE:  BPG11:        (Use with floppy disk drives.)

   EXAMPLE:  :BPG4:BPG11:  (Use when saving data to a
                            hard disk or local area
                            network.)

Enter path for DECISION and REPORT files:

      BPG11:_____        ┌──────────┐
                                   │    OK    │
                                   └──────────┘
                                   ┌──────────┐
                                   │  Cancel  │
                                   └──────────┘
```

For a floppy disk drive, designate:

    BPGcw:

where c = Company number, w = World number

```
┌─────────────────────────────────────────────┐
│               IMPORTANT NOTE                  │
│ Be sure to include the correct company and    │
│ world number. Since BPG11 is the name of a    │
│ disk, it is not preceded by a colon. Only     │
│ folder names need to be preceded by a colon.  │
│ Both disk and folder names should be followed │
│ by a colon.                                   │
└─────────────────────────────────────────────┘
```

For a hard drive, designate:

    HARD DRIVE:BPG4:BPG11:

This designates folder BPG11 nested in folder BPG on the hard drive named, quite originally, Hard Drive. If the simulation administrator asks you to enter your decisions on a LAN, the decision and data files may be included in the same folder with the program files and spreadsheet templates. Then the designation for both the program folder and the decision/data folder would be HARD DRIVE:BPG11:.

2. <u>File</u>. You will use the File menu most often. When you click on File, the pull-down menu will display the following choices.

```
File
-------------
New Decision Set
Open Decision Set
Save Decision Set
-------------
View Reports
Print Reports
-------------
Graph Variables
-------------
Quit
```

Each of these menu items will be described below. Your first task will be to examine the reports for Year 2, Quarter 4. Thus, you might want to skip down to the View Reports section.

a. **New Decision Set**. The decision-entry window which appears is nearly identical to the decision forms in this manual. The default entries in the window are values from your last quarter's decision set. For your first set of decisions, Year 3, Quarter 1, the default values in the window should match the decision set that was used to generate the reports for Year 2, Quarter 4. See Report E (in Appendix C) for the Year 2, Quarter 4 decision set.

Decision values are entered by clicking on a variable field in the decision-entry window and entering the new value for that variable. Click on the desired field using the mouse. Other cursor-movement keys may be used to move around the input window. They are as follows:

                 \<ENTER\>   Forward one field
                 \<Tab\>   Forward one column

If you should enter a value outside of the range permitted by the rules of the game, an error message will appear in the middle of the window. The message will suggest the range of values that you may enter. If you have a question about the range of values for a particular decision variable, move the cursor to the numeric field for that variable and pull down the Help menu for context-sensitive help. Then, select Variable Information. Or hold down the Command key and press "H." A help window will open with information about that variable. For example, the help window for the Price variable is shown here. When you have finished reading the information, click OK to close the help window.

```
Help:
  PRICE
  Amount to be charged for your product.
  Enter dollars and cents for Areas
  1, 2, and 3.  Enter pesos for Sereno.
  If no sales office, value must be 0.
  Maximum Change: Areas 1,2,3: 30 Percent
  Maximum Change: Sereno:      40 Percent
  LIMITS:  1.00 to 99.99 (areas 1, 2, 3)
           1 to 99999    (Sereno)

                              Click  OK
```

When you have finished entering your set of decisions, carefully check the values in the window against the values on your decision form to make sure that you have entered all of the values and that they are correct. While you may have been called a "good kid," you do not want to become the team goat for entering an incorrect decision which causes your firm to lose thousands of dollars.

After you are satisfied that your firm's decision set has been entered correctly, pull down the File menu and select Save Decision Set. You may also hold down the Command key and press "S." There will be a short pause while all values in the decision-entry window are checked for conformation to the rules of the game. If any values fall outside of the permitted ranges, you will be returned to the decision-entry window with the cursor located in the field in question. A message at the middle of the window will identify the problem. Additional help can be obtained by using the Help menu. If all values pass the test, you will be returned to the opening window. If you return without saving the values, don't forget to run the program again, later.

There is additional help for data entry, which can be accessed by pulling down the Help menu and selecting Instructions for Data Entry, or the command key plus "I."

Good luck! May your decisions be wise and your entries be error free. But just in case you discover, too late, that you have entered incorrect values, or in case you change your mind about some of the decisions that you have entered, read the next section.

b. **Open Decision Set**. You may review or change your current-quarter decision set as many times as you like **prior** to the time designated by your administrator to run the simulation. **After the simulation has been run, it is too late**--you will have to live with the decision set that was entered. This option is available **only** if you already have entered a set of decisions for the current quarter. If no decisions have been entered previously, you will receive an error message. In this case, try the first item on the File menu, New Decision Set.

After selecting the Open Decision Set item, the decision-entry window showing your current decision set which has been previously entered for this quarter will appear. You may change any of the variable values shown in the window by clicking on the variable and entering the new value. The cursor is moved down by pressing <Enter> and is moved up by clicking on a field, using the mouse. Other cursor-movement keys are the same as those shown above under New Decision Set.

c. **Save Decision Set**. After you are satisfied that your firm's decision set has been entered correctly, pull down the File menu and select Save Decision Set. There will be a short pause while all values from the window are checked for conformation to the rules of the game. If any values fall outside of the permitted ranges, you will be returned to the decision-entry window with the cursor located in the field in question. A message at the middle of the window will identify the problem. Additional help can be obtained by pulling down the Help menu. If all values pass the test, you will be returned to the opening window.

IMPORTANT NOTE

A word of caution is in order. It is possible to overwrite a new decision file on your disk with old data. When you choose **New Decision Set** from the File menu, the default values in the decision-entry window are from the previous quarter. If you have already entered new decision values for the current quarter, they may be retrieved as default values **only** when you select **Open Decision Set**. If you wish to review them later but mistakenly select **New Decision Set,** you may have a problem. The default values on the window will **not** be the ones that you previously entered but rather the values that were used for the past quarter. Return to the opening window without saving and start over. Otherwise, you may inadvertently clobber your previously entered decision file. If, without changing any default values, you choose **Save Decision Set** from the File menu, the default values, last quarter's decision values, will be overwritten to your current-quarter's decision file. Any previously entered values will be overwritten and lost forever. **Be Careful!**

---

d. **View Reports**. After setting the data path, you will be ready to view or print your initial set of reports showing historical data for Years 1 and 2 and your company's position at the end of Year 2, Quarter 4. Initially, and after the simulation has been run each quarter, your report files will be returned on your Decision/Data Disk (or placed in your directory on a LAN). To view or print the reports, select this item. Sample reports for Year 2, Quarter 4 may be found in Appendix C, or you may be asked to view or print copies from your disk. If the copies on your disk are different from those in the appendix, you should rely on the files from your Decision/Data Disk.

You may use *The Business Policy Game* Report Viewer to view any of the reports that have been placed on your data disk or folder. Click on View Reports and the BPG Report Viewer and Notepad window will appear. Click on Reports to choose from the list of reports that are available on your disk. You may print the displayed report from the File menu. To return to the opening window, select Quit from the File menu.

e. **Print Reports**. Reports also may be printed directly from the opening window. Select Print Reports from the File menu, and the dialog box for printing company reports will open. Some of the reports are defaulted to Print. Make any changes in the default settings you desire by entering "Y" for Yes or "N" for No. Indicate the desired number of copies if greater than 1. Then click <OK> to begin printing. Your printer must be on-line, and the paper should be positioned to start printing at the top of the page. When all reports have been printed, the dialog box will close.

```
┌─────────────────────────────────────────┐
│          PRINT COMPANY REPORTS           │
│   Enter choices. Click on OK to continue:│
│                                          │
│    Print Company Reports (Y/N)?     Y    │
│    Print Industry Report (Y/N)?     Y    │
│    Supplementary Reports (Y/N)?     N    │
│    How many copies?                 1    │
│                                          │
│     Be sure that printer is on and       │
│       set to the top of the page         │
└─────────────────────────────────────────┘
```

f. **Graph**. The graphing utility allows you to examine the performance of teams in your industry world over time. Each simulated firm is shown as one line on a graph. You have a choice of creating graphs using quarterly data or yearly data. Quarterly data provide more detail. Yearly data provide a clearer picture of trends in the world.

Pull down the File menu and select Graph. A data selection dialog box will appear allowing you to select yearly or quarterly data. Then click OK.

A variable selection dialog box will appear with the following list of variables that may be graphed:

> Assets (total)
> Bonds/equity
> Dividends/share
> Earnings/share
> Equity
> Market share
> Net income
> Net income/equity
> Net income/sales
> Production cost (unit)
> ROI (investor's)
> Sales (dollars)
> Selling costs (unit)
> Stock price

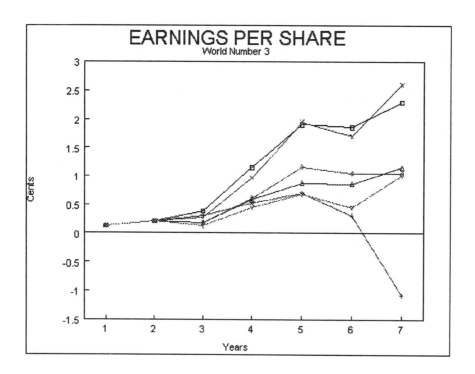

Select a variable and then click on Graph. A line graph of the variable you have chosen will appear. If you wish to print the graph, pull down the File menu and select Print. When you have finished examining the graph, click on Return. The variable selection dialog box will reappear so that you may select another variable to graph. When you have finished graphing variables for the time period (year or quarter) you selected in the data selection dialog box, click Return.

The data selection dialog box will reappear. You may select the other time period (quarterly or yearly) and select OK to return to the variable selection dialog box. You can then create additional graphs. If you are finished graphing, pull down the File menu and select Quit.

That is all there is to it. It takes longer to read than to do. The program is designed to give you a quick and easy way to analyze the performance of the teams in your industry world over time. Hopefully the pictures are worth 1,000 words.

g. **Quit**. Select Quit from the File menu when you have finished entering decisions and/or printing and viewing reports.

More Floppy Disk User Instructions

After you have received the message that your current session has ended, and your disk is visible on the desktop, move the disk icon to the trash can to eject it from the computer. If you want to shut the computer off, pull down the Special menu and select Shut Down. In a minute, a message will appear indicating that it is safe to turn off the computer, or the computer may turn itself off, depending upon the Macintosh model you are using.

Return the disk to the security of your firm's records area. Arrange for delivery of the disk to the administrator prior to the simulation run!

IMPORTANT NOTE

Your firm is responsible for providing the administrator with a disk containing the current quarter's decision set prior to the simulation run time. Failure to do so will result in the previous quarter's decision set being used for your current decision set.

Past Quarter's Reports

Each quarter, the report files on your Decision/Data Disk will be updated with the current quarter's reports. That means that the reports from last quarter will be gone forever! If you would like to keep copies of the files, create a storage disk and copy the files onto the storage disk. You may use a separate storage disk for each quarter. Alternatively, you may decide to rename the report files after you copy them to the storage disk so that you do not overwrite the files next quarter when you copy that quarter's files to the disk.

The report files are in text (ASCII) format. Thus, you can read them with any word processor. If the files have been renamed, you can read them with the BPG Report Viewer by using the Open item on the File menu.

The Business Policy Game, 4th Edition

APPENDIX B

DECISION SUPPORT SYSTEMS

Basic Decision Support Systems (DSS) have been provided in a form which can be easily modified and improved upon. Specifically, we have developed spreadsheet templates for the DSS work sheets from Appendix D. The files containing the templates are on the disk that came packaged with this manual. The templates, containing formulas where appropriate, may be used with Lotus 1-2-3 and compatible spreadsheets such as Quattro or Quattro Pro. They also may be used with Excel. The templates do not contain macros and thus will likely work in a variety of other spreadsheets with little modification.

The template file names on your disk and their associated work sheets are shown below, along with the chapter in which they are discussed.

1. FORECAST.WK1   - Sales Forecast Work Sheet (Chapter 6)
2. PRODPLAN.WK1   - Production Plan Work Sheet (Chapter 7)
3. CAPBUD.WK1   - Capital Budget Work Sheet (Chapter 9)
4. FINANCE.WK1   - Pro Forma Income Statement (Chapter 10)
                           - Pro Forma Cash Flow Work Sheet (Chapter 10)
                           - Pro Forma Balance Sheet (Chapter 10)

We decided not to put all of the work sheets in one large template file as several members of a management team may want to use the templates at the same time. For example, the person in charge of production scheduling may want to develop the production plan while another member is evaluating the capital budget.

We did include three work sheets in the FINANCE.WK1 template, however, as the work sheets have a number of common elements. These work sheets are linked in the template so that numbers appearing in more than one of the statements will only need to be entered once. The Pro Forma Income Statement should be completed first. The common data are automatically transferred to the Pro Forma Cash Flow Work Sheet and the Pro Forma Balance Sheet. The Pro Forma Cash Flow Work Sheet should be completed second with the Pro Forma Balance Sheet being finished last. The work sheets appear in the template in the order in which they should be completed.

The spreadsheet templates greatly simplify the process of planning, when using the work sheets provided for *The Business Policy Game*. The spreadsheet program handles all of the calculations. Your management team is left with the more interesting and educational task of providing input data based upon forecasts, experience and assumptions. The templates save your team the work of re-creating the work sheets in spreadsheet format.

To use the templates, first load the spreadsheet program into computer memory. This is normally done, when using a computer that is not connected to a network, by first going to the disk drive and/or directory [folder] containing the spreadsheet program. If your program resides in a directory named SPREADSHEET on your C: drive, the command is:

```
cd C:\SPREADSHEET <ENTER>
```

The spreadsheet program then is loaded. Use the command that is required to start your spreadsheet program. Enter one of the following, for example:

```
123          (for Lotus 1-2-3)
q or q123    (for Quattro)
qpro         (for Quattro Pro)
```

When the spreadsheet window appears on the screen, set the file directory to the one that contains the spreadsheet templates If the templates are on a floppy disk in Drive A, for example, enter:

```
/fd A: <Enter>
```

or, if they are located in the BPG4 directory on Drive C:

```
/fd C:\BPG4 <Enter>
```

Then load the desired template by entering

```
/fr{TEMPLATE NAME}<Enter>
```

The work sheet should appear on the screen in a form almost identical to that shown on the same work sheet in Appendix D.

Each spreadsheet template begins with a set of instructions in the top left screen. A consolidated work sheet begins one screen below (press PgDn). The consolidated work sheet is several screens long. The first screen to the right contains the first-quarter work sheet (press Ctrl + right arrow). Enter your world, company year and quarter in this work sheet. The quarter should be the quarter for which you are planning a decision. These data fields then will automatically appear correctly numbered on all of the work sheets in the file. The second screen to the right contains the second-quarter work sheet, etc. The complete file contains four quarterly work sheets and a consolidated work sheet. You may print any combination you desire. The FINANCE.WK1 file begins with the Pro Forma Income Statement followed by the Pro Forma Cash Flow Work Sheet and the Pro Forma Balance Sheet. Each work sheet set includes four quarterly work sheets and one consolidated work sheet. For more information on completing the work sheets, see the related chapters in this manual.

The template cells are protected, except for those cells where data need to be entered. The protection is to prevent the user from accidentally writing over formulas in cells which contain calculated values from other cells. Protected cells are indicated by the abbreviation PR (for PRotected) shown in the far left of the descriptor line. Unprotected cells are indicated by a U (for Unprotected) in the far left of the descriptor line. It is quite easy for a user to unlock the template and modify any cell desired in either a positive or negative manner. Thus it is a good idea to keep a backup copy of the templates which can be used to replace damaged template files.

When the work sheet has been completed, a copy can be printed if desired. First make sure that your printer is turned on, and the paper is set to the top of the page. Then enter the following:

    /ppr{SET RANGE WHICH YOU WANT TO PRINT}agq

The work sheet also can be saved for future use. We recommend that it be saved with a different file name than the template so that the template remains available and unaltered, and without any data entered. The file can be saved by entering the following commands:

    /fa

(the a [for "save As"] calls a dialog box asking for a file name)

To exit the spreadsheet after saving the file, enter

    /qy

Note: If you want to save the work sheet file, be sure to do so prior to exiting the spreadsheet program If you exit the program without saving the file, the work sheet will be gone forever.

Summary of Template Use

1. Select the disk drive or directory [folder] containing the spreadsheet program. The command is the name of the disk drive, for a floppy disk: For disk drive A, enter:

    A:

or, for a directory on a hard disk enter the Change Directory command plus the name of the directory:

```
cd {DIRECTORY} <ENTER>
```

2. Load the spreadsheet program. The command is

```
123         (for Lotus 1-2-3), or
q or q123   (for Quattro)
qpro        (for Quattro Pro)
```

3. Set the file directory to the one containing template files. The command is:

```
/fd{DIRECTORY}<ENTER>
```

4. Load the desired template. The command is

```
/fr{TEMPLATE NAME}<ENTER>
```

5. Complete the template.

6. Print the template, if desired. The command is

```
/ppr{SELECT RANGE TO PRINT}agq
```

7. Save the work sheet file, if desired. The command is

```
/fa{FILE NAME}<ENTER>          (to save under a new name)
        or
/fs{FILE NAME]<ENTER>          (to save under the same name)
```

Do not save changes with the same file name as the spreadsheet template. Provide a new file name so that you do not overwrite the template file.

8. To load another template, the command is

```
/wey
```

Then go to number four above.

9. To exit the spreadsheet program, the command is

```
/qy
```

The Business Policy Game, 4th Edition

APPENDIX C

HISTORICAL DATA FOR YEARS 1 AND 2

```
World 1                                                            08-18-1994
J              CONSOLIDATED HISTORICAL DATA FOR YEARS 1 AND 2    20:36:08
                         THE BUSINESS POLICY GAME

                     --------Year 1---------    --------Year 2---------
                     Qtr 1 Qtr 2 Qtr 3 Qtr 4    Qtr 1 Qtr 2 Qtr 3 Qtr 4

GDP (Merica) Y2Q4=100   84.0  86.3  89.7  91.9     94.1  96.6  98.1 100.0
GDP (Sereno) Y2Q4=100   64.3  69.9  73.3  78.2     83.3  88.8  92.7 100.0
CPI (Merica) Y2Q4=100   85.8  86.5  88.2  90.0     92.1  94.1  97.2 100.0
CPI (Sereno) Y2Q4=100   74.8  78.0  81.0  84.9     87.8  91.5  94.4 100.0
Exchange Rate (Sereno)  5.98  6.00  5.94  5.97     5.99  5.97  5.97  6.00
Loan Interest Rate (%)  5.80  6.30  6.60  7.50     9.40  9.90  9.80 11.20
Bond Interest Rate (%)  8.20  8.00  8.00  8.10     8.50  8.40  9.60  9.10

  Stock Market:
Market Index           121.8 130.8 125.2 116.7    117.6 105.5 108.4 100.0
Company Stock Price($)  0.77  0.85  0.84  0.82     3.59  3.84  4.34  4.37
Company EPS      ($) 0.012 0.038 0.041 0.070    0.055 0.077 0.064 0.116

  Product Prices:
Home Area        ($) 10.00 10.10 10.20 10.40    10.40 10.20 10.10 10.00
Nonhome area     ($) 10.60 10.60 10.60 10.70    10.60 10.40 10.20 10.00
Nonhome area     ($) 10.60 10.60 10.60 10.70    10.60 10.40 10.20 10.00
Sereno          (Ps)    62    64    66    75       75    75    75    75

  Company Salespeople (#):
Home Area                 6     7     7     7        9    10    11    12
Nonhome area              6     7     7     7        7     8     9    10
Nonhome area              6     7     7     7        7     8     9    10
Sereno                    7     9     9     9       10    11    12    13

  Customer Orders (000s):
Home Area                52    61    59    77       69    89    86   121
Nonhome area             46    54    53    71       62    76    75   109
Nonhome area             46    54    53    71       62    76    75   109
Sereno                   42    53    51    58       57    73    75   108

  Company Sales (000s):
Home Area                52    61    59    77       69    89    86   121
Nonhome area             46    54    53    71       62    76    75   109
Nonhome area             46    54    53    71       62    76    75   109
Sereno                   42    53    51    58       57    73    75   108

  Advertising:
Home Area      ($000s)   30    32    33    37       45    45    46    46
Nonhome area   ($000s)   30    31    32    35       37    37    38    40
Nonhome area   ($000s)   30    31    32    35       37    37    38    40
Sereno        (Ps000s)   90    94    97   100      105   105   105   105

  R & D, Training ($000s):
Product R & D            40    42    46    51       56    62    68    72
Employee Training        40    42    45    49       54    58    64    68

  Other Items (000s):
Actual Output           208   250   312   260      312   312   312   312
Ending Inventory         22    50   146   129      191   189   190    55
Total Unit Sales        186   222   216   277      250   314   311   447
```

```
World 1                                                      08-18-1994
J                     FINANCIAL DATA FOR YEARS 1 AND 2         20:36:08
                         THE BUSINESS POLICY GAME

                      --------Year 1---------   --------Year 2---------
                      Qtr 1 Qtr 2 Qtr 3 Qtr 4   Qtr 1 Qtr 2 Qtr 3 Qtr 4

Consolidated Income Statement ($000s)

Gross Sales            1931  2325  2293  3050    2746  3405  3341  4740
Cost of Goods Sold      818   972   890  1220    1057  1399  1392  2152
Value Added Tax          43    56    57    73      71    92    94   135
Gross Profit           1069  1298  1347  1758    1618  1915  1855  2454

Selling Expenses        627   628   666   687     728   779   839   952
Admin and General Exp   322   313   281   386     357   384   397   378
Operating Profit        119   357   400   685     532   752   618  1125

Time CD Interest          0     0     0     6       7     9    14    19
Net Profit Before Tax   119   357   400   691     539   761   632  1144
Income Tax               46   128   156   269     210   297   246   446
Net Profit After Tax     73   229   243   421     329   464   386   698


-----------------------------------------------------------------------


Consolidated Cash Flow Statement ($000s)

Accounts Collected      922  2114  2312  2653    2897  3057  3369  3998
Less Production Cost    801   987  1242  1001    1226  1255  1281  1324
Less Operating Expense  887   879   885  1011    1023  1101  1174  1267
Less Taxes Paid          89   184   213   342     282   389   341   581
  Net Operating CF     -856    65   -27   300     366   313   573   827

Investment Receipts       0     0     0     6     507   509   514   719
Less Investment Expend    0     0     0   500     500   500   700  1000
  Net Investment CF       0     0     0  -494       7     9  -186  -281

Financing Receipts        0     0     0     0       0     0     0     0
Less Financing Expend    50    50    50    50      50    50    50    50
  Net Financing CF      -50   -50   -50   -50     -50   -50   -50   -50

Net CF for Quarter     -906    15   -77  -244     323   272   337   496


-----------------------------------------------------------------------


Consolidated Balance Sheet Items ($000s):

Cash                    694   709   632   387     711   984  1319  1814
Time CDs                  0     0     0   500     500   500   700  1000
Accounts Receivable    1009  1219  1203  1598    1445  1794  1766  2505
Inventory               115   264   750   663     964   954   976   281
Total Assets           9573  9800 10052 10468   10793 11262 11645 12337

Bank Loans                0     0     0     0       0     0     0     0
Bonds Outstanding      2000  2000  2000  2000    2000  2000  2000  2000
Total Equity           7573  7800  8052  8468    8793  9262  9645 10337
Total Liab and Equity  9573  9800 10052 10468   10793 11262 11645 12337
```

```
Company 1 World 1
Year 2 Quarter 4         CONSOLIDATED INCOME STATEMENT              08-18-1994
A                        BUSINESS POLICY GAME, 4TH EDITION              20:35:57
         Copyright (c) 1995 by Richard V. Cotter and David J. Fritzsche
-------------------------------------------------------------------------------
```

	Consoli- dated M$000s	Merica Area 1 M$000s	Merica Area 2 M$000s	Merica Area 3 M$000s	Sereno Ps000s
Net Sales:					
to Customers	4740	1210	1090	1090	8100
to Affiliates (cost + 20%)	1	1261	0	0	0
to Liquidators (at cost)	0	0	0	0	0
Less Cost of Goods Sold	2152	1608	603	603	3586
Less Value Added Tax	135	0	0	0	810
Gross Profit	2454	863	487	487	3704
Selling Expense:					
Advertising Expense	144	46	40	40	105
Sales Salaries	116	36	30	30	117
Sales Commissions	79	24	22	22	65
General Selling Expense	406	107	97	97	629
Transportation Expense	196	12	54	54	455
Sales Office Depreciation	12	3	3	3	19
Other Selling Expense	0	0	0	0	0
Total Selling Expense	952	228	246	246	1390
Admin and General Expense:					
Research and Development	72	72	0	0	0
Total Training Expense	68	68	0	0	0
Storage Expense	43	6	13	13	66
Executive Compensation	145	73	24	24	142
Loan Interest	0	0	0	0	0
Bond Interest	50	50	0	0	0
Other Expense	0	0	0	0	0
Total Adm & Gen Expense	378	269	37	37	208
Total Operating Expense	1329	497	283	283	1598
Operating Profit (Loss)	1125	366	204	204	2106
Other Income:					
CD Interest	19	19	0	0	0
Capital Gain (Loss)	0	0	0	0	0
Net Profit (Loss) Before Tax	1144	385	204	204	2106
Less Income Tax	446	149	80	80	821
Net Profit (Loss) After Tax	698	236	124	124	1285
Dividend from Subsidiaries	0	403	0	0	0
Dividends to Parent	0	0	124	124	931
Dividends to Shareholders	0	0	0	0	0
Added to Retained Earnings	698	639	0	0	354

```
-------------------------------------------------------------------------------
Notes:   Translation Exchange Rate      1.00      1.00      1.00      6.00
    Purchases from Affiliates is consolidated with Sales to Affiliates.
    Dividends to Parent is consolidated with Dividends from Subsidiaries.
    Minor differences in translation may be due to rounding errors.
```

```
Company 1 World 1
Year 2 Quarter 4        CONSOLIDATED CASH FLOW ANALYSIS          08-18-1994
B                       BUSINESS POLICY GAME, 4TH EDITION            20:35:57
        Copyright (c) 1995 by Richard V. Cotter and David J. Fritzsche
```

	Consoli- dated M$000s	Merica Area 1 M$000s	Merica Area 2 M$000s	Merica Area 3 M$000s	Sereno Ps000s
Operating Receipts:					
Accounts Collected	3998	1040	928	928	6615
Net Sales to Affiliates	1	1261	0	0	0
Sales to Liquidators	0	0	0	0	0
Operating Expenditures:					
Production Cost	1324	1324	0	0	0
Purchases from Affiliates	0	0	420	420	2522
Operating Expense	1267	444	280	280	1579
Taxes Paid	581	149	80	80	1631
Net Operating Cash Flow	827	384	148	148	883
Investment Receipts:					
CD Interest	19	19	0	0	0
CDs Matured	700	700	0	0	0
Subsidiary Dividends Rec'd	0	403	0	0	0
Fixed Assets Sold	0	0	0	0	0
Investment Expenditures					
CDs Purchased	1000	1000	0	0	0
New Equipment	0	0	0	0	0
Sales Office Investment	0	0	0	0	0
Plant Investment	0	0	0	0	0
Subsidiary Stock Purchased	0	0	0	0	0
Net Investment Cash Flow	-281	122	0	0	0
Financing Receipts:					
Loans from Bank	0	0	0	0	0
Stock Sold to Parent	0	0	0	0	0
Bond Sale	0	0	0	0	0
Stock Sale	0	0	0	0	0
Financing Expenditures:					
Interest Paid	50	50	0	0	0
Dividends Paid	0	0	0	0	0
Dividends to Parent	0	0	124	124	931
Bank Loans Repaid	0	0	0	0	0
Bonds Repurchased	0	0	0	0	0
Stock Repurchased	0	0	0	0	0
Net Financing Cash Flow	-50	-50	-124	-124	-931
Beginning Cash Balance	1318	911	116	116	1048
Net Cash Flow for Quarter	496	456	24	24	-48
Cash Balance End of Quarter	1814	1367	140	140	1000

```
-----------------------------------------------------------------------------
Notes:  Translation Exchange Rate       1.00      1.00      1.00      6.00
   Purchases from Affiliates consolidated with Sales to Affiliates.
   Dividends to Parent consolidated with Dividends from Subsidiaries.
   Stock sold to Parent consolidated with Stock Purchased in Subsidiaries.
   Minor differences in totals & translation may be due to rounding errors.
```

```
Company 1 World 1
Year 2 Quarter 4        CONSOLIDATED BALANCE SHEET            08-18-1994
C                       BUSINESS POLICY GAME, 4TH EDITION        20:35:57
            Copyright (c) 1995 by Richard V. Cotter and David J. Fritzsche
------------------------------------------------------------------------
                       Consoli-   Merica    Merica    Merica
                        dated     Area 1    Area 2    Area 3    Sereno
                        M$000s    M$000s    M$000s    M$000s    Ps000s

                       ----- ASSETS -----

Cash Balance             1814      1367       140       140      1000
Time Certificates of Deposit 1000  1000         0         0         0
Accounts Receivable      2505       605       545       545      4860
Inventory                 281       135        56        56       202

   Total Current Assets  5600      3107       741       741      6062

Net Sales Office         1501       376       376       376      2240
Net Manufacturing Plant  3092      3092         0         0         0
Net Manufacturing Equipment 2144   2144         0         0         0
Equity in Subsidiaries      0      3624         0         0         0

   Total Fixed Assets    6737      9236       376       376      2240

   Total Assets         12337     12343      1117      1117      8302


                       ----- LIABILITIES -----

Bank Loans                  0         0         0         0         0

   Total Current Liabilities 0        0         0         0         0

Bonds Outstanding        2000      2000         0         0         0

   Total Liabilities     2000      2000         0         0         0

Capital Stock            7500      7500       745       745      5762
Accumulated Earnings     2842      2842       373       373      2540
Cum. Translation Adjustment -5        0         0         0         0

   Total Equity         10337     10342      1118      1118      8302

   Total Liabilities & Equity 12337 12342     1118      1118      8302

------------------------------------------------------------------------
Notes:  Translation Exchange Rate     1.00      1.00      1.00      6.00
  Equity translated at historical exchange rates, others at current rates.
  Total Equity accts. of subs. are consolidated with parent's Equity in Subs.
  Minor differences in translation may be due to rounding errors.
```

```
Company 1 World 1
Year 2 Quarter 4          OPERATING INFORMATION REPORT          08-18-1994
D                       BUSINESS POLICY GAME, 4TH EDITION          20:36:03
        Copyright (c) 1995 by Richard V. Cotter and David J. Fritzsche
-----------------------------------------------------------------------------
                          PRODUCTION COST ANALYSIS

                       Consoli-   Merica    Merica    Merica
                        dated     Area 1    Area 2    Area 3    Sereno
                       M$000s     M$000s    M$000s    M$000s    Ps000s
Labor Cost               874       874        0         0         0
Materials Cost           374       374        0         0         0
Maintenance Cost          76        76        0         0         0
Temporary Layoff Costs     0         0        0         0         0
  Total Cash Expenditures 1324     1324       0         0         0

Equipment Depreciation   107       107        0         0         0
Plant Depreciation        26        26        0         0         0
  Total Production Cost  1457      1457       0         0         0
  Total Unit Production Cost 4.67  4.67     0.00      0.00        0
-----------------------------------------------------------------------------
              OUTPUT, INVENTORY, AND SALES ANALYSIS
                    (in thousands of units)

                       Consoli-   Merica    Merica    Merica
                        dated     Area 1    Area 2    Area 3    Sereno
Beginning Inventory      190        63        44        44        39
Normal Capacity          312       312         0         0         0
Actual Output            312       312         0         0         0
Sales Office Orders      312        87        75        75        75
Sales Office Purchases   225         0        75        75        75
Sold to Affiliates       225       225         0         0         0
Sold from Area Production 121      121         0         0         0
Customer Orders          447       121       109       109       108
Total Sales              447       121       109       109       108
Sold to Liquidators        0         0         0         0         0
Ending Inventory          55        29        10        10         6
Total Industry Sales    2682       678       678       678       648
-----------------------------------------------------------------------------
                       PRODUCTION CAPACITY STATUS

                             Merica    Merica    Merica
                             Area 1    Area 2    Area 3    Sereno
Production Lines Currently Producing  6    0         0         0
Space Available for New Lines         2    0         0         0
```

```
Company 1 World 1
Year 2 Quarter 4        OPERATING INFORMATION, Page 2         08-18-1994
E                       BUSINESS POLICY GAME, 4TH EDITION         20:36:05
        Copyright (c) 1995 by Richard V. Cotter and David J. Fritzsche
-------------------------------------------------------------------------
                        STANDARD COSTS PER UNIT
                          for Next Quarter

                              Merica    Merica    Merica
                              Area 1    Area 2    Area 3    Sereno
                                $         $         $         Ps

Model  1 Quality 2   Labor Cost    2.88      2.88      2.88      8.90
Savings Level  0     Material Cost 1.23      1.23      1.23      5.72

Note:  for Quality 1 add 10%.  For Quality 3 subtract 10%
-------------------------------------------------------------------------
                        SALES FORCE ANALYSIS

                              Merica    Merica    Merica
                              Area 1    Area 2    Area 3    Sereno

Active Salespeople (number of)    12        10        10        13
Salespeople in Training            0         0         0         0
Salespeople Resigned               0         0         0         0
Memo:  Sales Training Expense      0         0         0         0


---------------------CURRENT PERIOD DECISION SUMMARY--------------------
|         |         |          Salespeople        |                     |
|         | Price   Adv | Hire  Trans  Comm  Salary | Bank Loan       0 |
|Area 1 | 10.00    46 |   0     0     20   3000 | Bond Issue       0 |
|Area 2 | 10.00    40 |   0     0     20   3000 | Stock Issue      0 |
|Area 3 | 10.00    40 |   0     0     20   3000 | Dividends        0 |
|Sereno |    75   105 |   0     0     60   8971 | Time CDs      1000 |
------------------------------------------------------------------------
|         |        |        |          |              |                  |
|R&D/Trng|        |        |Production | Capacity Adjustment| Construction |
|--------|        |Sales |-----------|                    |              |
|R&D   72|        |Office| Schedule  | Lay  Deac-  Reac-| New  New  New |
|Trng  68|        |Orders|Lines Hours| Off  tivate tivate| Lines Add Plant|
|--------| Area 1 |  87  | 6    40   |  0    0     0 |  0    0    0  |
| Model  | Area 2 |  75  | 0     0   |  0    0     0 |  0    0    0  |
|--------| Area 3 |  75  | 0     0   |  0    0     0 |  0    0    0  |
|Model  1| Sereno |  75  | 0     0   |  0    0     0 |  0    0    0  |
|Qual   2| 2d Shft|      | 0     0   |  0    0     0 |  0            |
------------------------------------------------------------------------
```

```
World 1                    QUARTERLY INDUSTRY REPORT              08-18-1994
Year 2 Quarter 4       BUSINESS POLICY GAME, 4TH EDITION             20:36:07
F1        Copyright (c) 1995 by Richard V. Cotter and David J. Fritzsche
-----------------------------------------------------------------------------
                          FINANCIAL MARKET DATA
                      Merica  Sereno  |              ---Credit Rating---
GDP Index (Nominal)   100.00  100.00  | Interest Rates:  No. 1  No. 2  No. 3
Consumer Price Index  100.00  100.00  |   Long-Term       8.40   9.10  10.60
Stock Market Index    100.00          |   Short-Term     11.00  11.20  12.30
3-Month Time CD Rate    9.50          |
-----------------------------------------------------------------------------
                   REAL GROSS DOMESTIC PRODUCT FORECAST
            Actual Values, Last 4 Quarters    Forecast Values, Next 4 Quarters
            Qtr  5  Qtr  6  Qtr  7  Qtr  8    Qtr  9   Qtr 10    Qtr 11   Qtr 12

Merica  102.17  102.66  100.93  100.00      99.67    97.94     98.79    94.46
Sereno   94.87   97.05   98.20  100.00     104.76   107.08    109.14   115.87
-----------------------------------------------------------------------------
                         EXCHANGE RATE FORECAST

Sereno    5.99    5.97    5.97    6.00      6.09     6.02      6.08     6.18
-----------------------------------------------------------------------------
                         Inves-
      Stock  Earn-  Divi-    tor  Shares         Bank           Time  Credit
Co.   Price  ings   dends    ROI  Issued  Bonds  Loans   Cash   CDs   Rating

 1    4.37   0.116  0.000    0.0   6000    2000      0    1814   1000     2
 2    4.37   0.116  0.000    0.0   6000    2000      0    1814   1000     2
 3    4.37   0.116  0.000    0.0   6000    2000      0    1814   1000     2
 4    4.37   0.116  0.000    0.0   6000    2000      0    1814   1000     2
 5    4.37   0.116  0.000    0.0   6000    2000      0    1814   1000     2
 6    4.37   0.116  0.000    0.0   6000    2000      0    1814   1000     2
-----------------------------------------------------------------------------
                               Income Income  Income  Sales  Bonds  Int.
        Net   Fixed  Total  Total  to     to     to     to     to    Cover-
Co.  Income  Assets Assets Equity Assets Equity  Sales  Assets Equity  age

 1      698    6737  12337  10337   5.7    6.8   14.7   38.4   19.3   23.9
 2      698    6737  12337  10337   5.7    6.8   14.7   38.4   19.3   23.9
 3      698    6737  12337  10337   5.7    6.8   14.7   38.4   19.3   23.9
 4      698    6737  12337  10337   5.7    6.8   14.7   38.4   19.3   23.9
 5      698    6737  12337  10337   5.7    6.8   14.7   38.4   19.3   23.9
 6      698    6737  12337  10337   5.7    6.8   14.7   38.4   19.3   23.9
-----------------------------------------------------------------------------
Key:    Company 1
        Company 2
        Company 3
        Company 4
        Company 5
        Company 6
```

```
World 1                 QUARTERLY INDUSTRY REPORT, Page 2        08-18-1994
Year 2 Quarter 4        BUSINESS POLICY GAME, 4TH EDITION            20:36:07
F2        Copyright (c) 1995 by Richard V. Cotter and David J. Fritzsche
------------------------------------------------------------------------------
      Sales   Market  ----Sales (in 000s)-----  --Sales Office Orders---
Co.   $000s   Share   Tot  M1   M2   M3    S    Tot   M1   M2   M3    S

1     4740    16.7    447  121  109  109  108   312   87   75   75   75
2     4740    16.7    447  109  121  109  108   312   75   87   75   75
3     4740    16.7    447  109  109  121  108   312   75   75   87   75
4     4740    16.7    447  121  109  109  108   312   87   75   75   75
5     4740    16.7    447  109  121  109  108   312   75   87   75   75
6     4740    16.7    447  109  109  121  108   312   75   75   87   75
------------------------------------------------------------------------------
      ------Product Price-------  No. of Salespeople  Estimated Advertising
Co.   M1($)  M2($)  M3($)  S(Ps)  M1   M2   M3    S    M1   M2   M3   S(Ps)

1     10.00  10.00  10.00    75   12   10   10   13    40   40   40    110
2     10.00  10.00  10.00    75   10   12   10   13    40   40   40    100
3     10.00  10.00  10.00    75   10   10   12   13    40   40   50    110
4     10.00  10.00  10.00    75   12   10   10   13    50   40   40    100
5     10.00  10.00  10.00    75   10   12   10   13    40   50   40    110
6     10.00  10.00  10.00    75   10   10   12   13    40   40   50    100
------------------------------------------------------------------------------
      ------Production-------    -----Inventory-----   Plant Expansion
      Tot   M1   M2   M3    S    Tot   M1   M2   M3   S   M1   M2   M3   S

1     312  312    0    0    0    55   29   10   10   6    0    0    0    0
2     312    0  312    0    0    55   10   29   10   6    0    0    0    0
3     312    0    0  312    0    55   10   10   29   6    0    0    0    0
4     312  312    0    0    0    55   29   10   10   6    0    0    0    0
5     312    0  312    0    0    55   10   29   10   6    0    0    0    0
6     312    0    0  312    0    55   10   10   29   6    0    0    0    0
------------------------------------------------------------------------------
                                  Unit   Unit   Unit   Product  Total
      Model  Qual.  Model  New   Prod   Sell   Admin    R&D    Training
      No.    No.    Avail  Lines Cost   Exp    Exp      Exp    Expense

1      1      2      1      0    4.67   2.13   0.85     72       68
2      1      2      1      0    4.67   2.13   0.85     72       68
3      1      2      1      0    4.67   2.13   0.85     72       68
4      1      2      1      0    4.67   2.13   0.85     72       68
5      1      2      1      0    4.67   2.13   0.85     72       68
6      1      2      1      0    4.67   2.13   0.85     72       68
------------------------------------------------------------------------------
Key:  Company 1
      Company 2
      Company 3
      Company 4
      Company 5
      Company 6
```

APPENDIX D

BLANK FORMS AND WORK SHEETS

Corporate Charter (located at the front of this manual)
Peer Evaluation Form (1)
Decision Forms (5)
Sales Forecast Work Sheet (4)
Production Plan Work Sheet (4)
Capital Budget Work Sheet (4)
Pro Forma Income Statement (4)
Pro Forma Cash Flow Work Sheet (4)
Pro Forma Balance Sheet (4)

THE BUSINESS POLICY GAME
PEER EVALUATION FORM

Team Evaluation: Please rank the company teams according to the way you judge their overall performance in *The Business Policy Game*. (1 is highest, 8 is lowest). A low rank does not necessarily mean poor performance, but rather a lower **relative** performance than the team with the next highest rank.

Rank	Company	Rank	Company
1		5	
2		6	
3		7	
4		8	

Team Member Evaluation: Please rate the members of your company team according to the way that you judge their contribution to your team's performance. Rate the following factors:

Factors:
1. Attendance at team meetings
2. Constructive participation in team meetings
3. Effort shown outside of team meetings
4. Ability and willingness to work in a group
5. Overall average

Ratings:
9 to 10 = Excellent
7 to 8 = Good
4 to 6 = Fair
0 to 3 = Poor

Name	Atten-dance	Partici-pation	Effort	Contri-bution	Overall Average
Self:					

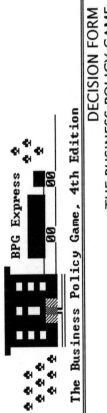

The Business Policy Game, 4th Edition

BPG Express

DECISION FORM
THE BUSINESS POLICY GAME, 4th Edition

Company _____ World _____ Year _____ Quarter _____ Company Name _____

	Marketing		Salespeople					Finance (000s)	
	Price	Adv(000s)	Hire	Transfer	Comm	Salary			
Area 1	$.	$	#	#	¢	$	Bank Loan	$	
Area 2	$.	$	#	#	¢	$	Bond Issue	$	
Area 3	$.	$	#	#	¢	$	Stock Issue	#	
Sereno	Ps	Ps	#	#	¢	Ps	Dividends	$	
							Time CDs	$	

R&D/Training (home currency)		Sales Office Orders (000s)	Production Schedule		Capacity Adjustment			Construction		
			Lines	Hours	Layoff	Deac-tivate	Reac-tivate	New Lines	New Add'n	New Plant
R&D	$	Area 1 #	#	#	#	#	#	#	#	#
Trng	$	Area 2 #	#	#	#	#	#	#	#	#
Model/Quality		Area 3 #	#	#	#	#	#	#	#	#
Model	#	Sereno #	#	#	#	#	#	#	#	#
Quality	#	2nd Shift	#	#	#	#	#	←	←	←

Copyright © 1995 by Richard V. Cotter and David J. Fritzsche

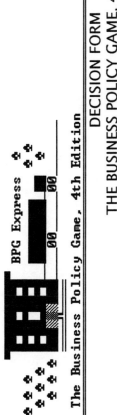

BPG Express

The Business Policy Game, 4th Edition

DECISION FORM
THE BUSINESS POLICY GAME, 4th Edition

Company _____ World _____ Year _____ Quarter _____ Company Name _____

Marketing

	Price	Adv(000s)
Area 1	$.	$
Area 2	$.	$
Area 3	$.	$
Sereno	Ps	Ps

Salespeople

	Hire	Transfer	Comm	Salary
Area 1	#	#	¢	$
Area 2	#	#	¢	$
Area 3	#	#	¢	$
Sereno	#	#	¢	Ps

Finance (000s)

Bank Loan	$
Bond Issue	$
Stock Issue	#
Dividends	$
Time CDs	$

R&D/Training (home currency)

R&D	$
Trng	$

Sales Office Orders (000s) / Production Schedule

	Sales Office Orders (000s)	Lines	Hours
Area 1	#	#	#
Area 2	#	#	#
Area 3	#	#	#
Sereno	#	#	#
2nd Shift		#	#

Model/Quality

Model	#
Quality	#

Capacity Adjustment

Layoff	Deac-tivate	Reac-tivate
#	#	#
#	#	#
#	#	#
#	#	#

Construction

New Lines	New Add'n	New Plant
#	#	#
#	#	#
#	#	#
#	#	#
#	↓	↓ ↓

Copyright © 1995 by Richard V. Cotter and David J. Fritzsche

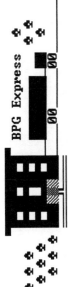

BPG Express

The Business Policy Game, 4th Edition

DECISION FORM
THE BUSINESS POLICY GAME, 4th Edition

Company _____ World _____ Year _____ Quarter _____ Company Name _____

Marketing

	Price	Adv(000s)
Area 1	$.	$
Area 2	$.	$
Area 3	$.	$
Sereno	Ps	Ps

Salespeople

	Hire	Transfer	Comm	Salary
Area 1	#	#	¢	$
Area 2	#	#	¢	$
Area 3	#	#	¢	$
Sereno	#	#	¢	Ps

Finance (000s)

Bank Loan	$
Bond Issue	$
Stock Issue	#
Dividends	$
Time CDs	$

R&D/Training (home currency)

R&D	$
Trng	$

Model/Quality

Model	#
Quality	#

Production Schedule

	Sales Office Orders (000s)	Lines	Hours
Area 1	#	#	#
Area 2	#	#	#
Area 3	#	#	#
Sereno	#	#	#
2nd Shift	#	#	#

Capacity Adjustment / Construction

	Layoff	Deac-tivate	Reac-tivate	New Lines	New Add'n	New Plant
	#	#	#	#	#	#
	#	#	#	#	#	#
	#	#	#	#	#	#
	#	#	#	#	#	#
	#	#	#	#	←	←
						←

Copyright © 1995 by Richard V. Cotter and David J. Fritzsche

BPG Express

The Business Policy Game, 4th Edition

DECISION FORM
THE BUSINESS POLICY GAME, 4th Edition

Company _____ World _____ Year _____ Quarter _____ Company Name _____

	Marketing		Salespeople			
	Price	Adv(000s)	Hire	Transfer	Comm	Salary
Area 1	$.	$	#	#	¢	$
Area 2	$.	$	#	#	¢	$
Area 3	$.	$	#	#	¢	$
Sereno	Ps	Ps	#	#	¢	Ps

Finance (000s)	
Bank Loan	$
Bond Issue	$
Stock Issue	#
Dividends	$
Time CDs	$

R&D/Training (home currency)	
R&D	$
Trng	$

Model/Quality	
Model	#
Quality	#

	Sales Office Orders (000s)	Production Schedule		Capacity Adjustment			Construction		
		Lines	Hours	Layoff	Deactivate	Reactivate	New Lines	New Add'n	New Plant
Area 1	#	#	#	#	#	#	#	#	#
Area 2	#	#	#	#	#	#	#	#	#
Area 3	#	#	#	#	#	#	#	#	#
Sereno	#	#	#	#	#	#	#	#	#
2nd Shift	#	#	#	#	#	#	←	←	←

Copyright © 1995 by Richard V. Cotter and David J. Fritzsche

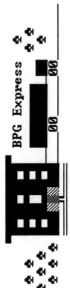

The Business Policy Game, 4th Edition

BPG Express

DECISION FORM
THE BUSINESS POLICY GAME, 4th Edition

Company _____ World _____ Year _____ Quarter _____ Company Name _____

Marketing

	Price	Adv(000s)
Area 1	$.	$
Area 2	$.	$
Area 3	$.	$
Sereno	Ps	Ps

Salespeople

	Hire	Transfer	Comm	Salary
Area 1	#	#	¢	$
Area 2	#	#	¢	$
Area 3	#	#	¢	$
Sereno	#	#	¢	Ps

Finance (000s)

Bank Loan	$
Bond Issue	$
Stock Issue	#
Dividends	$
Time CDs	$

R&D/Training (home currency)

R&D	$
Trng	$

Model/Quality

Model	#
Quality	#

Production Schedule

Sales Office Orders (000s)	Lines	Hours
Area 1 #	#	#
Area 2 #	#	#
Area 3 #	#	#
Sereno #	#	#
2nd Shift	#	#

Capacity Adjustment

Layoff	Deac-tivate	Reac-tivate
#	#	#
#	#	#
#	#	#
#	#	#

Construction

New Lines	New Add'n	New Plant
#	#	#
#	#	#
#	#	#
#	↓	↓
↓	↓	↓

Copyright © 1995 by Richard V. Cotter and David J. Fritzsche

THE BUSINESS POLICY GAME
SALES FORECAST WORK SHEET

World ___ Company ___ Year ___ Quarter ___	Consoli-dated	Merica Area 1	Merica Area 2	Merica Area 3	Sereno
Forecasted GDP Change (percent)	----------	%	%	%	%
Sales, Previous Quarter, thousands of units					
Estimated Sales Increments (thousands of units)					
From GDP Change					
Seasonal Factors					
Price Change					
Advertising Change					
Sales Salary Change					
Sales Commission Change					
Number of Salespersons Change					
New Model Introduction					
Competitors' Actions					
Total Incremental Change					
Total Sales Forecast (thousands of units)					
Expected Average Price (per unit)	$.	$.	$.	$.	Ps
Expected Sales Revenue (thousands of local currency)	$	$	$	$	Ps

Copyright © 1995 by Richard V. Cotter and David J. Fritzsche

THE BUSINESS POLICY GAME
SALES FORECAST WORK SHEET

World ___ Company ___ Year ___ Quarter ___	Consoli-dated	Merica Area 1	Merica Area 2	Merica Area 3	Sereno
Forecasted GDP Change (percent)	----------	%	%	%	%
Sales, Previous Quarter, thousands of units					
Estimated Sales Increments (thousands of units)					
From GDP Change					
Seasonal Factors					
Price Change					
Advertising Change					
Sales Salary Change					
Sales Commission Change					
Number of Salespersons Change					
New Model Introduction					
Competitors' Actions					
Total Incremental Change					
Total Sales Forecast (thousands of units)					
Expected Average Price (per unit)	$.	$.	$.	$.	Ps
Expected Sales Revenue (thousands of local currency)	$	$	$	$	Ps

Copyright © 1995 by Richard V. Cotter and David J. Fritzsche

THE BUSINESS POLICY GAME
SALES FORECAST WORK SHEET

World ___ Company ___ Year ___ Quarter ___	Consoli-dated	Merica Area 1	Merica Area 2	Merica Area 3	Sereno
Forecasted GDP Change (percent)	----------	%	%	%	%
Sales, Previous Quarter, thousands of units					
Estimated Sales Increments (thousands of units)					
From GDP Change					
Seasonal Factors					
Price Change					
Advertising Change					
Sales Salary Change					
Sales Commission Change					
Number of Salespersons Change					
New Model Introduction					
Competitors' Actions					
Total Incremental Change					
Total Sales Forecast (thousands of units)					
Expected Average Price (per unit)	$.	$.	$.	$.	Ps
Expected Sales Revenue (thousands of local currency)	$	$	$	$	Ps

Copyright © 1995 by Richard V. Cotter and David J. Fritzsche

THE BUSINESS POLICY GAME
SALES FORECAST WORK SHEET

World ___ Company ___ Year ___ Quarter ___	Consoli-dated	Merica Area 1	Merica Area 2	Merica Area 3	Sereno
Forecasted GDP Change (percent)	----------	%	%	%	%
Sales, Previous Quarter, thousands of units					
Estimated Sales Increments (thousands of units)					
From GDP Change					
Seasonal Factors					
Price Change					
Advertising Change					
Sales Salary Change					
Sales Commission Change					
Number of Salespersons Change					
New Model Introduction					
Competitors' Actions					
Total Incremental Change					
Total Sales Forecast (thousands of units)					
Expected Average Price (per unit)	$.	$.	$.	$.	Ps
Expected Sales Revenue (thousands of local currency)	$	$	$	$	Ps

Copyright © 1995 by Richard V. Cotter and David J. Fritzsche

THE BUSINESS POLICY GAME
PRODUCTION PLAN WORK SHEET

World ___ Company ___ Year ___ Quarter ___	Consoli-dated	Merica Area 1	Merica Area 2	Merica Area 3	Sereno

OUTPUT, INVENTORY, AND SALES ANALYSIS
(in thousands of units)

Sales Forecast					
Safety Stock					
Total Units Required					
Beginning Inventory					
Sales Office Orders					
Production Scheduled					
Local Sales Office Purchases					
Local Sales Office Shortage					
Goods Available to Affiliates					
Affiliate Sales Office Purchases					
Sales to Affiliates					
Goods Available for Sale					
Sold to Customers					
Sold to Liquidators					
Ending Inventory					

TOTAL PRODUCTION COST ANALYSIS
(total cost in thousands of dollars or pesos)

Labor Cost					
Materials Cost					
Maintenance Cost					
Layoff Cost					
Total Cash Expenditures					
Equipment Depreciation					
Plant Depreciation					
Total Production Cost					

UNIT PRODUCTION COST ANALYSIS
(cost per unit in dollars or pesos)

Unit Labor Cost					
Unit Materials Cost					
Unit Maintenance Cost					
Unit Layoff Cost					
Total Unit Cash Expenditures					
Unit Equipment Depreciation					
Unit Plant Depreciation					
Total Unit Production Cost					

Copyright © 1995 by Richard V. Cotter and David J. Fritzsche

THE BUSINESS POLICY GAME
PRODUCTION PLAN WORK SHEET

World ___ Company ___ Year ___ Quarter ___	Consoli-dated	Merica Area 1	Merica Area 2	Merica Area 3	Sereno
OUTPUT, INVENTORY, AND SALES ANALYSIS (in thousands of units)					
Sales Forecast					
Safety Stock					
Total Units Required					
Beginning Inventory					
Sales Office Orders					
Production Scheduled					
Local Sales Office Purchases					
Local Sales Office Shortage					
Goods Available to Affiliates					
Affiliate Sales Office Purchases					
Sales to Affiliates					
Goods Available for Sale					
Sold to Customers					
Sold to Liquidators					
Ending Inventory					
TOTAL PRODUCTION COST ANALYSIS (total cost in thousands of dollars or pesos)					
Labor Cost					
Materials Cost					
Maintenance Cost					
Layoff Cost					
Total Cash Expenditures					
Equipment Depreciation					
Plant Depreciation					
Total Production Cost					
UNIT PRODUCTION COST ANALYSIS (cost per unit in dollars or pesos)					
Unit Labor Cost					
Unit Materials Cost					
Unit Maintenance Cost					
Unit Layoff Cost					
Total Unit Cash Expenditures					
Unit Equipment Depreciation					
Unit Plant Depreciation					
Total Unit Production Cost					

Copyright © 1995 by Richard V. Cotter and David J. Fritzsche

THE BUSINESS POLICY GAME
PRODUCTION PLAN WORK SHEET

World ___ Company ___
Year ___ Quarter ____

	Consoli-dated	Merica Area 1	Merica Area 2	Merica Area 3	Sereno

OUTPUT, INVENTORY, AND SALES ANALYSIS
(in thousands of units)

	Consoli-dated	Merica Area 1	Merica Area 2	Merica Area 3	Sereno
Sales Forecast					
Safety Stock					
Total Units Required					
Beginning Inventory					
Sales Office Orders					
Production Scheduled					
Local Sales Office Purchases					
Local Sales Office Shortage					
Goods Available to Affiliates					
Affiliate Sales Office Purchases					
Sales to Affiliates					
Goods Available for Sale					
Sold to Customers					
Sold to Liquidators					
Ending Inventory					

TOTAL PRODUCTION COST ANALYSIS
(total cost in thousands of dollars or pesos)

	Consoli-dated	Merica Area 1	Merica Area 2	Merica Area 3	Sereno
Labor Cost					
Materials Cost					
Maintenance Cost					
Layoff Cost					
Total Cash Expenditures					
Equipment Depreciation					
Plant Depreciation					
Total Production Cost					

UNIT PRODUCTION COST ANALYSIS
(cost per unit in dollars or pesos)

	Consoli-dated	Merica Area 1	Merica Area 2	Merica Area 3	Sereno
Unit Labor Cost					
Unit Materials Cost					
Unit Maintenance Cost					
Unit Layoff Cost					
Total Unit Cash Expenditures					
Unit Equipment Depreciation					
Unit Plant Depreciation					
Total Unit Production Cost					

Copyright © 1995 by Richard V. Cotter and David J. Fritzsche

THE BUSINESS POLICY GAME
PRODUCTION PLAN WORK SHEET

World ___ Company ___
Year ___ Quarter ___

OUTPUT, INVENTORY, AND SALES ANALYSIS
(in thousands of units)

	Consoli-dated	Merica Area 1	Merica Area 2	Merica Area 3	Sereno
Sales Forecast					
Safety Stock					
Total Units Required					
Beginning Inventory					
Sales Office Orders					
Production Scheduled					
Local Sales Office Purchases					
Local Sales Office Shortage					
Goods Available to Affiliates					
Affiliate Sales Office Purchases					
Sales to Affiliates					
Goods Available for Sale					
Sold to Customers					
Sold to Liquidators					
Ending Inventory					

TOTAL PRODUCTION COST ANALYSIS
(total cost in thousands of dollars or pesos)

	Consoli-dated	Merica Area 1	Merica Area 2	Merica Area 3	Sereno
Labor Cost					
Materials Cost					
Maintenance Cost					
Layoff Cost					
Total Cash Expenditures					
Equipment Depreciation					
Plant Depreciation					
Total Production Cost					

UNIT PRODUCTION COST ANALYSIS
(cost per unit in dollars or pesos)

	Consoli-dated	Merica Area 1	Merica Area 2	Merica Area 3	Sereno
Unit Labor Cost					
Unit Materials Cost					
Unit Maintenance Cost					
Unit Layoff Cost					
Total Unit Cash Expenditures					
Unit Equipment Depreciation					
Unit Plant Depreciation					
Total Unit Production Cost					

Copyright © 1995 by Richard V. Cotter and David J. Fritzsche

THE BUSINESS POLICY GAME
CAPITAL BUDGET WORK SHEET

World ___ Company ___
Year ___ Quarter ___

	Consoli-dated M$000s	Home Area M$000s	Merica Area___ M$000s	Merica Area___ M$000s	Sereno Ps 000s

CAPITAL EXPENDITURES (enter number of lines and cost by area):

	M1	M2	M3	S	Exchange Rate → →				
Plant									
Addition									
Lines									
Total Expenditures									

SOURCES OF FUNDS:

Quarterly Earnings					
Stock Sold to Parent	----------				
Sale of Bonds			----------	----------	----------
Sale of Common Stock			----------	----------	----------
Short-Term Bank Loan			----------	----------	----------
Total Sources					
Less Loan Repayment			----------	----------	----------
Total Available Sources					
Surplus/Deficit					

Copyright © 1995 by Richard V. Cotter and David J. Fritzsche

THE BUSINESS POLICY GAME
CAPITAL BUDGET WORK SHEET

World ___ Company ___ Year ____ Quarter _____					Consoli-dated M$000s	Home Area M$000s	Merica Area___ M$000s	Merica Area___ M$000s	Sereno Ps 000s

CAPITAL EXPENDITURES (enter number of lines and cost by area):

	M1	M2	M3	S		Exchange Rate → →			
Plant									
Addition									
Lines									
Total Expenditures									

SOURCES OF FUNDS:

Quarterly Earnings									
Stock Sold to Parent					----------				
Sale of Bonds							----------	----------	----------
Sale of Common Stock							----------	----------	----------
Short-Term Bank Loan							----------	----------	----------
Total Sources									
Less Loan Repayment							----------	----------	----------
Total Available Sources									
Surplus/Deficit									

Copyright © 1995 by Richard V. Cotter and David J. Fritzsche

THE BUSINESS POLICY GAME
CAPITAL BUDGET WORK SHEET

World ___ Company ___
Year ____ Quarter _____

	Consolidated M$000s	Home Area M$000s	Merica Area___ M$000s	Merica Area___ M$000s	Sereno Ps 000s

CAPITAL EXPENDITURES (enter number of lines and cost by area):

	M1	M2	M3	S	Exchange Rate → →			
Plant								
Addition								
Lines								
Total Expenditures								

SOURCES OF FUNDS:

	Consolidated	Home Area	Merica Area	Merica Area	Sereno
Quarterly Earnings					
Stock Sold to Parent	----------				
Sale of Bonds			----------	----------	----------
Sale of Common Stock			----------	----------	----------
Short-Term Bank Loan			----------	----------	----------
Total Sources					
Less Loan Repayment			----------	----------	----------
Total Available Sources					
Surplus/Deficit					

Copyright © 1995 by Richard V. Cotter and David J. Fritzsche

THE BUSINESS POLICY GAME
CAPITAL BUDGET WORK SHEET

World ___ Company ___ Year ____ Quarter _____					Consoli- dated M$000s	Home Area M$000s	Merica Area___ M$000s	Merica Area___ M$000s	Sereno Ps 000s
CAPITAL EXPENDITURES (enter number of lines and cost by area):									
	M1	M2	M3	S		Exchange Rate → →			
Plant									
Addition									
Lines									
Total Expenditures									
SOURCES OF FUNDS:									
Quarterly Earnings									
Stock Sold to Parent						----------			
Sale of Bonds							----------	----------	----------
Sale of Common Stock							----------	----------	----------
Short-Term Bank Loan							----------	----------	----------
Total Sources									
Less Loan Repayment							----------	----------	----------
Total Available Sources									
Surplus/Deficit									

Copyright © 1995 by Richard V. Cotter and David J. Fritzsche

THE BUSINESS POLICY GAME
PRO FORMA INCOME STATEMENT (000s)

World ___ Company ___ Year ___ Quarter ___	Consoli-dated	Home Area	Merica Area ___	Merica Area ___	Sereno
Net Sales: to Customers					
to Affiliates (cost + 20%)	----------				
to Liquidators (at cost)					
Total Sales					
Beginning Inventory					
Goods Manufactured					
Purchases from Affiliates	----------				
Goods Available for Sale					
Ending Inventory					
Cost of Goods Sold					
Less Value Added Tax		----------	----------	----------	
Gross Profit					
Advertising Expense					
Sales Salaries					
Sales Commissions					
General Selling Expense					
Transportation Expense					
Sales Office Depreciation					
Other Selling Expense					
Total Selling Expense					
Research & Development			----------	----------	----------
Total Training Expense					
Storage Expense					
Executive Compensation					
Loan Interest			----------	----------	----------
Bond Interest			----------	----------	----------
Other Expense					
Total Admin. and Gen. Expense					
Total Operating Expense					
Operating Profit					
CD Interest			----------	----------	----------
Capital Gain (Loss)					
Net Profit (Loss) Before Tax					
Less Income Tax					
Net Profit (Loss) After Tax					
Dividends from Subsidiaries	----------		----------	----------	----------
Dividends to Parent	----------	----------			
Dividends to Shareholders			----------	----------	----------
Added to Retained Earnings					

Copyright © 1995 by Richard V. Cotter and David J. Fritzsche

THE BUSINESS POLICY GAME
PRO FORMA INCOME STATEMENT (000s)

World ___ Company ___ Year ___ Quarter ___	Consoli-dated	Home Area	Merica Area ___	Merica Area ___	Sereno
Net Sales: to Customers					
to Affiliates (cost + 20%)	----------				
to Liquidators (at cost)					
Total Sales					
Beginning Inventory					
Goods Manufactured					
Purchases from Affiliates	----------				
Goods Available for Sale					
Ending Inventory					
Cost of Goods Sold					
Less Value Added Tax		----------	----------	----------	
Gross Profit					
Advertising Expense					
Sales Salaries					
Sales Commissions					
General Selling Expense					
Transportation Expense					
Sales Office Depreciation					
Other Selling Expense					
Total Selling Expense					
Research & Development			----------	----------	----------
Total Training Expense					
Storage Expense					
Executive Compensation					
Loan Interest			----------	----------	----------
Bond Interest			----------	----------	----------
Other Expense					
Total Admin. and Gen. Expense					
Total Operating Expense					
Operating Profit					
CD Interest			----------	----------	----------
Capital Gain (Loss)					
Net Profit (Loss) Before Tax					
Less Income Tax					
Net Profit (Loss) After Tax					
Dividends from Subsidiaries	----------		----------	----------	----------
Dividends to Parent	----------	----------			
Dividends to Shareholders			----------	----------	----------
Added to Retained Earnings					

Copyright © 1995 by Richard V. Cotter and David J. Fritzsche

THE BUSINESS POLICY GAME
PRO FORMA INCOME STATEMENT (000s)

World ___ Company ___ Year ____ Quarter ____	Consoli-dated	Home Area	Merica Area ___	Merica Area ___	Sereno
Net Sales: to Customers					
to Affiliates (cost + 20%)	----------				
to Liquidators (at cost)					
Total Sales					
Beginning Inventory					
Goods Manufactured					
Purchases from Affiliates	----------				
Goods Available for Sale					
Ending Inventory					
Cost of Goods Sold					
Less Value Added Tax		----------	----------	----------	
Gross Profit					
Advertising Expense					
Sales Salaries					
Sales Commissions					
General Selling Expense					
Transportation Expense					
Sales Office Depreciation					
Other Selling Expense					
Total Selling Expense					
Research & Development			----------	----------	----------
Total Training Expense					
Storage Expense					
Executive Compensation					
Loan Interest			----------	----------	----------
Bond Interest			----------	----------	----------
Other Expense					
Total Admin. and Gen. Expense					
Total Operating Expense					
Operating Profit					
CD Interest			----------	----------	----------
Capital Gain (Loss)					
Net Profit (Loss) Before Tax					
Less Income Tax					
Net Profit (Loss) After Tax					
Dividends from Subsidiaries	----------		----------	----------	----------
Dividends to Parent	----------	----------			
Dividends to Shareholders			----------	----------	----------
Added to Retained Earnings					

Copyright © 1995 by Richard V. Cotter and David J. Fritzsche

THE BUSINESS POLICY GAME
PRO FORMA INCOME STATEMENT (000s)

World ___ Company ___ Year ___ Quarter ___	Consoli-dated	Home Area	Merica Area ___	Merica Area ___	Sereno
Net Sales: to Customers					
to Affiliates (cost + 20%)	----------				
to Liquidators (at cost)					
Total Sales					
Beginning Inventory					
Goods Manufactured					
Purchases from Affiliates	----------				
Goods Available for Sale					
Ending Inventory					
Cost of Goods Sold					
Less Value Added Tax		----------	----------	----------	
Gross Profit					
Advertising Expense					
Sales Salaries					
Sales Commissions					
General Selling Expense					
Transportation Expense					
Sales Office Depreciation					
Other Selling Expense					
Total Selling Expense					
Research & Development			----------	----------	----------
Total Training Expense					
Storage Expense					
Executive Compensation					
Loan Interest			----------	----------	----------
Bond Interest			----------	----------	----------
Other Expense					
Total Admin. and Gen. Expense					
Total Operating Expense					
Operating Profit					
CD Interest			----------	----------	----------
Capital Gain (Loss)					
Net Profit (Loss) Before Tax					
Less Income Tax					
Net Profit (Loss) After Tax					
Dividends from Subsidiaries	----------		----------	----------	----------
Dividends to Parent	----------	----------			
Dividends to Shareholders			----------	----------	----------
Added to Retained Earnings					

Copyright © 1995 by Richard V. Cotter and David J. Fritzsche

THE BUSINESS POLICY GAME
PRO FORMA CASH FLOW WORK SHEET

World ___ Company ___ Year ___ Quarter ___	Consoli-dated	Home Area	Merica Area	Merica Area	Sereno
Operating Receipts:					
Collect from Last Quarter Sales					
Collect from Current Quarter Sales					
Net Sales to Affiliates	----------				
Sales to Liquidators					
Operating Expenditures:					
Production Cost					
Purchases from Affiliates	----------				
Operating Expense					
Taxes Paid					
Net Operating Cash Flow					
Investment Receipts:					
CD Interest			----------	----------	----------
CDs Matured			----------	----------	----------
Subsidiary Dividends Received	----------		----------	----------	----------
Fixed Assets Sold					
Investment Expenditures:					
CDs Purchased			----------	----------	----------
New Equipment					
Sales Office Investment					
Plant Investment					
Subsidiary Stock Purchased	----------		----------	----------	----------
Net Investment Cash Flow					
Financing Receipts:					
Loans from Bank			----------	----------	----------
Stock Sold to Parent	----------	----------			
Bond Sale			----------	----------	----------
Stock Sale			----------	----------	----------
Financing Expenditures:					
Interest Paid			----------	----------	----------
Dividends to Shareholders			----------	----------	----------
Dividends to Parent	----------	----------			
Bank Loans Repaid			----------	----------	----------
Bonds Repurchased			----------	----------	----------
Stock Repurchased			----------	----------	----------
Net Financing Cash Flow					
Beginning Cash Balance					
Net Cash Flow for Quarter					
Cash Balance End of Quarter					
Required Loan (+ interest)			----------	----------	----------

Copyright © 1995 by Richard V. Cotter and David J. Fritzsche

THE BUSINESS POLICY GAME PRO FORMA CASH FLOW WORK SHEET					
World ___ Company ___ Year ___ Quarter ___	Consoli- dated	Home Area	Merica Area ___	Merica Area ___	Sereno
Operating Receipts:					
Collect from Last Quarter Sales					
Collect from Current Quarter Sales					
Net Sales to Affiliates	----------				
Sales to Liquidators					
Operating Expenditures:					
Production Cost					
Purchases from Affiliates	----------				
Operating Expense					
Taxes Paid					
Net Operating Cash Flow					
Investment Receipts:					
CD Interest			----------	----------	----------
CDs Matured			----------	----------	----------
Subsidiary Dividends Received	----------		----------	----------	----------
Fixed Assets Sold					
Investment Expenditures:					
CDs Purchased			----------	----------	----------
New Equipment					
Sales Office Investment					
Plant Investment					
Subsidiary Stock Purchased	----------		----------	----------	----------
Net Investment Cash Flow					
Financing Receipts:					
Loans from Bank			----------	----------	----------
Stock Sold to Parent	----------	----------			
Bond Sale			----------	----------	----------
Stock Sale			----------	----------	----------
Financing Expenditures:					
Interest Paid			----------	----------	----------
Dividends to Shareholders			----------	----------	----------
Dividends to Parent	----------	----------			
Bank Loans Repaid			----------	----------	----------
Bonds Repurchased			----------	----------	----------
Stock Repurchased			----------	----------	----------
Net Financing Cash Flow					
Beginning Cash Balance					
Net Cash Flow for Quarter					
Cash Balance End of Quarter					
Required Loan (+ interest)			----------	----------	----------

Copyright © 1995 by Richard V. Cotter and David J. Fritzsche

THE BUSINESS POLICY GAME
PRO FORMA CASH FLOW WORK SHEET

World ___ Company ___ Year ___ Quarter ___	Consoli-dated	Home Area	Merica Area__	Merica Area__	Sereno
Operating Receipts:					
Collect from Last Quarter Sales					
Collect from Current Quarter Sales					
Net Sales to Affiliates	----------				
Sales to Liquidators					
Operating Expenditures:					
Production Cost					
Purchases from Affiliates	----------				
Operating Expense					
Taxes Paid					
Net Operating Cash Flow					
Investment Receipts:					
CD Interest			----------	----------	----------
CDs Matured			----------	----------	----------
Subsidiary Dividends Received	----------		----------	----------	----------
Fixed Assets Sold					
Investment Expenditures:					
CDs Purchased			----------	----------	----------
New Equipment					
Sales Office Investment					
Plant Investment					
Subsidiary Stock Purchased	----------		----------	----------	----------
Net Investment Cash Flow					
Financing Receipts:					
Loans from Bank			----------	----------	----------
Stock Sold to Parent	----------	----------			
Bond Sale			----------	----------	----------
Stock Sale			----------	----------	----------
Financing Expenditures:					
Interest Paid			----------	----------	----------
Dividends to Shareholders			----------	----------	----------
Dividends to Parent	----------	----------			
Bank Loans Repaid			----------	----------	----------
Bonds Repurchased			----------	----------	----------
Stock Repurchased			----------	----------	----------
Net Financing Cash Flow					
Beginning Cash Balance					
Net Cash Flow for Quarter					
Cash Balance End of Quarter					
Required Loan (+ interest)			----------	----------	----------

Copyright © 1995 by Richard V. Cotter and David J. Fritzsche

THE BUSINESS POLICY GAME
PRO FORMA CASH FLOW WORK SHEET

World ___ Company ___ Year ___ Quarter ___	Consoli-dated	Home Area	Merica Area ___	Merica Area ___	Sereno
Operating Receipts:					
Collect from Last Quarter Sales					
Collect from Current Quarter Sales					
Net Sales to Affiliates	----------				
Sales to Liquidators					
Operating Expenditures:					
Production Cost					
Purchases from Affiliates	----------				
Operating Expense					
Taxes Paid					
Net Operating Cash Flow					
Investment Receipts:					
CD Interest			----------	----------	----------
CDs Matured			----------	----------	----------
Subsidiary Dividends Received	----------		----------	----------	----------
Fixed Assets Sold					
Investment Expenditures:					
CDs Purchased			----------	----------	----------
New Equipment					
Sales Office Investment					
Plant Investment					
Subsidiary Stock Purchased	----------		----------	----------	----------
Net Investment Cash Flow					
Financing Receipts:					
Loans from Bank			----------	----------	----------
Stock Sold to Parent	----------	----------			
Bond Sale			----------	----------	----------
Stock Sale			----------	----------	----------
Financing Expenditures:					
Interest Paid			----------	----------	----------
Dividends to Shareholders			----------	----------	----------
Dividends to Parent	----------	----------			
Bank Loans Repaid			----------	----------	----------
Bonds Repurchased			----------	----------	----------
Stock Repurchased			----------	----------	----------
Net Financing Cash Flow					
Beginning Cash Balance					
Net Cash Flow for Quarter					
Cash Balance End of Quarter					
Required Loan (+ interest)			----------	----------	----------

Copyright © 1995 by Richard V. Cotter and David J. Fritzsche

THE BUSINESS POLICY GAME
PRO FORMA BALANCE SHEET (000s)

World ___ Company ____ Year ____ Quarter _____	Consoli- dated	Home Area	Merica Area ___	Merica Area ___	Sereno
ASSETS:					
Cash Balance					
Time Certificates of Deposit			----------	----------	----------
Accounts Receivable					
Inventory					
Total Current Assets					
Net Sales Office					
Net Manufacturing Plant					
Net Manufacturing Equipment					
Equity in Subsidiaries	----------		----------	----------	----------
Total Fixed Assets					
Total Assets					
LIABILITIES AND EQUITY:					
Bank Loans			----------	----------	----------
Total Current Liabilities			----------	----------	----------
Bonds Outstanding			----------	----------	----------
Total Liabilities					
Capital Stock					
Accumulated Earnings					
Cumulative Translation Adjustment		----------	----------	----------	----------
Total Equity					
Total Liabilities and Equity					

Copyright © 1995 by Richard V. Cotter and David J. Fritzsche

THE BUSINESS POLICY GAME
PRO FORMA BALANCE SHEET (000s)

World ___ Company ___ Year ___ Quarter ___	Consoli-dated	Home Area	Merica Area__	Merica Area__	Sereno
ASSETS:					
Cash Balance					
Time Certificates of Deposit			----------	----------	----------
Accounts Receivable					
Inventory					
Total Current Assets					
Net Sales Office					
Net Manufacturing Plant					
Net Manufacturing Equipment					
Equity in Subsidiaries	----------		----------	----------	----------
Total Fixed Assets					
Total Assets					
LIABILITIES AND EQUITY:					
Bank Loans			----------	----------	----------
Total Current Liabilities			----------	----------	----------
Bonds Outstanding			----------	----------	----------
Total Liabilities					
Capital Stock					
Accumulated Earnings					
Cumulative Translation Adjustment		----------	----------	----------	----------
Total Equity					
Total Liabilities and Equity					

Copyright © 1995 by Richard V. Cotter and David J. Fritzsche

THE BUSINESS POLICY GAME
PRO FORMA BALANCE SHEET (000s)

World ___ Company ____ Year ___ Quarter ____	Consoli- dated	Home Area	Merica Area___	Merica Area___	Sereno
ASSETS:					
Cash Balance					
Time Certificates of Deposit			----------	----------	----------
Accounts Receivable					
Inventory					
Total Current Assets					
Net Sales Office					
Net Manufacturing Plant					
Net Manufacturing Equipment					
Equity in Subsidiaries	----------		----------	----------	----------
Total Fixed Assets					
Total Assets					
LIABILITIES AND EQUITY:					
Bank Loans			----------	----------	----------
Total Current Liabilities			----------	----------	----------
Bonds Outstanding			----------	----------	----------
Total Liabilities					
Capital Stock					
Accumulated Earnings					
Cumulative Translation Adjustment		----------	----------	----------	----------
Total Equity					
Total Liabilities and Equity					

Copyright © 1995 by Richard V. Cotter and David J. Fritzsche

THE BUSINESS POLICY GAME
PRO FORMA BALANCE SHEET (000s)

World ___ Company ____ Year ____ Quarter _____	Consoli- dated	Home Area	Merica Area___	Merica Area___	Sereno
ASSETS:					
Cash Balance					
Time Certificates of Deposit			----------	----------	----------
Accounts Receivable					
Inventory					
Total Current Assets					
Net Sales Office					
Net Manufacturing Plant					
Net Manufacturing Equipment					
Equity in Subsidiaries	----------		----------	----------	----------
Total Fixed Assets					
Total Assets					
LIABILITIES AND EQUITY:					
Bank Loans			----------	----------	----------
Total Current Liabilities			----------	----------	----------
Bonds Outstanding			----------	----------	----------
Total Liabilities					
Capital Stock					
Accumulated Earnings					
Cumulative Translation Adjustment		----------	----------	----------	----------
Total Equity					
Total Liabilities and Equity					

Copyright © 1995 by Richard V. Cotter and David J. Fritzsche

INDEX

QUICK-REFERENCE GUIDE
DECISION-VARIABLE DEFINITIONS AND LIMITS

PRICE Amount to be charged for your product Maximum change, Areas:1 to 3: 30 percent Maximum change: Sereno: 40 percent Limits, Areas 1 to 3: 1.00 to 99.99 (dollars and cents) Limits, Sereno: 1 to 99999 (pesos) If there is no sales office, price must be 0	**ADVERTISING** Amount to be spent for advertising in each marketing area Limits, Areas 1 to 3: 0 to 999 (thousands of dollars) Limits, Sereno: 0 to 9999999 (thousands of pesos)
HIRE NEW SALESPEOPLE Number of new salespeople to be hired. Those hired now will be in training for one quarter, then become active salespeople in the following quarter. Limits: 0 to 99	**TRANSFER OR DISCHARGE SALESPEOPLE** Number to be transferred or discharged Negative values: discharge or transfer out. Positive values: transfer in. A negative balance will be discharged. Maximum: Number available minus 1 Limits: -99 to 99
CLOSING A SALES OFFICE Transfer **out** or discharge of **all** salespeople will cause the sales office in that area to be closed and executives discharged. Maximum negative entry: Number of active salespeople Limits: -99 to 0	**OPENING (REOPENING) A SALES OFFICE** Transfer **in** of one or more salespeople to an area where there is no sales office will cause an office to be built and executives to be hired. Limits: 0 to 99
COMMISSION Commission per unit to be paid to each sales person Limits, Areas 1 to 3: 1 to 99 (cents per unit) Limits, Sereno: 1 to 99999 (centavos per unit) If there is no sales office in an area, the value must be 0.	**SALARY** Quarterly salary to be paid to each salesperson Limits, Areas 1 to 3: 1 to 9999 (dollars) Limits, Sereno: 1 to 9999999 (pesos) If there is no sales office in an area, the value must be 0.
BANK LOAN Short-term loan to parent company, for one quarter. Maximum: 50% of consolidated receivables plus inventory Maximum: 0, if loan outstanding in each of the last 3 quarters. Limits: 0 to 2500 (in thousands of dollars)	**BOND ISSUE** Sold in million-dollar lots by parent company Positive numbers: sell new 10-year bonds Maximum: the lesser of 50% of equity or 75% of net fixed assets Limits: 0 to 9000 (in thousands of dollars)
BOND REPURCHASE Redeem outstanding bonds in lots of $100,000 Negative numbers: amount of bonds to repurchase. Limits: -500 to 0 (in thousands of dollars)	**STOCK ISSUE** Sold in 100,000-share lots by parent company Positive numbers: Number of common shares to be issued, Minimum issue: enough shares to total $1,000,000 Limits: 0 to 9000 (in thousands of shares)
STOCK REPURCHASE Repurchased in lots of 100,000 shares Negative numbers: Number of shares to repurchase Maximum repurchase: to leave at least 3 million shares with positive accumulated retained earnings. Limits: -500 to 0 (in thousands of shares)	**DIVIDENDS** Declared and paid by parent company Amount to pay external shareholders from profits Maximum: Consolidated net income in last 4 quarters, minus dividends paid in last 3 quarters. Limits: 0 to 9999 (in thousands of dollars)
TIME CERTIFICATES OF DEPOSIT (CDs) Short-term 3-month investments by parent company, purchased in $100,000 lots. Limits: 0 to 9900 (in thousands of dollars)	**PRODUCT RESEARCH & DEVELOPMENT** Amount for parent company to spend on developing new models Limits: 1 to 999 (in thousands of dollars)

QUICK-REFERENCE GUIDE (Continued)
DECISION-VARIABLE DEFINITIONS AND LIMITS

TRAINING OF EXISTING PRODUCTION EMPLOYEES Amount for parent company to spend on training of existing production employees (to reduce production costs). Limits: 1 to 999 (in thousands of dollars)	**MODEL NUMBER** For production this quarter. Goes on sale next quarter. Minimum: Same model number as last quarter Maximum: Highest number reported to be available Limits: 1 to 12
QUALITY (of product) May be changed only on introduction of a new model. Enter 1 for deluxe quality Enter 2 for standard quality Enter 3 for economy quality	**SALES OFFICE ORDERS** Number of units to be shipped to each sales office. Units will be held there for resale. Unsold units will be placed in inventory. Limits: 0 to 999 (in thousands of units)
SCHEDULING PRODUCTION LINES (First Shift) Number of lines scheduled for production. Any lines not scheduled must be Idled or deactivated. New lines must be purchased and installed one quarter before they may be scheduled. Limits: 0 to number of lines available	**SCHEDULING PRODUCTION HOURS** (First Shift) Number of hours to schedule production per week. Number of lines must also be scheduled. Limits: 0, 40 to 48 (hours)
SECOND-SHIFT LINES (Home area plant only) Number of lines scheduled for second shift First-shift lines also must be scheduled. New lines must be prepared one quarter before production may be scheduled. Limits: 0 to number of first-shift lines scheduled for production.	**SECOND-SHIFT HOURS** (Home area plant only) Number of hours scheduled per week Number of lines must also be scheduled. Limits: 0, 40 to 48
TEMPORARY LAYOFF–IDLED (one quarter only) Number of lines to shut down for temporary layoff of employees . Lines subject to temporary layoff are automatically available for production one quarter later. Limits: 0 to number of lines available for production Lines that are available for production but not scheduled must be Idled(temporary layoff) or deactivated.	**DEACTIVATE PRODUCTION LINES** (Permanent Layoff) Number of lines to be deactivated (and not available for production until reactivated). If a plant is closed all lines must be deactivated, and none will be available for reactivation later. Limits: 0 to number of lines available Lines not scheduled for production must be Idled or deactivated.
REACTIVATE PRODUCTION LINES Number of previously deactivated 1st or 2nd-shift lines to be prepared for production next quarter. 1st-shift lines must be available in order to reactivate 2nd-shift lines. 1st and 2nd-shift lines may be reactivated at the same time. Limits: 0 to number of previously deactivated lines	**NEW PRODUCTION LINES** Number of new lines to be purchased and installed, ready to begin production the following quarter 1st-shift lines must be available to install new 2nd-shift lines. Limits (1st shift): 0 to space reported as available Limits (2nd shift): 0 to number of 1st-shift lines
NEW ADDITION Number of lines capacity to add to the plant Construction takes 2 quarters. This is an addition to the building in which new lines may be installed. Only one new 2-line addition may be started in any quarter, but another could be started the following quarter so that two additions are under construction at the same time. New lines must be installed separately during the last quarter of construction (or later). Limits: 0 or 2 (to a maximum capacity of 12 lines)	**NEW PLANT** Number of lines capacity for a new plant to be constructed May only be built in areas where there is no existing plant. This is a new building in which production lines may be installed during the last quarter of construction (or later). New lines must be installed separately. New additions may be built later, to a maximum capacity of 12 lines in any area. An entry of -1 causes the plant to be closed and sold for 90% of book value. All lines must then be deactivated at the same time. No further production in such a plant is possible. Limits: -1 (to close plant) 0, 2, 4, 6, 8 or 10 (number of lines capacity)